John Birch:
A Life

JOHN BIRCH: A LIFE

TERRY LAUTZ

OXFORD
UNIVERSITY PRESS

OXFORD
UNIVERSITY PRESS

Oxford University Press is a department of the University of
Oxford. It furthers the University's objective of excellence in research,
scholarship, and education by publishing worldwide.
Oxford is a registered trademark of Oxford University Press
in the UK and certain other countries.

Published in the United States of America by
Oxford University Press
198 Madison Avenue, New York, NY 10016

© Oxford University Press 2016

Cataloging-in-Publication Data is on file at the Library of Congress.
ISBN 978–0–19–026289–1

1 3 5 7 9 8 6 4 2
Printed in the United States of America
on acid-free paper

For Ellen Stromberg Lautz

CONTENTS

Part Three Encountering Communists

Part Four Making A Martyr

PREFACE

I FIRST HEARD THE name of John Birch when I was a high school student in Michigan during the 1960s, but I had no idea who he actually was. The John Birch Society's founder, Robert Welch, seemed like a fusty old fanatic—a misguided relic of the past—and the Birchers' paranoia about communists was an easy target for ridicule. Anti-communist witch-hunts of the early Cold War years had been discredited as the product of hysteria; even those who defended Joseph McCarthy's goals agreed that his means were wrong. Novels and films like *The Manchurian Candidate* and *Seven Days in May* warned about the dangers of demagogues who would manipulate extremist fears as an excuse to seize power. The times were changing with the civil rights movement, women's liberation, and protests over the Vietnam War. Yet President Eisenhower's warning about the dangers of a military-industrial state was worrisome, and Barry Goldwater's nomination as the Republican Party's candidate for president in 1964 suggested that suspicions about an elite group working to co-opt the U.S. Constitution and subvert individual freedoms rang true for many Americans.

It was many years later that I came across the name of John Birch while researching the fate of Americans living in China when the Communists rose to power during the 1940s. Much to my surprise, I found that Birch had been a Baptist missionary who joined the U.S.

Army in China during the Second World War. He lost his life at the hands of Chinese Communists in 1945 soon after the war ended, and thirteen years later his name was adopted for a right-wing political cause in the United States. Needless to say, he had nothing to do with the John Birch Society.

Birch's story fascinated me because it seemed so colorful and implausible, but I was also intrigued for personal reasons. During my first two years of high school, I lived in Taiwan where I met American and British missionaries, some of whom had been forced out of China after Mao's victory in 1949. I was curious as well because my uncle Bill Lautz was a Protestant minister who lived in Japan with his wife and my four cousins. I learned more about the influential and contentious history of missionaries when I went to work for the Yale-China Association, which had its origins as a mission society at Yale University during the early twentieth century, and still more when I joined the staff of the Henry Luce Foundation, whose founder was the famous son of China missionaries.

Birch's role as a soldier and military intelligence officer in China also interested me. My father, who met my mother in Australia during the Second World War, served in the Pacific Theater in New Guinea and the Philippines. He made his career in the U.S. Army and was posted to Taiwan as a member of the Military Assistance Advisory Group (MAAG). It was at Taipei American School that I was introduced to Chinese history and started to think about Cold War politics in Asia. In those days, the mainland—as China proper was called—was a strange, hostile place where Americans were not permitted to visit. My parents, sister, and I peered into China from across the border during a visit to Hong Kong. Even to an American teenager, it was clear that Chiang Kai-shek's annual speeches about overthrowing the Communists and recovering the mainland were empty rhetoric. Nevertheless, our family had a primitive bomb shelter in our back yard in Taiwan, just in case the island was invaded.

After college, I served with the Army in Vietnam, working with a medical evacuation helicopter unit and then with an intelligence outfit, analyzing the medical capabilities of the Vietnamese Communists. The American government was tied to a deeply corrupt anti-communist regime in South Vietnam, while the Communists in North Vietnam were able to claim the mantle of anti-imperialist nationalism. The parallels between the civil wars in Vietnam and China were obvious. In both conflicts, the United States found itself tied to regimes with ebbing legitimacy, while the Communists preached egalitarianism and practiced repression. Recriminations heard after South Vietnam's collapse in 1975 were disturbingly similar to charges over the "loss" of China to the Communists in 1949. Had the United States only done more, it was argued, the outcome would have been different. My experience in Vietnam convinced me that Americans needed to learn more about Asia, a conclusion that led me to graduate school and made me an advocate for better understanding between Asia and the United States.

As I delved into John Birch's biography, I discovered an adventure story, murder mystery, romance tale, and political thrilller. I also began to see his life and death as a commentary on America's well-meaning idealism and misguided adventurism. He seemed to personify a long-standing American ambition to save and defend the Chinese, and in his afterlife, a sense of fear and loathing when that dream collapsed. My goal in writing this book is neither to vilify nor glorify but rather to encourage an honest understanding of this complicated past.

MAIN CHARACTERS

John Morrison Birch, an American missionary and soldier, was killed by Communist soldiers in China in August 1945.

Ethel Ellis Birch and George Snider Birch, the parents of John Birch, were missionaries to India when John was born. After returning to the United States, they raised their family in New Jersey and Georgia.

Robert H. W. Welch Jr., a Boston businessman who marketed candy, founded the anti-communist John Birch Society in 1958.

J. Franklin Norris, an Independent Baptist preacher from Fort Worth, Texas, sent John Birch to China as a missionary.

Claire Lee Chennault, commanding general of the U.S. 14th Air Force in China, recruited Birch to set up radio intelligence networks in China.

Albert C. Wedemeyer, commanding general of U.S. forces in China, confronted Mao Zedong with information about the death of Birch and the detention of other American soldiers.

William F. Knowland, a Republican senator from California, revealed the story of John Birch on the floor of the U.S. Senate in September 1950.

Audrey Mair, Marjorie K. Tooker, and Dorothy Yuen lived and worked in China during the Second World War. Birch had romances with each of them.

NOTE ON CHINESE NAMES AND PLACES

THE LETTERS AND DOCUMENTS quoted in this book use the old Wade-Giles and, occasionally, other systems for converting Chinese characters into words using the Roman alphabet. In some cases, I have therefore retained the traditional spelling instead of the contemporary *pinyin* spelling system, especially where the original rendering is more familiar. The most important names and places (followed here by the *pinyin* version in parentheses) are: Chiang Kai-shek (Jiang Jieshi), Chungking (Chongqing), Kuomintang (Guomindang), Soong Ching-ling (Song Qingling), Soong Mei-ling (Song Meiling), Sun Yat-sen (Sun Zhongshan), Yenan (Yan'an), and the Yangtze (Yangzi) River.

MAPS

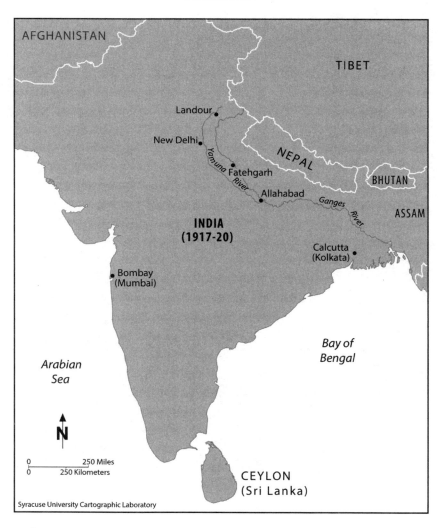

India, circa 1917–20

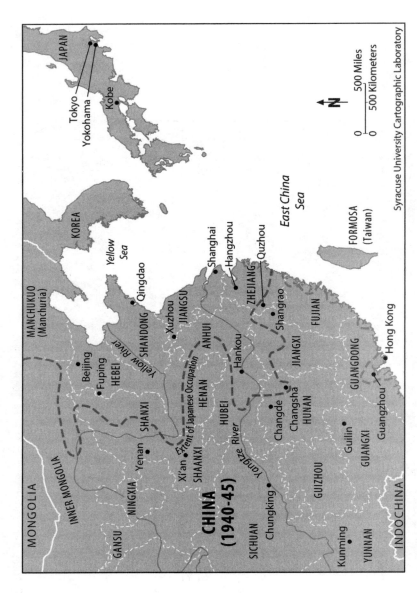

China and Japan, circa 1940–45

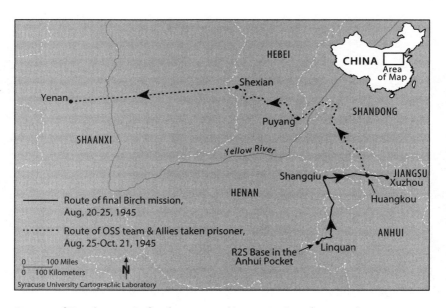

Route of Birch team's final mission (August–October 1945)

John Birch:
A Life

Introduction

ON THE MORNING OF September 12, 1945, a young woman driving a taxi came to the home of Ethel and George Birch at 1305 Ridge Avenue in Macon, Georgia, to deliver a Western Union telegram. Ethel hastily signed and tore open the envelope, hoping to find that her eldest son John was coming home from China, now that the war was over. It had been five years since she had seen him. Instead the telegram informed her that Captain John M. Birch was dead.

She immediately wrote to her three sons away from home serving in the military. Herbert was with the Navy in South Carolina, George Stanley was on Guam repairing aircraft for the Army Air Forces, and Robert was shipping out to China with the Navy from San Bruno, California. Robert reached China a few weeks later and was assigned duty as a truck driver in the north. Fearing the loss of a second son, Ethel wrote to her congressman, Carl Vinson, who arranged for him to be assigned to ship duty off the Chinese coast.[1]

She told her boys that John's death was "the hardest experience of our lives . . . Our family circle is broken for the first time, but John is safe in the Lord and we can praise His name who makes no mistakes."[2] Her husband did not yet know the news; he was on the road doing anti-typhus work for the state of Georgia. It was their twenty-eighth wedding anniversary.

A letter from the War Department in Washington soon followed, confirming the telegram: "The official casualty report states that your son was killed on August 25, 1945 en route to Suchow [Xuzhou], China on the

Lunghai Railway, as a result of stray bullets." General Edward Witsell, who signed the letter, expressed his deepest sympathy and the hope that "in time you may find sustaining comfort in knowing that he served his country honorably." The unit commander or chaplain would provide further detail.[3]

A subsequent letter from Major General Charles B. Stone, Commander of the 14th Air Force in China, praised Captain Birch's work as an intelligence liaison officer, "performed to a great extent behind enemy lines and often under hazardous conditions, in circumstances of extreme personal hardship and immediate danger. His unassuming manner, unswerving loyalty and personal courage earned him the respect and admiration of officers and enlisted men among both American and Chinese units alike . . . You can well be proud of your son's overseas record and contribution to victory."[4]

The Army later returned some personal articles to Mrs. Birch, including John's 35 mm Kodak camera and $211.45 he had left for safekeeping in Xi'an when he went on his final mission.[5] Because he "loved China" and wanted to stay there as a missionary after the war, she decided to leave her son's body where he had been buried in the city of Xuzhou, rather than bringing him back to Georgia. Yet she was determined to do whatever she could to ensure that his life would be recognized.

John Birch was better known in death than life. During the Cold War, his name was synonymous with right-wing extremism, and millions of Americans believed he was "a rabid communist-hater who would stop at nothing," as one journalist put it. There were those who disagreed and thought he was a hero who willingly gave up his own life to warn about the evils of communism in China. And there were even some who doubted that Birch ever existed. A high school teacher in Georgia told one of her students that he was just a figment of someone's imagination.[6] Most people did not realize that Birch had nothing to say about the use of his name by Robert Welch, a retired businessman who founded the John Birch Society (JBS) in 1958. Few knew that he was an American missionary and soldier during the Second World War in China, killed in a quarrel with Chinese Communist troops in 1945. He was twenty-seven.

Following in the footsteps of Senator Joseph McCarthy, Welch tapped into deep-seated fears of socialism, collectivism, and communism. During a period of mounting social change, he connected with a longing to restore traditional, albeit idealized, American values. He and other conservatives believed, then as now, that the growing centralized power of government threatened individual liberties guaranteed by the U.S. Constitution. A communist takeover would come not through military invasion but from creeping internal conspiracy. The antidotes for this metastasizing cancer, said Welch, were education and mass action.

The JBS mobilized nationwide campaigns to abolish the federal income tax, get the United States out of the United Nations, stop foreign aid, and support local police. Bircher billboards along highways throughout the country exclaimed "Save Our Republic—Impeach Earl Warren," the Chief Justice of the Supreme Court who supported desegregation of public schools. Despite the Society's radicalism, tens of thousands of Americans were members, most of them solid, middle-class citizens. Even if they disagreed with Welch on some issues, they were attracted by the Society's goal of "less government, more responsibility, and a better world." The JBS was one of the most influential and polarizing groups of its time. Its grassroots populism was a precursor of today's Republican Tea Party movement.[7]

This part of the JBS narrative is reasonably well-known, yet there are several unanswered questions about the Society's namesake: Why did Robert Welch choose an obscure missionary-soldier to represent his cause? Who really was Birch and how did he become the icon for a right-wing organization? What was he doing in China and how did he die? Was he truly a hero and martyr? Was there a conspiracy to cover up his death? And, if he had been alive, would he have agreed to join the JBS?

John Birch was, by all accounts, a brilliant student, a Christian fundamentalist, and a dedicated soldier. High-spirited and single-minded, he marched to his own drummer. Even those who disagreed with his strict religious beliefs respected his courage and commitment. A sensitive, steadfast young man, he was driven by a quest to share his faith with others. Brimming with idealism and self-confidence, he had thrown himself into an unknown country and culture in the midst of war. As a missionary, he strove to save the Chinese people from ignorance and superstition. As a soldier, he sought to protect China from a ruthless Japanese enemy.

Welch reinvented this story, transforming the fallen hero into a martyr. He saw in Birch not only a man of conviction and purpose but also a selfless soldier-patriot who courageously defended American values. Welch claimed that the resolute young Army officer understood the threat of socialist tyranny long before others and was willing to sacrifice his own life to *prove* the Communists were enemies who only pretended to be allies of the United States at that time. Murdered by Chinese Communists soon after Japan's surrender, he was not simply a victim of circumstances. He was memorialized as the first casualty of World War III—the Cold War.

Welch also believed Birch's death dramatized a larger narrative of deception and defeat. The devastating "loss" of China to the Communists, charged Welch and other critics, was not due to the ineptitude and corruption of Chiang Kai-shek's Nationalist government, nor to Communist policies of land reform and wealth redistribution. It was not the result of the success of the Chinese Communist Party (CCP) in harnessing anti-Japanese nationalism. Based on 'this reading of the past, Chiang collapsed because Washington had turned its back on his government in its hour of greatest need. History would have been different—China would have been America's Cold War partner and a bulwark against the Soviet Union—if only President Truman and Secretary of State Acheson had stayed the course.

Confusion, uncertainty, and ambiguity marked U.S. relations with China at the time of Birch's death in 1945. The United States, moreover, saw China mainly through the lenses of missionaries and soldiers, both of whom represented American idealism and ambition, not the brutal realities of the Chinese revolution. With the Communist victory, China suddenly was on the wrong side of a world divided between allies and enemies, good and evil, capitalism and communism. In this age of confrontation, it was easy to second-guess the motives of those who had warned that Chiang Kai-shek's collapse was inevitable.

The Chinese Communist victory produced anger, bewilderment, and scapegoating in American politics. Accusations over the collapse of U.S. policy in Asia mounted in the post-World War II period, starting with revelations about Roosevelt's secret agreements with Stalin at Yalta, growing when Beijing and Moscow signed a security alliance, and reaching a crescendo when Truman relieved General Douglas MacArthur of his command during the Korean War. Cold War paranoia gave birth to McCarthyism and then to the rise of the John Birch Society.

America's failure to rescue China was not a matter of ignorance, according to Welch. It was a case of duplicity, appeasement, and betrayal. It was a failure reflected in the untold story of John Birch. Beyond his purity and patriotism, there was an even more compelling reason to commemorate Birch. Welch was convinced that information about his murder was intentionally concealed from the American public by senior figures within the U.S. government—people who were sympathetic to the communist cause. To the conspiracy-minded founder of the JBS, the idea that the brutal murder of so heroic a young man had been suppressed was evidence of nothing less than treason. The fate of John Birch was one indication of a carefully orchestrated plan for worldwide domination directed from Moscow.

Welch's thinking was shaped by assumptions common to all conspiracy theories: nothing is as it seems, nothing happens by accident, and everything is connected.[8] All three elements were present in America's China narrative: the Communists actually were the foes of the United States, not friends or "agrarian reformers" as some claimed; the death of Birch was intentional, not random, because he was a threat to Mao Zedong's plans to take over China; and the suppression of information about his death was evidence of a larger pattern of betrayal within the U.S. government. Welch's unyielding belief in the hidden logic of events took his ideas to extremes not because he sought infamy or was psychotic, but because he was convinced the unknown and unseen could be explained.

The Birch Society has received renewed attention in recent years as scholars have investigated the origins of the modern conservative movement in U.S. politics and the more recent advent of the Tea Party. But these accounts typically give only the briefest summaries of John Birch. Robert Welch wanted to rescue him from obscurity, asking "why was so heroic, brilliant, and consecrated a patriot so completely unknown in America?" He laid the blame with "our Communist enemies" for "consigning him to temporary oblivion."[9] But instead of revealing Birch, Welch politicized his name and reputation, making him infamous instead of real.

Given Welch's reputation as an irresponsible right-wing fanatic, it was easy to dismiss Birch as his surrogate. Some observers who looked into his background reached the conclusion that his religious fundamentalism was every bit as ideological and radical as Welch's politics, and decided that the Society was aptly named. Defenders of the JBS, on the other hand, eulogized Birch for his unyielding religious principles and praised him as a patriot who was willing to give up his life to oppose atheistic communism.[10]

Certainly Birch was not the key to understanding an alleged communist conspiracy, and clearly his death did not explain the future course of United States-China relations. Had it not been for the torturous twists and turns of domestic American politics, almost no one would have heard of Birch's name. The saga would have ended quietly after his death, relegated to a historical footnote and overshadowed by far more momentous events in a chaotic postwar world. When the U.S. government finally released the details of his death in 1972, the information was treated as a minor addendum to early Cold War history. No one was inspired to write a well-documented, objective study to explain who Birch was and why the John Birch Society posthumously adopted his name.[11] Yet as metaphor and myth, the life of John Birch is a story worth telling because it offers a window to the fanaticism of religion, the absolutism of war, and the extremism of politics.

This is a book about the use and misuse of history, a cautionary tale about America's complex and important relationship with China. Part One explains how John Birch was shaped by his parents and siblings, his religious faith, and his upbringing in New Jersey and Georgia. We learn of his determination to become a missionary and his decision to go to China, a nation fighting for its survival in a war against Japan. In Part Two, we see how Birch reinvented himself as an intelligence officer after joining the U.S. Army in China, working for Claire Chennault, the famous leader of the Flying Tigers. In letters to three women he reveals his innermost thoughts in his search for love during this phase of his life. Part Three presents the circumstances of Birch's unexpected death, which was the subject of a heated conversation between Mao Zedong, leader of the Chinese Communists, and Albert Wedemeyer, commander of American forces in China. It foreshadowed a dramatic shift from ally to enemy in U.S. relations with China.

Part Four shows how Birch became the namesake for the controversial John Birch Society, after Senator William Knowland identified Birch as a martyr for the cause of anti-communism. The book concludes with an assessment of the "real" John Birch and what his legacy says about American politics and U.S. perceptions of China.

Part One

Saving Souls

JOHN BIRCH BELONGED TO a long-standing tradition of American missionaries, diplomats, businessmen, and soldiers who believed it was their God-given duty to remake China into a Christian, capitalist, democratic nation that looked like the United States. That lofty goal seemed almost within reach when China achieved a degree of unity, stability, and prosperity under the Nationalist (Kuomintang or KMT) Party during the early 1930s. Generalissimo Chiang Kai-shek, who led the government, and Madame Chiang, his American-educated wife, were Christians. Americans saw opportunities and felt an obligation to enlighten the Chinese people.

The concept of the United States as exemplar was shared to some extent on the Chinese side. After the once proud and mighty dynastic system collapsed in 1911, China's leaders desperately sought ways to restore the country's wealth, power, and prestige. America proved to be an attractive model; it was a young nation that had freed itself from British colonialism and rapidly become a major power. Perhaps the secrets of success could be unlocked by sending China's best and brightest to study science and technology in the United States. Perhaps

American-style democracy and its culture, including religion, could reveal the answers for overcoming China's backwardness.[1]

Yet hopes for recovery of greatness turned into a nightmare, with tens of millions of deaths in more than a decade of war and civil war from 1937 to 1949. China's plight during the war against Japan evoked an outpouring of sympathy in America. The U.S. government mounted a major campaign to portray the Chinese people as heroic allies and China as a progressive, democratic nation that shared basic American values and goals. *Why We Fight: The Battle of China*, a wartime propaganda film, equated Sun Yat-sen, founding father of the Republic of China, with George Washington. As the film's narrator explained, "The oldest and the youngest of the world's great nations, together with the British Commonwealth, fight side by side in a struggle that is as old as China itself—the struggle of freedom against slavery, civilization against barbarism, good against evil. Upon their victory depends the future of mankind."[2]

Time and *Life* magazines, published by Henry R. Luce, the son of Presbyterian missionaries to China, portrayed a people in desperate need of American help. Luce was heavily involved with United China Relief, a humanitarian agency created in 1941 to coordinate the work of eight different agencies ranging from the American Bureau for Medical Aid to China to the American Committee for Chinese War Orphans. Money was raised for medical needs, child welfare, construction of schools, and disaster relief. These widely publicized efforts drew upon an image of China as supplicant and ward. Saving China became a moral imperative for Americans.[3]

Pearl Buck, famous for her novel *The Good Earth* about peasant life in China, acknowledged the financial success of United China Relief but took Luce to task for perpetuating an image of virtuous benevolence: "Why does the relationship between the Americans and Chinese always take the shape of patronage? Why are we forever telling the Chinese to remember all our good deeds toward them? The Chinese feel that these good deeds have been to our advantage,—as they have—and it ill becomes us to insist upon our own goodness. Yet again and again the American mind reverts to this feeling of righteousness toward China."[4]

It was in this context—armed with righteousness, resolute in his faith, and determined to save the Chinese from themselves—that John Birch became a foreign missionary. He journeyed to China, blissful and unknowing, in search of souls and his own destiny. His quest was sanctioned by God, blessed by his parents, and enabled by a Texas preacher. The intense fire burning inside him would purge any doubts. With clarity and certainty of purpose, he was determined not to fail.

I

Missionary to China

IN THE SUMMER OF 1940, John Birch and his colleague Oscar Wells—aware that China was at war with Japan, but knowing little more—set out for the Far East. Crossing the country by train from Texas to San Francisco, they visited the Golden Gate International Exposition on Treasure Island before boarding another train to Seattle. There they picked up their visas and sailed from U.S. shores on July 1, 1940, on the *Hie Maru*, a passenger-cargo ship of Japan's NYK shipping line. Birch had no misgivings about traveling on a Japanese ship. It was the least expensive option for crossing the Pacific.

After a stop in Vancouver, they traveled north along the Canadian coast and then headed south of the Aleutian Islands, awaking one night to find the sea splashing in through an open porthole in their second-class cabin. They spent time with other passengers (including missionaries returning to Japan, Korea, and India), attended religious services, updated their inoculations for cholera and typhoid, watched newsreels and a film about Japan, took photographs, and played shuffleboard. Birch declined an invitation to a dance in first class, and wrote a letter to his Grandma Bertie in New Jersey instead.

When the ship reached Yokohama about two weeks later, the eager young men took in the sights for the next two days. They toured the famous shrines at Nikko, Lake Tyuzenzi, the Imperial Palace gardens, and Hibiya Park. Birch was pleased that the Japanese they met, including a young cavalry lieutenant, were cordial and willing to accept the Bible tracts placed in their hands. He admired Japan's beauty but was reminded of the lines of the English hymn *From Greenland's Icy Mountains*, which captured the evangelical mood of the day:

> From Greenland's icy mountains, from India's coral strand,
> Where Afric's sunny fountains roll down their golden sand,
> From many an ancient river, from many a palmy plain,
> They call us to deliver their land from error's chain.
>
> What though the spicy breezes blow soft o'er Ceylon's isle;
> Though every prospect pleases, and only man is vile:
> In vain with lavish kindness the gifts of God are strown;
> The heathen in his blindness bows down to wood and stone.
>
> Shall we, whose souls are lighted with wisdom from on high,
> Shall we to those benighted the lamp of life deny?
> Salvation! O salvation! The joyful sound proclaim,
> Till earth's remotest nation has learned Messiah's Name.
>
> Waft, waft, ye winds, His story, and you, ye waters, roll
> Till, like a sea of glory, it spreads from pole to pole;
> Till o'er our ransomed nature the Lamb for sinners slain,
> Redeemer, King, Creator, in bliss returns to reign.[1]

Wells returned to the ship alone, Birch lost track of time, and the *Hie Maru* sailed from Yokohama without him. Fortunately, the NYK office gave him a free railway ticket down the coast to Kobe where he could rendezvous with his companion. In the meantime, he went to see the movie *Stanley and Livingstone*. That night from the train window, he watched the magnificent sight of Mt. Fuji shining in the moonlight. In Kobe, he and Wells transferred to another ship, the *Taiyou Maru*, which set course for China. It was not a dangerous voyage; China's modest navy had been devastated, and the Americans and European powers were still neutral. In Shanghai, Fred Donnelson from the Fundamental Baptists met the newly minted missionaries at the docks.[2] A photo taken soon after their arrival shows Birch and Wells standing with their white pith helmets, grinning widely, and fashionably dressed in white summer suits with white shoes.

Shanghai's days of colonial privilege were numbered by the time the two Americans arrived. The city's Chinese districts had been bombed, shelled, and then occupied when the Japanese invaded eastern China in 1937. The Soviet Union provided Chinese forces with ammunition, supplies, airplanes, and pilots, but it was not enough to alter the equation. (The Chinese Communists, isolated in the northwest, were not a military factor at this point.) Chiang Kai-shek's army fought tenaciously, but after three months had suffered about 187,000 casualties.

Oscar Wells (left) and John Birch soon after their arrival in Shanghai in July 1940. Credit: Arlington Baptist College Heritage Collection.

Trading territory for time, his remaining troops were forced to retreat inland, eventually making their way to the landlocked southwest beyond the reach of enemy ground troops but still vulnerable to aerial bombardments.[3]

Until the United States and its allies declared war on Japan in December 1941, Shanghai's International Settlement and French Concession were treated as safe havens. With "extraterritorial" status derived from treaties imposed on the Qing dynasty in the nineteenth century, these neutral zones were exempt from Chinese—and now Japanese—legal control. Shanghai had been a place of sanctuary in the past, during the massive mid-nineteenth-century civil war with the Taipings, the 1911 Revolution that overthrew the imperial system, and conflicts between warlord factions. By June 1938, there were 170,000 Chinese refugees living in the city's foreign areas, and that winter thousands of men, women, and children (many of them Jewish) arrived from Central Europe, in part because no visa was required to enter Shanghai.

Birch understood hardship and poverty from his youth, but the suffering from war, disease, and hunger could not be compared with anything he had witnessed before. "Starving and horribly diseased or wounded beggars line the streets," he wrote to his parents.[4] One grim measure of desperation was the "exposed corpse index"—the number of dead bodies found on the streets. A total of 72,857 dead were reported found in the International Settlement in 1939. Yet despite the threat of worldwide war, thousands of foreign businessmen, merchants, journalists, diplomats, and missionaries continued living and working in Shanghai. Due to the low cost of Chinese labor, the city still prospered as a center of industry, commerce, and investment.[5] It was a place where anything could be bought, anything could be sold.

Surrounded by uncertainty, with virtually no understanding of China and very little money, Birch was undaunted. He preached through an interpreter to about six hundred people on his first Sunday in Shanghai—fifty-nine came forward and were "saved"—and later he spoke on the radio of the Shanghai Christian Broadcasting Association.[6] His immediate job, though, was to learn Chinese. The written language is essentially uniform throughout the country, but various dialects and sub-dialects are mutually unintelligible, which posed a dilemma for him. Should he study Mandarin (*Guoyu* or *Putonghua)*, the standard national language, which was not yet widespread in 1940, or concentrate on mastering the language spoken in the area where he would live and work? (To this day, people born in east China use the local Wu dialect as their first language.) Birch opted for Mandarin, which his teachers almost certainly would have spoken with a strong Shanghai flavor. Enrolled at the Shanghai Language School, the diligent young man reported after two weeks that he could speak over 300 words and read about 150 characters.

Birch was modest about his Chinese language skills, although others observed that he became a flawless speaker. Donald Willmott, the son of China missionaries, told me that Birch, whom he met toward the end of the war, "had excellent Chinese and did not need an interpreter." Bryan Glass, a U.S. intelligence officer who grew up in China,

Effie Donnelson, John Birch, Oscar Wells, Charlie Qi, and Fred Donnelson, (front center, left to right) with a congregation in Shanghai, summer 1940. The Chinese characters read, "Believe in Jesus and you and your family will be saved." Credit: Arlington Baptist College Heritage Collection.

recalled Birch was so accomplished that he could discuss Chinese opera and was good at translating American humor for Chinese colleagues. While Birch developed considerable ability during his five years in China, he nonetheless would have been challenged by local accents and regional dialects, just like any native speaker. Paul Frillmann, a former missionary who also spoke Chinese and worked with Birch in the U.S. Army, observed that he spoke with a very strange accent.[7] This most likely was a reflection of his initial studies in Shanghai and Hangzhou.

At the Missionary Home Annex on Bubbling Well Road where Birch and Wells first stayed, they met a number of missionaries who were beginning or ending vacations or furloughs. "They were for the most part old, pessimistic, tired, and quarrelsome," wrote Birch.[8] The disgruntled old-timers made him appreciate Fred Donnelson's optimism all the more. Donnelson, who showed Birch and Wells the ropes, had come to China in 1933 with his wife and two children. A genial, round-faced 42-year-old, he had been pastor of the Plainfield, Illinois First Baptist Church, which had recently broken away from the Northern Baptist Convention to become independent. One day a missionary named Josephine Sweet visited and convinced him to give up everything and follow her to Asia where "999 out of every thousand Chinese were tripping into eternal hell!" Unlike some others, observed Donnelson, Mrs. Sweet "had not gone from the extreme of modernism to the extreme of Pentecostalism and fanaticism." She was just an old-fashioned Baptist with snow-white hair.[9]

Known to all as Mother Sweet, she first went to China in 1893 with her husband, William S. Sweet. He taught at the Wayland Academy in Hangzhou, but did not get along with the headmaster, E. H. Clayton, and in 1914 decided to cash in his life insurance policy and become an independent missionary, free of any denominational ties. After his death three years later, Josephine Sweet founded a girls' school and went on to build four chapels in Hangzhou and fifteen churches in the countryside. She gave the girls Western names of flowers and the boys names from the Bible. The first neon sign ever seen in the city was placed over the entrance to her Central Church. Its Chinese characters read: "Jesus Saves!" A bell for the church tower was ordered from the Montgomery Ward catalogue.[10] After hearing of her success in teaching and training young Chinese to become Christians, Frank Norris, a Texas preacher who saw tremendous opportunities for evangelism in China, enthusiastically adopted Sweet's mission under the auspices of the Fundamental Baptist Missionary Fellowship and his churches in Fort Worth and Detroit.

"What a need and what an opportunity!"

Birch was asked to carry on Mother Sweet's work in Hangzhou since she was not in good health and was now living in Shanghai. He made an initial trip to Hangzhou with Wells, Donnelson, and Beauchamp Vick, pastor of Detroit's Temple Baptist Church, on August 20, 1940. It was a hot, dirty five-hour train ride from Shanghai. A pass was required and Japanese soldiers rode in every car with rifles and bayonets at the ready. Pastor Du Qingshen [Du Wah-sen] met the three Americans at the station and they rode in several rickshaws to Sweet's Central Church. They were rowed around the West Lake and toured the city in rented cars. The "main business section seemed almost deserted," reported Vick. Many people "looked like walking skeletons. . . . I've never seen so many beggars or such persistent ones as in these Chinese cities."[11]

Hangzhou—the capital of Zhejiang Province and a center for tea, silk, and rice—is about 150 miles southwest of Shanghai. On December 24, 1937, an "orgy of looting, raping and killing" took place following the Japanese occupation of the city, according to a Canadian insurance man who was there at the time. Soldiers raided wine shops and then went on a drunken rampage. There were no mass executions as there were in Nanjing, where tens of thousands of civilians and prisoners were murdered, but women and girls in both cities were raped and killed by Japanese soldiers. Many smeared their faces with mud to make themselves unattractive, while "hundreds of others hid in churches and the homes of foreigners" in Hangzhou, reported the *New York Times*. Retreating Chinese troops looted rice shops, and Japanese soldiers carried off what was left in trucks and on horses or donkeys.[12]

Birch wrote that he arrived in Hangzhou "in the midst of gathering gloom."[13] He described the scene with a mixture of excitement and dismay:

Once China's most beautiful city, and still quite lovely in its hills and lakes, rivers and canals, it now lies in blackened ruins in many sections, thanks to the war. Most of its million people have fled, and the several hundred thousand who remain are starved for food, as well as for the Gospel. Many missions, churches and schools have been abandoned. What a need and what an opportunity! The Japanese will never conquer these people.[14]

Where some only saw desperation and despair, Birch was certain that the Gospel's message about salvation in the life to come would bring hope. He would later realize that ordinary people who had been skeptical of Christianity now welcomed the church not only for its message but also because it provided protection and medical care. As historian Timothy Brooks writes, "The visible service that Chinese Christians rendered to their country did much to indigenize this foreign religion: the church was earning its right to a place in Chinese society."[15]

After three months of language study in Shanghai, Birch returned to Hangzhou, where about ten American and twenty British as well as a few French Catholic missionaries were still living. He taught in a boys' school and led religious services with the help of Pastor Du. The foreigners worked together in relief and social welfare efforts, offering their neutral mission compounds as safe zones. Birch wrote, "We are feeding eighty-some Christians here ... to keep them from starving; they are mostly widows, orphans, and very old people." He observed that his colleagues evidenced "quite a bit of lukewarm modernism," meaning they were not conservative fundamentalists.[16]

Amid shrinking financial support back in the United States, there were growing doubts about the moral justification for the missionary enterprise. In 1932, John D. Rockefeller Jr., a devout Baptist and generous sponsor of missions, commissioned William Ernest Hocking, a Harvard philosopher, and his colleagues to study the work of seven Protestant denominations in China, Japan, Burma, and India. They spelled out various misgivings in their report, *Re-Thinking Missions*, advising that there should be greater respect for local religions in other parts of the world: "It is clearly not the duty of the Christian missionary to attack the non-Christian systems of religion—it is his primary duty to present in positive form his conception of the way of life and let it speak for itself." Proclaiming the Gospel and "expounding single-mindedly the Christianity and culture of the West" was not effective, stated the report. "Ministry to the secular needs of men in the spirit of Christ . . . *is* evangelism, in the right sense of the word; to the Christian no philanthropy can be mere secular relief." Furthermore, each mission should plan for "the transfer of its responsibility to the hands of the nationals." Hocking pointedly asked, "Have these missions in some measure finished their work?"[17]

Pearl Buck fanned the flames of the fire ignited by the Hocking report when she addressed a large audience of Presbyterian women at the Hotel Astor in New York City in December 1932. She spoke on the topic with considerable authority, as she had been raised by missionary parents in China. She was, she confessed, deeply disillusioned with the narrowness and bigotry she saw in some Americans who were "scornful of any civilization except their own" and "lacking in sympathy for the people they were supposed to be saving." Among those sent to China, too many were ignorant, mediocre, arrogant people who only preached hell and damnation. It was time to face the fact that "the old reasons for foreign missions are gone from the minds and hearts of many of us, certainly from those of us who are young." Many Chinese had told her, "Preach to us no more, but share with us that better and more abundant life which your Christ lived." If there was a case to be made for foreign missions, said Buck, "it would depend on selecting more highly qualified persons with more specific training and experience, suited to some particular place of need."[18]

The skepticism that threatened to undermine the mainline mission establishment did not seem to faze hardcore evangelists. In their eyes, the millenarian conviction that Christ's return was imminent made the task of sharing Christ's message of redemption that much more urgent. The impending day of the Last Judgment, as revealed in the book of Revelation, compelled them to make saving souls a priority over rescuing temporal society. There was no time for delay. Focusing on individual conversions rather than more visible, expensive institutions like colleges and hospitals, they dismissed the likes of William Hocking and Pearl Buck as voices of liberalism and modernism.[19] Only one or two persons ran many faith missions, as they were called, so their overhead was minimal.

Birch's commitment to old-fashioned, Bible-believing mission work did not waver. The Independent Baptists, he explained, "stand apart from others because we cannot have fellowship with those who abandon the fundamentals of the Faith, or who fail to observe Scriptural Baptism, or who deny the doctrine of grace." He whole-heartedly embraced the credo of end-time prophecies, and was convinced that the war in China "and the ensuing federations will set the world stage, as never before, for the rise of anti-Christ!" He wrote to his Aunt May that he was using her money "to buy New Testaments, food for starving Christians, evangelistic trips to the countryside, and my daily bread."[20]

Fred Donnelson reassured supporters back home that the work of the Fundamental Baptist Missionary Fellowship "is primarily devoted to the simple, direct method of preaching the Gospel." He also admitted, "in this hour of China's distress, we feel that to close our eyes to the physical suffering of the people would be heartless." There are people "who had never known want before and who are even now too proud to beg, are penniless, without food and clothing and in many cases their homes have been completely destroyed. With the thought of helping a little to alleviate this suffering, our Mission is providing one good meal a day for a hundred needy people in Hangchow [Hangzhou]." Quilts would be helpful gifts, as would be medicines such as aspirin, quinine, and various kinds of salves. But there was constant pressure to show donors that evangelism was paramount in order to keep the dollars flowing. How many revival meetings were held? How many baptisms performed? Donnelson described China as "a great harvest field."[21]

After the December 1937 assault on Hangzhou, Donnelson, his wife Effie, and their two children left for the United States, frightened and dispirited. The Japanese had confiscated Donnelson's prized Ford V-8 sedan, which he had used to transport his tent for revival meetings in the countryside where he conducted baptisms in canals, creeks, and ponds. Despite the dangers, they returned to China one year later to open a church and Bible institute in Shanghai, where the war was still held in abeyance. Mornings were devoted to study and the afternoons and evenings to preaching the Gospel.

Beyond Shanghai, the war raged on. Kepler Van Evera, a Presbyterian missionary in Hangzhou, conveyed an especially bleak picture of conditions in the region. "For the past two or three weeks," he wrote in May 1941, "airplanes have been humming above us daily on their way to their destructive work along the railway leading into Kiangsi [Jiangxi]." The eastern provinces of occupied China were "ridden by the fear of banditry and guerrilla warfare, the cruelty of soldiers and the various puppet regimes." Many people held no hope for the future. Poverty and despair, epidemics and diseases of malnutrition "prey[ed] upon the bodies of the poor and undernourished." Inflation was rampant and it was sometimes necessary to use as many as four different types of currency because of overlapping political jurisdictions. Poppies were cultivated in districts under Japanese control to raise money through the sale of opium and heroin.

Van Evera and his wife, Pauline, spent their time managing refugee centers; feeding children; distributing grain and clothing; and teaching skills like knitting, weaving, tailoring, gardening, and cooking. Corn, beans, and vegetables made up the diet of children in welfare programs. "On holidays we try to give them a treat of a bit of bean curd. Only those who are wealthy or hold government jobs eat rice these days." The Hangzhou Red Cross Committee, composed of representatives from Protestant and Catholic missions and churches, was able to provide cracked wheat for nourishment and quinine for malaria.[22]

"Joy in the midst of sorrow"

Anyone entering deeply into another culture is caught on the horns of a dilemma. Outsiders arrive with their own ideas and a particular version of reality. If you hold fast to these preconceptions without compromise and refuse to accept the idea that a new realm may have different but equally valid answers, you place yourself in a position of isolation which will likely result in confusion, frustration, and anger. Why can't the local people see the light and understand the proper way to do things? Why are they so ignorant and backward? If, on the other hand, you uncritically embrace the strange new world, proclaiming its wisdom and virtue, you run the risk of losing your bearings and may be tempted to jettison your values and beliefs. The price of such enlightenment, or "going native," can be steep.

Instead of confronting the challenge of how to adapt, some Westerners literally walled themselves off from China by living in compounds, eating Western food, and buying Western clothing from mail-order catalogues. Such women and men learned only enough Chinese to communicate with their servants in pidgin. Yet there were others who engaged with Chinese society wholeheartedly, becoming proficient in the language, eating Chinese food, and adopting Chinese dress. They were optimistic that not only were Western and Chinese cultures compatible, but that there could be a convergence of ideas and a melding of both traditions. It was a longstanding idea beginning with the Jesuit missionaries led by Matteo Ricci in the seventeenth century. Some of their nineteenth century successors took China so seriously that they became experts in the country's history, philosophy, linguistics, literature, and other fields. These "missionaries in reverse" helped to establish the modern academic study of China when they returned to North America and Europe.

Birch combined the two contrasting approaches for adapting to his new environment. On the one hand, he held fast to his own beliefs and resisted the idea that Chinese religions should be equated with Christianity. At the same time, he was curious, adventurous, and quickly accepted many aspects of the Chinese way of doing things. Rather than retreating to the relative comfort of Shanghai, he sought out the poorest, most benighted Chinese in Hangzhou and beyond.

Many Chinese were ambivalent if not hostile to Westerners who sought to impose their thinking on them. They resented the privileges granted to foreigners under the unequal treaties forced on the Qing government and the racist immigration policies of Western countries. Yet there were always those Chinese who were willing to work as interpreters, interlocutors, collaborators, colleagues, and partners. It was a practice going back to the earliest days of the Canton trading system when Westerners were assigned compradors—men who were responsible for managing the outsiders. The foreigners' ability to identify such intermediaries was a key to their success.

Not all missionaries were as forthright in admitting how much they depended on their Chinese coworkers to negotiate language and culture as Fred Donnelson. He said of his early days in Hangzhou, "It was almost like being a child again, so strange were the habits and customs, but we loved it. We would go up and down the streets on a Sunday evening, using the few words that we had learned to invite people to come to the Gospel services." Because he was not born and raised in China like some missionaries, Donnelson quickly realized that becoming fluent in Chinese would take many years. After watching young Chinese preachers and Bible women—"how zealous they were for the Lord and for souls and how able they were in reaching their own people with a little help from foreign friends"—he wisely decided that delegating authority to Chinese workers was the most efficient and effective way to operate.[23]

Pastor Du Qingshen and a Chinese evangelist named Wu Meng'en played the go-between role for Birch, showing him how to negotiate and survive. On one occasion Birch and Wu visited a humble rural church some sixty miles south of Hangzhou in the town of Huangshan. "The roof is thatch, the walls are mud, and the floor is the earth, but the glory of the Lord of Hosts is there," wrote Birch. Located in a kind of no-man's land, the local Christians lived "in the midst of fighting, burning, looting, and all the other horrors of war, along with all sorts of persecutions from the unbelievers." They were stopped along the way by a Japanese sentry who threatened to tear up Wu's pass, but otherwise had no trouble. "I gave out tracts and a word or two of testimony at villages and crossroads along the way," noted Birch. During another trip to a village, Pastor Du preached and Birch led a communion service in a house made of bamboo and straw. The Japanese had burned everything else to the ground.[24]

Despite the dangers and travails, Birch was full of enthusiasm for his new life, writing to members of a church back in Macon, Georgia, "There is war, starvation, disease, sin, idolatry, superstition, suffering and death on every side, but our wonderful Savior keeps saving souls, answering prayers, and giving joy in the midst of sorrow."[25]

2

Evangelizing the World

FROM HIS MOTHER, JOHN Birch would learn courage, determination, and leadership. From his father, he would gain stubbornness and a fear of failure. As so often happens with firstborn sons, John would grow up striving for excellence, eager to realize the ambitions his parents had for him.

Ethel May Ellis, his mother, was smart and able. She was born in 1890 in the southern New Jersey town of Vineland, where her father owned an orchard. After graduating second in her class from Vineland High School in 1908, she took a stenography and typing course in Camden, New Jersey, and for the next two years was secretary to Henry Goddard, director of the Training School of the Psychological Research Laboratory in Vineland. It was one of the first centers in the country for children with intellectual and developmental disabilities.[1] With the money she earned, Ethel enrolled in the College of Wooster, a well-respected liberal arts school in central Ohio, affiliated with the Presbyterian Church. The college yearbook praised her as someone who "never says an unkind, cutting, or cruel thing about anyone." Graduating with a BS in biology and a minor in education, she planned to attend Women's Medical College in Philadelphia, a dream that was not achieved. Later in life she told a reporter, "I always said that if I had been a man, I'd be a preacher, a lawyer or a medical missionary."[2]

John's father, George Snider Birch Jr., two years younger than Ethel, was born and raised on a farm near Macon, Georgia, where cotton was the principal crop. When he failed the first year of high school, he was sent to a military boarding school in north Georgia. "My parents thought the mountain climate, the military discipline, and the change of educational environment would work together for my good." He then entered Emory College in Oxford, Georgia (the original campus of Emory University), but left after only one semester. In his application for missionary service, George admitted to going astray when he allowed fraternity life to interfere with his studies. But he had reformed: "I have smoked less than a dozen times, having used pipe, cigars, and cigarettes. Alcoholic beverages and narcotic drugs do not tempt me. I have never taken a cup of coffee, and quit tea several years since." He also confessed, "My temper used to get from under control, and the sex passion has been hard to keep in its bounds," but "neither has ever caused me any serious trouble."[3] After his bumpy start at Emory, George entered the University of Georgia. "My studies were rather difficult to master the freshman year, and I spent a large part of my remaining waking hours in Bible study, YMCA work, and choir practice." He also taught Sunday school and was doing "some social investigation among Negroes." Eventually he found his stride and graduated with a BS in agriculture in 1915.[4]

Religion was central to social and intellectual life on American campuses during the early twentieth century, and Ethel and George were active in various Christian youth organizations. Ethel was secretary and, in her senior year, president of the Young Women's Christian Association (YWCA) at Wooster College. George was secretary, missionary chairman, and then president of the Young Men's Christian Association (YMCA) at University of Georgia. Ethel represented Wooster at the YWCA conference in Eagles Mere, Pennsylvania, and was active in Christian Endeavor, a popular evangelical society. George attended a YMCA Conference in the Blue Ridge Mountains of North Carolina.

These hubs for group activities organized retreats, sponsored big sister and brother programs for incoming freshmen, held Bible and mission study classes, raised money for local community projects, and invited inspirational speakers to campus. When two prominent preachers visited Wooster in November 1914, their impassioned entreaties for Christian values struck a chord. According to the *Cincinnati Enquirer*, "improper literature and immoral pictures, among which were several prints of 'September Morn,' were given up to the flames of a bonfire at the college gymnasium Saturday night as a climax to a week of prayer for students, during which was reached a religious fervor never equaled at Wooster College."

Many of Wooster's young men confessed to wrongdoing and adopted resolutions "promising to refrain from profanity, from late hours and from inattention to college work." The college's athletic authorities declared that "confessions of football players explain the poor showing of the varsity team during the season." Ethel Ellis, representing the YWCA, said the women adopted no resolutions, but their meetings featured "scores of voluntary confessions." It seems that female students—who had a 10:30 p.m. curfew and could be punished for smoking—had less leeway for mischief.[5]

After graduating in 1915, Ethel applied to teach at the Berry Schools in northwest Georgia, and it was there that she met George when he arrived the year after. The Berry Schools, situated near the Oostanaula River in the foothills of the Appalachian Mountains, were founded by Martha Berry, a remarkable woman who devoted her life to educating the sons and daughters of sharecroppers and tenant farmers from the region. She was at the vanguard of a social reform movement that

Members of the Young Women's Christian Association at Wooster College in 1915. Ethel Ellis, second from the left in the front row, was president in her senior year. Credit: The College of Wooster Libraries, Special Collections.

combined education and work. A boys' school was founded in 1902, and a school for girls was established in 1909. Both were "positively Christian in spirit and methods" but nonsectarian and nondenominational. Their purpose was to provide disadvantaged young people with "a thorough, liberal, practical education at small cost." The schools grew rapidly, attracting poor children from several southern states. Theodore Roosevelt, who admired Berry's ideas, invited her to the White House in 1907, and after leaving the presidency visited the schools on a rainy day in October 1910.[6]

Martha Berry was a model of independence and enterprise, a formidable organizer and fundraiser. Her energy and dedication must have been an inspiration for Ethel, who led an extremely active life at the girls' school: teaching English to elementary and high school students, coaching plays, advising the YWCA, teaching Sunday school classes, and chaperoning girls at parties. She was also secretary to the principal, Miss Brewster, for two hours a day.[7] George came in 1916 to teach in the agricultural department, which had a dairy herd of seventy cows for milk, butter and beef, and a large truck garden with a variety of vegetables.

The Berry Schools' ethos of learning through labor was something Ethel and George embraced and passed down to their own children. Students had classes in the morning and five hours of work in the afternoon to pay their school fees. The boys made furniture and did plumbing, painting, road work, farming, and woodcutting. They also cared for trees, shrubs, flowers, and lawns. The girls learned "the preparation and service of meals, simple nursing, sewing, laundering, household management, house decoration—in a word, the making of a cheerful, comfortable home." Students learned dairying, poultry-raising, and gardening. Graduates became farmers, mechanics, carpenters, cooks, preachers, teachers, and homemakers.[8]

But yearning to see more of the world and inspired by a commitment to helping others, Ethel and George decided to exchange their busy and well-ordered existence at the Berry Schools for the uncertainty of far-off lands. "Working with girls who live way back in the country or mountains for the past two years has been fulfilling," Ethel wrote to her Wooster classmates. "I have grown to love the girls and the work very much, but if an opportunity for greater service comes I want to be ready for it."[9] Her religious beliefs had grown stronger. During the summer of 1916 she returned to Vineland and experienced a spiritual epiphany when she took a course in Biblical prophecy, "especially the prophecies yet to be fulfilled." Through this and her father's influence, her "whole Christian life was changed: there came a greater infilling of the Holy Spirit, an awakening to the realization of God's plan for each of His children, and a peace and joy" she had never known before. Along with this came a greater desire to witness for Him."[10] By the following summer, she was engaged to George and was applying to go with him to India as a foreign missionary.

Missionaries to India

George and Ethel were recruited to serve as foreign missionaries through the Student Volunteer Movement (SVM), an organization that emerged from the YMCA during the late nineteenth century. George signed his pledge to become a missionary at a World Student Volunteer Convention in Kansas City in 1914 with three other delegates from the University of Georgia. He hoped to study at the Yale School of Religion after graduation, and then to become a preacher or teacher overseas, possibly in Africa or India. Ethel made the decision to become a foreign missionary during her junior year in college when she signed the Student Volunteer declaration.[11] Mr. and Mrs. W. T. Mitchell, missionaries on furlough at Wooster, encouraged her to consider going to India. Convinced that there was an immediate need in that vast land, she decided to put aside her plans for medical school for the time being.[12]

Promising the "evangelization of the world in this generation," the SVM had chapters on campuses across America, tapping into the energy and idealism of young Americans and sending them overseas with minimal preparation to proselytize and to build schools and hospitals. Typical candidates were earnest, trusting, and naive. Except for the daughters and sons of missionaries, virtually none of them had any international experience or spoke languages like Hindi or Chinese. It was the same type of youthful altruism and self-confidence that inspired young people to join the U.S. Peace Corps in the 1960s.

Small denominational colleges like Wooster and Oberlin (another Presbyterian school in Ohio)—where a number of missionary children (known as mish kids or MKs) were enrolled—were especially fertile grounds for recruiting. Missionaries on furlough from Asia, Africa, Latin America, and the Middle East would visit these campuses and exhort students to follow Christian lives and consider dedicating themselves to the foreign mission cause. Working at home in the United States was a worthy cause, they argued, but the need for service was so much greater in other countries. Traveling and living abroad was an exciting prospect, despite the very real risks of disease and other hazards. Few careers promised more by way of self-fulfillment and adventure during the late nineteenth and early twentieth centuries. Missionary life was especially attractive to young women whose professional options were otherwise limited to teaching, nursing, and secretarial work. For this reason, a high percentage of Protestant missionaries were single women.[13]

Ethel had taken a mission study class on China and India at Wooster, and in December 1916 inquired with the Woman's Foreign Missionary Society of the Presbyterian Church in Philadelphia about an opening at Huai Yuan, a mission station in central China's Anhui Province. (Ironically, it was the same area where John Birch would spend his final days.) She was informed that the position had been filled and was encouraged to spend a year taking courses at the Moody Bible Institute in Chicago. "We want you to have all the Bible training you can get," wrote the board secretary. "At the same time, as you know, you need experience in teaching and to give special attention to the problem of education."[14]

A few months later, George was informed by Mr. Orville Reed at the Presbyterian mission office in New York City that "as a general rule we prefer to have our missionaries go out married," because married men generally are more stable.[15] Encouraged by this policy, George proposed to Ethel—much to her surprise—and she accepted. They resigned from the Berry Schools, submitted their medical examinations and vaccination certificates, and applied for U.S. passports and Indian visas.

The Student Volunteer secretary at the University of Georgia recommended George to the Presbyterian Mission Board specifically for agricultural work at a new college in India. He was interested, but was concerned that he lacked enough experience for the job and worried about his parents' age and their declining health. Because of college debts, he might instead work one or two years in farm demonstration work, possibly as a county agent. He was also unsure about the military draft, since America was now at war in Europe. After weighing all of these considerations, he finally decided that his knowledge of agriculture "may be of use in the field, as an opening wedge into the hearts of some." The Army did not select him, nor did he volunteer for military service, stating that the call to be a missionary was a higher duty. Because the second coming of Christ is a "vital reality," he wrote to the Presbyterian board, the critical purpose of this age must be to spread the Gospel in the "dark corners" of the world. He hoped to take the Scofield Correspondence Course to improve his knowledge of the Bible, but never had this opportunity.[16]

In the photograph accompanying his missionary application, George Birch poses in a dark suit jacket with wide lapels, a high-collared white

George Snider Birch studied agriculture at the University of Georgia. Credit: Presbyterian Historical Society, Presbyterian Church (U.S.A.) (Philadelphia, PA).

shirt, and a white tie. His carefully quaffed pompadour hairdo is brushed up and back from his forehead. His clear eyes are set below prominent eyebrows. There is an air of uncertainty in his expression. A recommendation letter from Mr. R. M. Guess, general secretary of the YMCA at University of Georgia, described him as "quiet and unassuming." Guess did not consider him a forceful leader nor an effective public speaker, but asserted that "he can be depended upon in every detail of work placed on him." Other testimonials said he was a good farmer and a religious, upright, honest, conscientious youth. Martha Berry praised him for having "one of the sunniest, sanest dispositions I have ever known. He is absolutely fearless when a question of right or wrong comes up; and he is tolerant and gentle toward other people's opinions, though a man of exceptionally firm convictions."[17]

In her photograph, Ethel looks beyond the camera with a confident, composed gaze. Her light brown hair is short and tousled, and the most striking features of her oval face are her expressive eyes and full lips. A large pendant hangs from her neck on an open-necked white blouse. The letters supporting her application to become a missionary were uniformly enthusiastic. They describe her as a cheerful, bright, and capable leader; full of energy, considerate of others, and an earnest Christian. The dean of Wooster College rated her intellectual ability as "quite above medium of graduates" and was also very keen on her "executive ability and fertility of resource." "During her two years with us we have learned to love Miss Elllis," wrote the dean of Berry School. "She is most unselfish and so enthusiastic that it is a real joy to work with her."[18]

Their wedding took place at Ethel's parents' home in Vineland on September 12, 1917. The local newspaper announced, "The bride was given away by her father at the front of a bower of white clematis. She was daintily attired in a gown of white Georgette crepe over silk and wore orange blossoms."[19] After a few days honeymoon on the Jersey shore, they visited George's relatives in Georgia and crossed the country by train to San Francisco. They boarded the steamship SS *China* on October 11, 1917, and sailed across the Pacific for their new life in India. After stopping on the way at Yokohama and Shanghai, they reached Calcutta (Kolkata) on India's northeast coast in November.[20] From there they took a train westward to the city of Allahabad in a densely populated region of north central India.

Ethel May Ellis majored in biology at the College of Wooster and hoped to attend medical school. Credit: Presbyterian Historical Society, Presbyterian Church (U.S.A.) (Philadelphia, PA).

Not long after their arrival in Allahabad, the Birches encountered the Kumbh Mela festival, the single largest religious gathering in the world. Once every twelve years, Hindu pilgrims converge on the banks of the *sangam*—the confluence of the Ganga (Ganges), the Yamuna, and the mythical Saraswati rivers—where they bathe in these holy waters to be cleansed of all sins. Millions of people from all over India, including thousands of absolutely naked holy men called *sadhus*, came to Allahabad in January and February 1918, not long after the young missionary couple arrived.[21] The scale and intensity of this massive convergence of men and women, young and old, rich and poor—all in search of spiritual redemption—must have led the young missionary couple to reflect on their own beliefs and their role in India's deeply spiritual and religious society.

Ethel, twenty-seven years old, was pregnant with her first child. In the spring, she escaped from the heat of the plains to the temperate hill station of Landour, some five hundred miles northwest of Allahabad at an altitude of seven thousand feet. Settled by the British military, the area was popular with American missionaries, and they built schools for their children there, the most prominent being the Woodstock School.

Ethel gave birth to John Morrison Birch in Landour on May 28, 1918. She wrote to her college classmates that he was a "fine, strong little boy."[22] Her son was a source of great pride and joy. Back in Allahabad, she would take her baby in his little bassinet, going "from house to house with my Hindustani Bible to women in the villages." Hindi phrases, learned from servants, were among his first words. She remembered that he would astonish the people who crowded the streets of the marketplace by speaking in the local language. Because the Birches had no refrigerator and little or no ice, John was over a year old before he ate ice cream. After the first taste, he said in Hindi, "This is hot!" "John was always obedient. When we took him to church he didn't fuss or wiggle," remembered Ethel. "When candy was put within reaching distance, he would not take any without permission. Vases or other breakables were safe even though in easy reach."[23]

Their second child, Walter Ellis, named for Ethel's father, was born on February 10, 1920, in Fatehgarh, a city some two hundred miles up the Ganges from Allahabad. Unlike John, he was "into everything and never still a waking minute. Had it not been for Ellis," wrote Ethel, "I would have been egotistical enough to take the credit for having a very well-trained child."[24]

The Birches had arrived in India full of enthusiasm and hope, but instead encountered frustration and disappointment. Their nemesis was Sam Higginbottom, head of the newly established Allahabad Agricultural Institute. He was an imposing, heavy-set man originally from Manchester, England, and educated at Princeton University. He joined the North India Mission of the Presbyterian Church to teach economics at Allahabad Christian College in 1903, and became aware of "the difficulty of handling illiterate people, with fear-ridden imaginations, whose whole lives were shadowed by the superstition that the very air they breathed was filled with evil spirits." The hunger, poverty, filth, and illiteracy of India's peasants—not to mention the opium dens and lepers in the streets—convinced him that food was more important than salvation. In 1909, at the age of thirty-five, he made a "drastic decision," as he put it, to study agriculture at Ohio State University. Three years later with a master's degree in hand, he was ready to teach villagers how to plow, irrigate, grow crops, and raise animals.[25] At the time, however, teaching agriculture was not an acceptable activity for a Christian school. The head of Ewing College, C. A. R. Janvier, a minister from Philadelphia, rejected Higginbottom's plan. His project was hived off from Ewing, and he had no choice but to direct and raise money for the Allahabad Agricultural Institute by himself.[26]

George Birch was responsible for dairy work and animal husbandry, and the Institute's priorities were made clear. Evangelical work was not important; the sole purpose was to help raise the standard of living in India. After all, what was the point of preaching to people about their souls if their stomachs were empty? Christianity would be demonstrated through good works, not through sermons. "The Agricultural Institute was doing the work of the Church just as much as the preacher in the pulpit," declared Higginbottom.[27] But the idea that a missionary would ignore proselytizing for the sake of improving the livelihoods of native peoples was still anathema in those days. Farming and food production was a worthy cause, but someone else's job.

Higginbottom would persist and make it acceptable for missionaries to teach agriculture. "I am more than ever convinced that with scientific farming and with the proper care and use of India's resources, the threat of famine should cease to cause terror to this people," he wrote in 1930.[28] With single-minded focus, he imported cattle from the United States to breed more productive dairy cows, and became an international pioneer in soil reclamation, turning barren earth into productive land. Eventually, he won the support of funders, including John D. Rockefeller Jr., and gained the attention and support of maharajahs as well as Mahatma Gandhi and Jawaharlal Nehru, leaders of India's independence movement.

In the early days, however, the domineering Higginbottom promised more than he could deliver to his young staff. The Birches were not alone in their discontent. The director's overbearing personality led seven of the eight American teachers he had recruited to leave for other jobs during 1919 and 1920. Housing was a problem and so were the Institute's finances. In addition to everything else, the behavior of Higginbottom's demanding and opinionated wife, Ethelind (a cousin of William "Buffalo Bill" Cody), only exacerbated the situation.[29]

After sticking it out for nearly three years, George and Ethel resigned in disillusion. They were fed up with Higginbottom's demands, disagreed with his ideas about missions, and saw little hope for the dairy industry in India. Ethel was told not to organize Bible classes for local women; no use was made of her background in science, her talents as a teacher, or her experience as a secretary.[30] Their commitment to the Presbyterian board to "enter the foreign missionary work for life, if God wills," was shattered.

Abandoning their lives in India was a wrenching decision for the young couple, not only emotionally but also financially. Because they had failed to finish their five-year term, they were obliged to borrow money to pay for their passage back home. With broken dreams, the Birches sailed from Calcutta on the SS *Trafford Hall*, a British passenger cargo ship, with two-and-a-half-year-old John and six-month-old Ellis. Stopping in Colombo, Ceylon (Sri Lanka), and Port Said (Egypt)—after passing through the Suez Canal—they reached Boston on October 10, 1920, after nearly a month at sea.[31]

Despite their bitter disappointment in India, two of the Birch children would become missionaries, following in their parents' footsteps, helping to achieve their unfulfilled goals. John would go to China and his brother George Stanley and his wife Alice to Nigeria and the Caribbean. They would serve not as educators or agricultural specialists but as Christian evangelists.

3

Old-time Religion

THE BIRCHES RETURNED FROM their India sojourn facing an uncertain future. After spending the winter with George's family in Macon, Georgia, they moved to Vineland, New Jersey, where Ethel had grown up. George needed work, so his father-in-law, who owned the Blue Spruce Fruit Farm—specializing in peaches, pears, and apples—gave him a job managing a large apple orchard.

There would be seven Birch children—three boys, a girl, and three more boys. Arriving at regular two-year intervals were John, Walter Ellis, George Stanley (named for his father and Ethel's brother, who died in a motorcycle accident), Elizabeth, Herbert, Robert, and Douglas (named after a medical missionary the Birches knew in India). When the family went to church, they filled the whole pew.

Vineland, with a population of about twenty thousand when the Birches arrived, was a center for agriculture and poultry farming. Founded in 1861 as a "model town of the world" by a young lawyer named Charles Landis, it was one of several utopian communities across the country where the sale of alcohol was prohibited. Landis said he "had never known of a sober man to be a pauper."[1] The terrain was a flat wilderness of oaks, pines, and brush thirty-four miles south of Philadelphia. Landis believed the soil and temperate climate would make it a good place for growing fruit—hence the town's name. Swampland was drained, roads and houses built, a railway constructed, and churches and schools organized. Landis Avenue, one hundred feet wide, bisected the city's one-mile-square grid.

Vineland's most famous resident was Thomas Bramwell Welch (no relation to Robert Welch), who arrived with his family in 1865 to set up a dental practice. An entrepreneurial man who was opposed to the use of wine in communion services, he set about inventing a pasteurization process that prevented the fermentation of grapes. Marketed as a non-alcoholic "natural tonic," the beverage became a booming business. In the 1890s, he and his son Charles moved the company to western New York, where Concord grape production was more bountiful. Before long, Welch's Grape Juice was being advertised as "The National Drink."[2]

The Birch family lived on East Chestnut Avenue, which was then on the outskirts of town, in a one-story house between the homes of two Italian families. Many of the streets were named for fruits and trees: Plum, Pear, Quince, Cherry, Almond, Maple, and Walnut. French and Germans were recruited as workers, followed by immigrants from southern Italy who mostly settled east of the city in an area called "New Italy." Trains carried produce—including fruits from the Blue Spruce orchard—to markets in Philadelphia and New York. By the 1920s, buyers drove their trucks to local farms to purchase produce directly from the fields.[3]

With a mortgage and a growing family, the Birches were not well off, but there was always food on the table. Ethel's brother Roland was a local dentist who took care of the children free of charge; he put in a bridge for John after his sister Betty threw a rock at him and knocked out his two front teeth when he was about fourteen. To supplement the family's income, Ethel Birch started her own business raising new and rare gladioli on open land behind their house. She was an excellent manager. All of the children had their assignments, helping to till and weed and dig up bulbs and store them in boxes before winter. A neighbor sold crates of the blooming red, white, pink, yellow, and purple flowers at one dollar per dozen in Trenton and Atlantic City from the back of his truck.[4]

Unable to afford her annual dues at Wooster College, Ethel wrote to the alumni secretary in 1926 asking if she might send flower bulbs instead: "For the last few years, in hopes of increasing the income from the land, I have been growing choice gladiolus bulbs . . . if you could use any of them in beautifying the Wooster grounds." The offer was graciously accepted and she sent a mixture of bulbs with instructions on how to plant them; her alumni account was credited with three dollars.[5] Eventually she made enough money to buy a big blue Buick sedan with cash. When she neglected to replace a worn-out muffler, the neighbors called the car—which could be heard for blocks around— "Mama Birch's Battle Boat."[6]

John and his siblings grew up during a decade of social, economic, and technological transformation: the Roaring Twenties. But they had little awareness of the big cities where jazz music, bobbed hair, and short dresses for women were all the rage. Nor was the powerful new political movement called Bolshevism—which spawned the Red Scare of 1919–1920—of great concern in small, relatively isolated places like Vineland. The lives of the Birch family revolved around the rhythms of work, school, and church.

John's face is brimming with curiosity and intelligence in a photo from these early years. May Cosman, Ethel's spinster schoolteacher aunt, took a special interest in the boy, giving him books and encouraging his academic pursuits. By age five, "he was reading everything he could get his hands on, asking the meaning of words he did not know," wrote his mother. "I remember particularly how he had read John Bunyan's *Pilgrim's Progress* and *Hurlbut's Story of the Bible* before he started school at seven."[7] His brother George Stanley described him as the scholar in the family. When his IQ was tested at age ten, he placed at the equivalent of age sixteen and was advanced two years into junior high. In high school he would borrow a textbook from a friend and earn a perfect score on the exam the next day.[8]

Modernists and Fundamentalists

A rapidly changing America opened up a great religious divide between "modernists," who embraced the new secular world, and "fundamentalists," who held to a strict moral code. A major dispute erupted within mainline Protestant churches—especially the Presbyterians and Baptists—over how to respond to new social and theological challenges. Despite their firsthand exposure to Martha Berry's progressive ideas about religion and education, Ethel and George Birch

Clockwise from the top are John, Ellis, Betty, and George Stanley—four of the seven Birch children—in Vineland, New Jersey, about 1925. Courtesy of Robert G. Birch.

now came down firmly on the conservative side of the debate. Sam Higginbottom's unconventional approach to Christian mission work in India had been dismaying to them, and perhaps the shock of India's religious and spiritual diversity also strengthened their commitment to Protestant orthodoxy. In any case, after returning to the United States, they gravitated toward an "old-time religion" that seemed reassuring and secure.

In part, their decision was due to the influence of one man. Not long after moving to Vineland, the Birches met William W. Rugh, an itinerant preacher with a weekly circuit through eastern Pennsylvania and southern New Jersey. This biblical Johnny Appleseed taught in churches, Christian associations, homes, schoolhouses, and Bible schools, and authored a series of pamphlets titled "Christ in the Bible: A Correspondence Course of Three Years for the Study of the Whole Bible by Books." He was a founder of the Bible Institute of Pennsylvania in 1913, known today as the Cairn University.[9] Impressed by his warmth, humility, and devotion, Ethel and George left the Presbyterians and joined Vineland's West Baptist Church, an independent, self-governing congregation. Armed with the ancient, inerrant truths of the Bible, the Birches resisted worldly temptations such as drinking, smoking, and dancing. It was an all-consuming, purifying brand of religion.

The so-called modernists advocated a reinterpretation of religion "to make it relevant to the needs of an urban-industrial society," as William Gatewood has explained. Modernists accepted "the rationality of the universe, an emphasis on science, and an optimistic faith in the ultimate triumph of goodness."[10] In their worldview, it was possible to retain the core tenets of Christianity while accepting new knowledge, including historical criticism of the Bible. Harry Emerson Fosdick, one of the leading voices for modernism, believed you "cannot keep your science in one compartment of your mind and your religion in another. All truth is God's truth and great discoveries, like evolution and the reign of law, if they are true for science are true for religion also."[11] For his outspoken words, Fosdick was forced to resign from the First Presbyterian Church in New York in 1924.

On the other side of the argument—the side favored by Ethel and George Birch—the fundamentalists charged that watering down Christianity would be the first step down a slippery slope to secularism and humanism, if not agnosticism and atheism. Modernism, wrote Gatewood, "discarded essential doctrines, stripped Christianity of its supernatural elements, and attempted to substitute sociology for the gospel."[12] What was needed was a revival of back-to-basics faith as revealed in the Bible through the divinely inspired word of God in order to achieve individual salvation. The fundamentals, based on the literal truth of the Bible, included the virgin birth of Jesus Christ, his sacrifice to atone for human sins, his bodily resurrection, and his second coming. Belief in Christ's return, known as pre-millennialism, made it imperative to save as many souls as possible before it was too late. Each side was convinced of its monopoly on truth and enlightenment. Modernists were branded as foolish and misguided, while fundamentalists were ignorant, narrow minded, and dogmatic. Modernism was perceived as a perversion of Christian values. Fundamentalism was stereotyped as a threat to rational thinking.

According to American fundamentalists, Christianity's truths were most accurately conveyed in the authorized King James Version of the Bible. The most popular version was the Scofield Reference Bible, published by Oxford University Press in 1909 and revised in 1917. Compiled by Cyrus I. Scofield, a contemporary of William Rugh, the edition's object was to provide "a clearer and more spiritual apprehension of the Word of God." Scofield's version, he explained, was heavily annotated with definitions, explanations of apparent discrepancies, references and cross-references, a chronology and index, and brief introductions to each of the Bible's sixty-six books. Important words were defined in "simple, non-technical terms." As one advertisement put it, "the difficult passages which formerly hindered your enjoyment are explained by foot-notes printed on the very pages where they are needed. No matter how many Bibles you have, you need this one, for it contains helps found in none other." The Bible was now presented as an integrated, coherent story, a "panoramic view" wherein "Christ, Son of God, Son of man, Son of Abraham, Son of David, thus binds the many books into one Book." Divinely inspired, it should be understood as one continuous story with "a progressive unfolding of the truth," moving from origins to deliverance to worship to prophecy to redemption.

Scofield was gratified to know that "the plain people of God in their homes, and far away missionaries in heathen lands have been helped to a clearer and more spiritual apprehension of the Word of God."[13] His interpretation represented another step in the Protestant crusade dating from Martin Luther to construct direct communion between the individual and God without the mediation of clergy. Baptists in particular believed the hierarchies of organized religion only obscured man's relationship with the Almighty.

Ethel Birch owned a Scofield, and in keeping with her creed she wanted to know about the standing of candidates for alumni trustees

at the College of Wooster in 1926. "Are they fundamentalist or leaning toward modernism?" she asked the alumni secretary. "I think for a
Christian College, and Presbyterian at that, that it is more important to
know something of their attitude religiously than even how successful
they are in the business world of today, tho that is of course necessary
too." The secretary politely replied, "As for the fundamentalist-modernist
angle, I do not know even that about the two whose church affiliation
I am familiar with. I am quite sure, however, that all of these men are
worthy in this particular."[14]

Wholeheartedly accepting their newfound convictions as
Independent Baptists, the Birches raised their children to believe in
the essential, inerrant, and infallible truths of the Bible. There was no
room for compromise or doubt. Everything was subordinated to the
idea of Christian redemption and Christ's mandate to share the message of salvation with all nations and peoples. Despite poverty—or
perhaps because of it—they found reassurance in a divine plan that
transcended the trials and tribulations of earthly life, promising better
days ahead. It was a faith that set the Birch family apart from America's
ever more secularized and urban culture. Most fundamentalists, moreover, abstained from politics, believing that church and state should be
kept in separate realms. It was not until the late 1970s that the religious
right would emerge as a political force in American politics as part of a
newly energized brand of conservatism that culminated with the election of Ronald Reagan as president.[15]

The confrontation between liberal and conservative theology—which
was by no means limited to the rural South—came to a head around
the theory of biological evolution. Fundamentalists believed that if
Darwin was correct about man's origins, it must mean the Bible was
wrong about God's role in the creation of the universe. As historian
Jeffrey Moran shows, the theory of natural selection (which was not
widely accepted by scientists until the 1930s and 1940s) "undermined the
Christian ideal of humanity's special relationship with God by lump-
ing humans in with all other animals." Even more troubling, Darwin's
ideas "seemed to make God, as Christians had long understood him,
not merely unknowable but unnecessary."[16] It was a twentieth-century
equivalent of the Copernican theory that the earth revolved around
the sun. For many deeply religious men and women, evolution was

linked to all the modern evils—communism, sexual immorality, and the disintegration of the family. Acceptance of evolution would lead to atheism. It was an existential threat to American democracy and the American way of life. It was un-American to believe in evolution.

The 1925 Scopes trial in Dayton, Tennessee, seized the nation's attention and crystallized the debate about whether science or scripture best explained human origins. John Scopes, a high school biology teacher, was charged with violating a Tennessee law that prohibited teaching evolution. William Jennings Bryan, known as the "silver-tongued orator," spoke for the fundamentalists, and Clarence Darrow defended Scopes, who was found guilty, but whose verdict was overturned on a technicality. The fundamentalist crusade peaked in the 1920s and declined after Bryan's death, just five days after the trial, but the movement never disappeared and fierce debates about creationism and evolution continue to this day.

A precocious John Birch was aware of the controversy over science and religion. In junior high school, several years after the Scopes trial, he received an "A" for a short paper titled "Evolution from the Standpoint of the Bible." Reflecting a fundamentalist point of view, he wrote: "The Bible is the positive proof against the theory of evolution. It is guaranteed by Almighty God to be true." He described the Bible as "the most wonderful and authentic History the World has ever known." His paper concluded with this tautology: "If the theory of evolution were true, there would be no need of a Savior to rescue man from his sinful state."[17]

Back to Georgia

Confronted by the Great Depression and a less than promising career working in his father-in-law's apple orchard, George Birch returned in 1930 to northwest Georgia, where he took a job teaching animal husbandry, horticulture, and agriculture at the Berry Schools. Martha Berry's vision for experimental education had flourished in the years since George and Ethel left for India. Berry Junior College was established in 1926, and Henry Ford and his wife, Clara, made generous gifts for several impressive English Gothic-style buildings, the first of which was a women's dormitory. But, for reasons that are unclear, George's teaching contract was not renewed after his first year, and he was given work as a groundskeeper, caring for the lawns, shrubs, flowers, trees, and a swimming pool at the new Ford buildings.[18]

His family had stayed behind in Vineland, where Ethel continued to raise the children and manage her gladiola business. In the summer of 1932, after two years apart, George drove with Ethel and their seven children in the big blue Buick from New Jersey to Georgia, traveling nearly one thousand miles in just two days. George found a position as principal of a small grammar school in Floyd Spring, and to help make ends meet, Ethel taught English at Armuchee High School in Floyd County, where John was one of her pupils. John attended three different schools near Rome, Georgia: one year at the Berry School, two years at Armuchee, and his final year at Gore High School in Chattooga County (which, unlike Armuchee, was accredited), where he graduated as the valedictorian.[19] A group photo on the front steps of a rural schoolhouse shows a smiling and confident John standing with his older and taller classmates. He won first place for a declamation on Patrick Henry's "Give me liberty or give me death" speech, but it must have been tough for a small boy from the north to make his way in a little southern town. George Stanley remembers being called a "damn Yankee." After he was wrongly punished for throwing a spitball at a teacher, he challenged the perpetrator to a fight after school. The boy was vanquished, and George Stanley became known as the "Jersey bull."[20]

Their father finally had some luck when he inherited a sizable parcel of land from his father, who had been quite successful raising cotton and corn. It was north of Macon in Bibb County on the western bank of the Ocmulgee River, on the fall line between the Atlantic coastal plain and the Piedmont plateau. (His sister Margaret was given property south of Macon, along with a house called "Breezy Point," where the family had been raised. A second sister, Beth, received another piece of land.) Neighbors had long since dismantled an old house on George's five hundred acres, but a formidable stone building, originally constructed for the superintendent of an abandoned rock quarry, stood on adjacent land. With $1,000 from Ethel's mother, the Birches bought an additional eighty-five acres, which included the stone structure.

John Birch stands on the far left in the second row in this school photo near Rome, Georgia, circa 1932. Courtesy of Robert G. Birch.

In 1934, the family moved from Rome to their new home, which they named Birchwood. John and Ellis, sixteen and fourteen respectively, went in advance of their mother and siblings driving a hand-cranked Model-T Ford that had been converted into a pickup truck. The two brothers traveled the 150 miles through Atlanta and on to Macon by themselves; no driver's licenses were required in those days. They set about building fences for thirty head of cattle. A series of Delco batteries provided electricity for pumping well water, lanterns lit the house, and there was a hand-cranked washing machine. The Buck Ice and Coal Company delivered ice. Ethel planted daffodils in the front yard.[21]

Situated in the rolling pine-forested hills about nine miles north of Macon, the property was bisected by Route 87, then a washboard dirt road at the end of the school-bus line. Eventually the Birches had a shared telephone line—a party line—with several other families. The Birch's signal was two long and two short rings, but the children would sometimes eavesdrop on other conversations to hear the local gossip. About one-quarter mile east of the house lay the tracks of the Southern

Railway, running between Macon and Atlanta, and just beyond the railway was the Ocmulgee River where the brothers and their sister enjoyed fishing, swimming, and boating. There were several natural springs on the property, and the boys once discovered a liquor still. Growing up close to the land—appreciating the value of hard work and without much in the way of material goods—would help prepare John for some of the deprivations he would face in China as a missionary and soldier.

It was a hardscrabble life during the Great Depression, but the family had their own cows for milk and chickens for eggs. They bought stale Merita bread—which sometimes included cinnamon rolls—for one dollar per bag. They slaughtered their own cattle and pigs for meat. "Nobody had any money in those days," remembers Douglas, "so we didn't know we were poor."[22] John introduced the family to chess, with a board and pieces made from cardboard. When his sister Betty was hospitalized, he gave his parents the money he was saving for a bicycle to help pay the bill.[23]

The Birch boys were enterprising. With an old dump truck, they hauled chunks of gray granite flecked with quartz from the quarry for five dollars a load. They set up chairs in the back of the truck and hauled "colored folk" to all-day church meetings for a fee. Each child had a vegetable plot for tomatoes, beans, and peanuts, although gardening was a challenge because of the rocks in the soil. The red dirt, however, was excellent for growing pine trees, and composted leaves from a nearby grove of oaks produced rich mulch. They marketed tomatoes for fifty cents a bushel and milk for ten cents a gallon. Cream was sold to the local Sealtest Company, and leftover skim milk was fed to the pigs. Down at the river they set out a trotline at night—a rope with several eighteen-inch fishing lines and hooks attached to it—and in the morning pulled out blue channel catfish, delicious for eating.

The only hired hand was a black man, Dan Gladden, who lived in one of the small houses down below the big stone house. He chopped wood, walked behind the mule plowing furrows, and did other chores. He also told stories to the Birch children and taught them how to cook cornbread on an open-hearth fire.[24] In a society where segregation was the norm, however, John was not without bias. He later admitted to a friend, "I have a lot of race prejudice in me, especially toward Negroes. . . . I believe this to be a wrong and unfair attitude, and I have always tried to repress it, but I know it's still there."[25]

Fascinated by radios, John developed a talent that would serve him well in China. He and Ellis collected the parts to build a crystal set with earphones and strung up an antenna from the house chimney across to some pine trees. This opened up the world beyond the confines of school, church, and farm. The boys heard broadcasts of Mussolini's attack on Ethiopia, the Hindenburg disaster, and Orson Welles's *The War of the Worlds*. John would recall listening to classical music broadcasts from Radio Berlin. Robert Birch remembers hearing the evangelist Charles A. Fuller, who hosted *The Old Fashioned Revival Hour* from Los Angeles every Sunday. The family's only magazine subscription was the *Saturday Evening Post*, but John was often found reading books from the Macon Public Library.[26]

Faced with an impoverished life and a less-than-happy marriage to a husband whose energy and ambition did not match her own, Ethel Birch found solace in her children. She was a talented organizer who

The Birch children on the family farm in Macon, Georgia, around 1935. From back to front are John, Ellis, George Stanley, Betty, Herbert, Robert, and Douglas, with their dog Lady. Courtesy of Robert G. Birch.

took charge of the family and the farm. "She had a knack for raising cattle and could have been a veterinarian," Douglas recalled. "Mother was as strong as an ox." If a cow had trouble delivering, she would reach into the womb to free the struggling calf. "To call Mother persuasive would be the understatement of the century," George Stanley told me. "She was a go-getter who knew her stuff."[27] She gave the children a firm sense of order and purpose, which included church on Sundays and a Bible reading and prayer every night after dinner. Her courage and determination in the face of scarcity and disappointment earned her the respect and devotion of her family. She was stalwart and fearless.

Her husband, on the other hand, had become lazy, spoiled, and ill-tempered. He considered himself a country gentleman and self-styled philosopher. Worse yet, he was sometimes cruel to the boys. One was forced to chop wood in the rain; another was whipped with a belt and, on another occasion, threatened with a cleaver when he couldn't spell correctly. "Father was always off and gone," George Stanley said, "and we older boys were responsible for farming and minding the younger children." Ethel would tell people that George had health problems to explain why he couldn't hold a job. John's decision to become a missionary fulfilled his mother's hopes; it also put distance between him and his absentee father.

"Strangely burdened"

John knew from an early age that he wanted to be a preacher and a missionary. He was only seven years old and his "heart was strangely burdened with sin" when he went to the front of the church in Vineland to accept the pastor's invitation to be "saved." Growing up, he listened to his parents talk about missionaries, and at age twelve heard Leonard Livingston Letgers describe the lives of indigenous peoples along Brazil's Amazon River basin. Letgers told how "there were more lost people in the world today than there ever was before." Hearing about the urgency for new translations of the Bible to reach these un-evangelized regions, the young Birch was inspired to think about the mission field for his own career.[28] His conviction never wavered, although he did not yet know that China was in his future.

Americans who aspired to become Christian missionaries often imagined serving in China. Being a missionary was a heroic and adventurous act of self-sacrifice for a greater cause, and certainly few places in the world were more challenging and exciting. The risks, and even the possibility of martyrdom, made it compelling. It was also a ticket out of the humdrum life of a small town or the monotony of living on a farm. Told that nowhere was the need greater than in China, children put their pennies, nickels, and dimes in collection plates every Sunday. Probably the most famous Southern Baptist missionary at the time was Lottie Moon, a woman from Virginia who spent forty years in Shandong Province. When her foreign mission board sent no funds in 1912, it was alleged that she starved herself to death during a famine and left what money she had to the Chinese people she loved. The apocryphal story became a legend, and she was enshrined as a martyr. Over the decades, the Lottie Moon Christmas Offering has raised over one billion dollars in support of Baptist missionaries.[29]

John Birch would have heard stories about Lottie Moon as well as the heroism of other Christian martyrs in China. During the Boxer Uprising in north China in the summer of 1900, some 250 foreigners, many of them Western missionaries and their children, and perhaps up to 30,000 Chinese Christians were killed. There were spine-chilling stories about their deaths; many were beheaded or burned alive. (About one-hundred of the missionaries were British, fifty-six Swedish, and thirty-two American.) In 1934, the horrifying fate of John and Betty Stam was widely publicized. The young American couple was in the city of Jingde in Anhui Province with the China Inland Mission when Communist soldiers who were fleeing from Nationalist troops arrived. In the throes of an anti-imperialist and anti-Christian campaign, the Reds beheaded John and Betty but spared their three-month-old daughter. The lurid tale made international headlines.[30] Examples of those who willingly made the ultimate sacrifice motivated many young Americans to volunteer for mission work. Yet becoming a missionary was something of a paradox. These American emissaries typically reflected conservative social values and shared a fear of radicalism, but at the same time they were internationalists who, for the most part, were deeply engaged with foreign cultures.

Birch was eager to find his destiny, but because he was younger than his peers when he graduated from high school, he waited for a year before entering Mercer University in 1935. In the meantime, he helped with chores and stringing barbed-wire fence at Birchwood. Somewhere he read that by lifting a calf every day you could become strong enough to lift a cow. This he did for many weeks before selling the animal to help pay for his college expenses.[31] Throughout his short life, Birch was both admired and criticized for this kind of resolve. He was obstinate, passionate, and headstrong. Even at an early age, it was this clarity of purpose and strength of character that either repelled or drew others to him.

4

Heresy Hunters

OF MEDIUM HEIGHT AND slender build, John Birch had grown into a handsome young man with wavy brown hair and hazel eyes. Yet it was his intensity, not his good looks, that impressed people. Many years later, Chauncey Daley, a Mercer University classmate called him "one of the most brilliant fellows I've ever met" and "one of the most dynamic personalities I ever knew. He had a personal magnetism, was a born leader, and was capable and gifted without measure." Beyond this, "he had a will of his own like few persons I ever met."[1]

Charles Drake, another fellow student, said Birch was "very scholarly and very much a loner. He was usually in the library studying the Bible, English literature, and American history." Drake's first impression of Birch was not good: "I thought he was a smart-egg, a person who knew it all, and very immature." Birch was a rebel and a radical who would interrupt almost any class to ask questions. "He did not care who disagreed with him or who he may have offended. He stood up for what he believed." In time they became friends, and Drake, who spent his career as a Baptist minister, respected Birch as "a very intelligent man of deep convictions, a man of God."[2]

Birch was not yet thinking about missionary work in China, but there was a notable China connection several miles down the road from Mercer at Wesleyan College, a Methodist institution chartered in 1836 as the Georgia Female College. All three of the famous Soong sisters studied at Wesleyan: Ai-ling, who married H. H. Kung, an influential

banker and politician; Ching-ling, who married Sun Yat-sen, first president of the Republic of China; and Mei-ling, wife of Chiang Kai-shek,
who led China from the mid-1920s until 1949. Mei-ling went on to
graduate from Wellesley College in Massachusetts, and became one of
China's most important interlocutors with American officials during
the Second World War.

The sisters came to Georgia because Charles Soong, their father
and a prominent Chinese businessman and devout Christian, had
met William Burke, a Macon native, when they both studied theology at Vanderbilt University in Tennessee. When Burke showed up in
China as a Methodist missionary, Soong asked for his help in sending
his eldest daughter Ai-ling to America for her education. Burke wrote
an enthusiastic letter to Wesleyan's president, who happily agreed to
accept her. Despite this welcome, there was considerable discrimina-
tion against Chinese at the time; when Ai-ling arrived in San Francisco
in 1904, traveling under a Portuguese passport, she was detained for
nineteen days while immigration officials questioned her visa.[3] The sisters left Macon by 1913, long before John Birch moved there, but he
would meet Soong Mei-ling—Madame Chiang—in China when he
joined the U.S. Army in 1942.

While attending Mercer University, Birch first lived at home, driving
to school, and later shared a house near campus with five or six other
students. He did some acting with the Mercer Players, a little writing
for a school publication, and plenty of debating as an active member of
the freshman and varsity teams. With a love for reasoning and argu-
mentation, he excelled at debate. He studied English and was a member
of the Ministerial Association, an organization that helped prepare students "to become efficient and spiritual religious workers." During his
senior year, he was appointed pastor for Benevolence Baptist Church,
a very small rural church in the peach country south of Macon. There
he conducted morning and evening services every Sunday. He was too
busy studying and preaching to have time for sports or dating.[4] He later
told a congregation in Fort Worth, Texas, that he read a lot of books on
psychology in college, and began to doubt the Word of God. "I stopped
trying to win souls . . . It was terrible, I wasn't happy."[5] After struggling
through his adolescent uncertainty, he became that much more steadfast in his Christian faith.

John Birch's 1939 yearbook photo at Mercer University, where he studied English and Christianity and was nominated for a Rhodes Scholarship. Credit: Special Collections, Jack Tarver Library, Mercer University.

Birch excelled academically and did so well that in his senior year Mercer selected him as its Rhodes Scholar candidate. A regional committee interviewed him in Atlanta with other finalists in December 1938. With quiet confidence he told a reporter he wanted to attend Oxford University to learn "as much as I possibly can about everything in order to accomplish my main purpose in life—to win people to God."[6] His bid for the Rhodes was unsuccessful—possibly because of rising uncertainty about the merits of the missionary enterprise—and before long the signal honor of being nominated would seem like a distant vision.

"Spanish Inquisition in Progress"

Birch had been a model student at Mercer, but found himself embroiled in a huge controversy over religious orthodoxy toward the end of his senior year. Years later, some journalists investigating his background noted that the absolutism of the young college student seemed to parallel the extremism practiced by Robert Welch. Jonathan Schoenwald, author of an influential book on American conservatism, subscribes to this view, writing that Birch had "a history of refusing to believe that others' opinions might be as valid as his own." Schoenwald believes Welch identified with Birch's "unbending personality, his refusal to admit defeat or wrongdoing, and his belief that he was the only one who could do what was necessary."[7] But this interpretation fails to account for the fact that Birch's thinking evolved and matured during the remaining years of his life. There was a significant difference between the callow young college student and the man who experienced so many challenges in China.

The depiction of Birch as an extremist was the result of an incident that unfolded just a few months before his graduation when he joined twelve other ministerial students who charged several of their own Mercer faculty with heresy—teaching ideas that contradicted Baptist beliefs. On March 9, 1939, the student protesters entered Macon's Bibb County Courthouse where they filed nine legally sworn affidavits with the notary public, Daisy L. Churchwell, making accusations against five faculty members. Reid Lunsford was credited as the ringleader—President Spright Dowell called him "the most active and bitter of them"—but Birch, with his remarkable memory for detail, authored and signed three of the affidavits. The students belonged to an organization called the Fellowship Group, whose membership, bound by secret oath, was based on acceptance of the articles of faith adopted by the Southern Baptist Convention in 1924. (After the Birch Society was founded, some critics would use the secrecy of the Fellowship Group to show that Birch, like Welch, was conspiratorial.)

There were precedents for heresy charges in American universities. The earliest case at Mercer was in 1900 when a professor of history and philosophy was pressured to resign after he left the Baptist church and became a Christian Scientist. Four professors accused of unorthodox beliefs left Mercer in 1905, and Henry Fox, a professor of biology, was dismissed in 1924. Fox was a widely admired teacher, not to mention an upstanding member of a Baptist church in Macon. Mercer's president, Rufus Weaver, was dismayed by the decision of the Georgia Baptist Convention and Mercer's board of trustees to dismiss Fox after they determined that he was teaching evolution not just as theory but as fact.[8] Academic purges such as these were rare by the late 1930s, but if the high tide of fundamentalism had subsided, the fires of religious rectitude were by no means extinguished.

One precipitating event for Birch and his colleagues was a lecture at Mercer University on "Science and Religion" given by Shirley Jackson Case from the University of Chicago on February 22. A. C. Baker, pastor of Macon's Baptist Tabernacle Church, seized on her words to prove that Mercer was on the wrong path. According to Baker, Case denied the miraculous, the account of creation in the book of Genesis, the idea that Eve was made out of Adam's rib, and the fall of humanity.

On March 14, Baker arranged for visiting Baptist ministers to meet the young ministerial students and to hear their complaints. Mimeographed copies of a letter from Baker, with the students' affidavits attached, were later sent to about one thousand Baptist preachers across Georgia. The letter lamented conditions at Mercer, particularly in the Christianity department, "where heresy, as we see it, has reared its head over a considerable period of time.... Such teachings have their consequential counterpart in the program of present degeneration of the moral and social life of the students. We are praying for a thorough investigation and we shall appreciate your prayers and cooperation in any effort to adjust this serious situation."[9]

The primary target was John D. Freeman, a professor who taught philosophy, biblical literature, and homiletics. The white-haired Freeman—who originally was from Canada and had been the pastor of a Baptist church in Leicester, England—had taught at Mercer since 1927. The dissident students claimed in their depositions that he had stated: "There were no such persons as Adam and Eve; you do not have to believe in Jesus Christ to be saved; the Bible contradicts itself; it was not necessary for Christ to die to free men from sin; [and] the Bible was not divinely inspired."[10] But Freeman was well-respected by the overwhelming majority of his students, some of whom testified in his defense that he "had not unsettled their faith but rather had helped and strengthened them." They signed statements that his teaching was "doctrinally sound, spiritually sane, and genuinely Christian."[11]

Four other teachers were accused of questioning the Bible's infallibility: Josiah Crudup, a physicist; W. T. Smalley, of the English department; John Allen, professor of journalism; and James Wallace, a biology laboratory assistant. Crudup had been voted the most admired professor on campus for three years in a row. "It turned out," he later recalled, "that the theology students in my class had found fault with my teaching about the solar system's evolution which didn't agree with their idea of the creation of the universe in six days." He called Birch "a dynamic fellow, a natural leader. He was the leader of the group."[12]

When President Dowell became aware of the situation, he invited the "small and disgruntled" group of students into his office for a discussion. Three days later, a group of preachers from the Macon Baptist Pastor's Union met with Dowell and the university's executive committee to present charges against the five faculty members and to call for a thorough investigation. Dowell quickly appointed a special committee of three lawyers and three ministers, all of them trustees, to look into the matter. Mercer faced a moral and ethical dilemma. Discrediting professors based on their personal beliefs would undermine academic freedom. But as a denominational institution, the university had to abide by certain basic tenets of the Baptist faith. Compelled to distinguish between these two principles, the committee concluded:

> We recognize the right of any American to hold any views of a religious nature he may wish; but we respectfully submit and insist that in all intellectual and moral honesty any professor in Mercer University should resign and seek a more congenial field of labor should he ever feel in his heart that he cannot subscribe to and teach as far as it is his province things believed by the Baptists of Georgia to be vital to the Bible truths as they interpret them.[13]

A hearing was convened in Roberts Chapel in the Theology Building on March 30, which lasted from 11:00 a.m. until 9:15 p.m. John Birch, called as the first witness, remained calm, respectful, and polite under a barrage of questions. Other speakers were less restrained. The eighty-five-page transcript of the proceedings, writes church historian Walter Shurden, reveals "rapier-like sarcasm, uncontrolled anger, rude interruptions, malicious innuendo, feigned courtesies, offensive insinuations, wily intimidations."[14] At one point, a speaker who supported the theory of evolution showed a human skeleton to prove that a tail could be the continuation of the spinal column. Observers were asked to refrain from cheering, laughing, demonstrating, or applauding.

One of the pastors representing the students broke down and sobbed. Following an afternoon recess, the meeting was opened to the public and students rapidly filled the room. Many stood in the rear or leaned through windows. Students applauded heartily as the accused professors took the stand in defense. The five faculty denied the remarks attributed to them, saying they must have been misunderstood.[15]

The fundamentalist students, dubbed the "unholy 13," had not made themselves welcome on campus. A small group waiting outside chapel doors posted a sign saying "Stay Out—Spanish Inquisition in Progress." Another read "The Second Scopes Trial." "Burly football players, bespectacled scholars, gay co-eds raced gleefully across the freshly green campus from point to point in the most sensational college demonstration here in many years," wrote a reporter for the *Macon Evening News*. The *Atlanta Constitution* ran the story on its front page under the headline "Mercer 'Heresy' Charge Causes Riot of Students." When the ten-hour marathon adjourned, "the enraged, but still jovial students made a rush for the accusers, yelling 'Lynch Saint Birch' and other cries." The police were called in to restore order, and Professor Crudup helped one of his accusers to escape from the jeering students in his automobile.[16]

The editors of Mercer's student newspaper, *The Cluster*, attacked the ministerial students for their intolerance: "We learn with amazement that such crass, medieval bigotry exists on the campus." The consensus of opinion, wrote the authors, was that "the students who instigated the charges against the faculty members for heresy are not qualified to represent the institution." A petition was circulated to demand that the thirteen be expelled from the university. The offending students claimed they were led by the Holy Spirit and made the charges after much prayer. *The Cluster* acidly observed that "the leaders of the Spanish Inquisition also thought they were led by the Holy Spirit—after ceaseless prayer."[17] At a chapel service the next morning, President Dowell urged all students to practice self-restraint and tone down their demonstrations. The president's special committee met that day and voted unanimously to dismiss all charges, although Freeman was chastised for failing to emphasize "some of the vital teachings of Christianity often and strongly enough" and admonished for using an unsound textbook. The board of trustees soon accepted the committee's recommendation, bringing the controversy to a close.[18]

In the aftermath of the hearing, one Baptist preacher told Mercer's president he should expel the thirteen students "regardless of where they came from and who they are." Another editorial in *The Cluster* called for them to be dismissed. The author did not propose to "stand idle and allow the administration and the student body to become laughing stocks of the entire nation because of a parochial, prejudiced group within Mercer's own constituency."[19] In their defense, the accusers sent a letter to a Georgia Baptist newspaper claiming that the trustees and administration had whitewashed the entire situation.[20]

Despite the outrage and impassioned pleas, none of offenders was expelled. Birch graduated magna cum laude from Mercer with the best academic record in his class. Willing to jeopardize his college career and gain the enmity of his fellow students, he paid a price for doing so. After the fiasco, Birch was with his mother one day in town and asked her, "Are you sure you want to be seen walking with me? I'm not very popular, you know."[21] "People shunned him and didn't care for his company," recalled classmate Charles Drake. "There was a stigma over the thirteen students that stayed with them for life."[22] Chauncey Daley, Birch's friend and fellow student, sat through the ten-hour hearing. "I heard the statements used by John against the religion professor. I thought the charges were untrue and unfair and still do, though I could not help admiring John for his convictions."[23]

While Birch had been reckless in labeling his professors as heretics, he was not seeking notoriety. The record shows he was not the instigator, had no reputation as a rabble-rouser, and only joined the accusing students because they implored him for his help. With the certainty of youth and the self-righteousness of a true believer, he thought he had no choice in the matter. When one of John's cousins complained to him about the negative attention generated by the controversy and asked why he did it, he asked in turn, "Are you a Christian?" That was the end of the conversation.[24]

Over time, these fiery theological disputes would fade and become a source of some regret for Birch. In his final letter to his parents in 1945 he referred to the "teacher episode" at Mercer: "I was just a fumbling college boy, scared of hurting people's feelings, and yet trying to tell them about the Lord Jesus Christ."[25] Baptist ministers in Macon, who long suspected liberalism at Mercer, had taken advantage of his youthful rectitude, and he had learned a painful lesson about politics, power, and public opinion. Yet if he had any second thoughts about the wisdom of the heresy trial, it was too late to turn back and undo the damage. He was looking ahead, eager to complete his parents' unfinished journey as foreign missionaries. To do so, he would hitch his star to a dynamic and controversial preacher from Texas by the name of J. Franklin Norris.

The Texas Tornado

Before Billy Graham, Oral Roberts, and Jerry Falwell; before there were mega-churches and televangelists; there was J. Franklin Norris, one of the most influential and divisive religious leaders of early twentieth-century America. He was preceded by Billy Sunday, an evangelical fundamentalist from the Midwest who attracted huge audiences across the country as he zealously promoted Prohibition and weighed in on the issues of the day. Another such personality, prominent during the 1930s, was the anti-communist, anti-Jewish, pro-fascist Father Charles Coughlin, a Michigan Catholic priest, whose radio broadcasts reached millions until he was silenced by the Vatican.

The tall, charismatic Norris was known variously as the "Texas tornado," the "gospel-of-dynamite preacher," and the "fighting fundamentalist." In 1926, he also became the "pistol-packing parson" after an irate man walked into his office in Fort Worth and threatened him with his life. Norris shot and killed him, was accused of murder, and was acquitted by a jury on grounds of self-defense. He was a pivotal figure who embodied the fusion of religion and social issues. He also had a profound influence on John Birch.

Norris was just as pretentious, abusive, and inflammatory as he was captivating, convincing, and compelling. In his rapid-fire Alabama-accented delivery, he would cajole and inspire, railing against the evils of dancing, gambling, saloons, houses of ill repute, and ungodly conduct "high and low, far and near." He vigorously denounced evolution, modernism, and socialism. His populist message was unflinching: "What America needs, what Georgia needs, what Atlanta needs, what Texas needs, what Michigan needs, what the world needs, is an old fashioned, heaven-sent, fire-baptized, brush-arbor, sin-convicting, mourners-bench revival of religion." The time had come for a great awakening: "Chaos, crime, loss of confidence, the abounding and increased iniquity—these are the very conditions that preceded and characterized every great revival in the history of the world," proclaimed Norris.[26]

His combative character won him a multitude of supporters as well as legions of enemies. The world for Norris was divided between light and darkness, heaven and hell, believers and unbelievers, the saved and the damned. There were those who were loyal to him and those who would have liked to see him hanged. He attacked the Southern Baptist Convention as an "ecclesiastical machine" and the Northern Baptist Convention as communists, because they preached the gospel of "social justice." After the 1922 Texas Baptist Convention censured him and the 1924 convention permanently expelled him and his First Baptist Church of Fort Forth from the denomination, Norris defiantly charted his own course as an Independent Baptist.

Before long he had congregations of thousands not only in Fort Worth but also in Detroit, at Temple Baptist Church, where many members were migrants from the South. He owned a weekly newspaper called *The Fundamentalist* and two radio stations—WJR in Detroit and KFQB in Fort Worth, where the call letters stood for "Keep Folks Quoting the Bible." He conducted huge revival meetings throughout the country, believing "with all my soul that future generations will write about this Fundamentalist Movement as historians now write up the Reformation and Wesley Revival and other great awakenings."[27]

Norris thrived on sensationalism. He once sat a monkey wearing a suit on a stool next to the pulpit while he was railing against evolution. From time to time he would turn to the monkey and ask, "Isn't that so?" Despite his folksy style, as biographer Barry Hankins shows, he aspired to be more than a backwoods preacher and never missed a chance to schmooze with movers and shakers. He attended Herbert Hoover's inauguration in 1928, knew the titans of Detroit's automobile companies, and met various world leaders, including David Lloyd George, Winston Churchill, Benito Mussolini, and Pope Pius XII. He heard Hitler speak in Nuremberg in 1939 and was in the audience when Madame Chiang Kai-shek addressed a joint session of the U.S. Congress in 1943.[28]

John Birch first met Norris when the preacher was barnstorming the southeast in January 1939. Norris was so well known that he was invited to speak to a joint session of the Georgia state legislature in Atlanta.[29] During this revival tour, he appeared one night at the Third Street Baptist Church in Cordele, seventy miles south of Macon. John, his brother Douglas, and their parents were in the audience. Birch and some of his fellow Mercer students attended another gathering in a town northeast of Atlanta. Norris recalled, "It was my pleasure to meet these young Fundamental ministerial students, or most of them, in my meetings through Georgia.... I have never met a finer, more heroic group of young ministers." He was especially taken with Birch.

After learning a few months later that Birch and other students had "unmasked the modernistic professors" for teaching heresy at Mercer University, he immediately featured the story on the front page of *The Fundamentalist* in a blazing red headline: "Hell Broke Loose in Georgia." He wired John's father: "Congratulations. Challenge University to expel your son. It will immortalize him. Let them do their worst and then we will have another day." Norris wrote to John, "I congratulate you! You have stirred the whole nation. You and your fellow ministerial students will take rank with Martin Luther, Roger Williams, and other worthies."[30] This was heady praise for the ardent young Birch.

The Texas preacher had considerable experience as a heresy hunter. In 1921, he assailed Baylor University's president, Samuel P. Brooks, for allowing professors to teach the theory of evolution: "If the powers are incompetent to prevent books being taught which destroy the faith of young men and women in the integrity of the Scripture, then the time has come for us to change administration." Baylor, which was Norris's alma mater, was harboring G. Samuel Dow, a sociology professor who had written a textbook describing prehistoric humans as "half way between the anthropoid ape and modern man."[31] Norris's attack forced Dow to resign.

Several years later, Norris convened a mock trial for three Methodist institutions accused of teaching evolution: Southern Methodist University, Southwestern University at Georgetown, Texas, and the

Texas Woman's College at Fort Worth. Students from these institutions appeared as witnesses for the prosecution before a sizable congregation. "Defense there was none. All the accused were convicted," exclaimed Norris.[32] In 1935, he charged that evolutionists were no different from communists who had infiltrated the universities and the headquarters of the Northern Baptist Convention. The purpose of the church was not to preach the social gospel, which simply was socialism and communism in disguise. Only through the inner individual transformation of accepting Christ as savior could basic human ills be cured.

After the heresy trail at Mercer University, Birch arranged for Norris to return to Georgia to speak in early May at Macon's Municipal Auditorium. The bombastic fundamentalist would set up a "trial" of the accused professors in absentia with Mercer students acting as witnesses. "We will try these modernistic infidels," Norris boasted to Birch, "and you can serve notice on that bunch of hyenas that they will not break up that meeting either. You have won a most notable victory." On a more pragmatic note, he added, "If any friend wants to help pay for the rent of this auditorium it will be greatly appreciated."[33]

Plans for the rally were quietly canceled, however, and Norris did not show up in Macon as planned. The university's swift response to the charges against the five faculty members had defused the situation. Norris must have realized that the moment for stirring up trouble had passed and decided to focus on more promising causes. Instead of hosting the Texas firebrand, Birch joined some young people in a citywide revival in Macon that spring, going house-to-house and holding prayer meetings. After graduating in June, he spent the summer as an associate pastor at the Woodlawn Baptist Church in Augusta, Georgia.

"A young minister of unusual powers"

Until Birch heard Norris speak about the work of the Sweet Baptist Mission in Hangzhou, he had been unsure about where to go as a missionary. After meeting the "fighting fundamentalist," he understood that a new day was coming in that "heathen country" which had a Christian leader in the person of Chiang Kai-shek. He realized the doors for Christian ministry had opened as never before. He confided to Norris, "I feel that God has laid His hand on me and called me to China."[34] Norris was delighted and promised to help Birch realize his calling. To prepare for the assignment, he would study for one year at Norris's newly established Fundamental Baptist Bible Institute in Fort Worth and then go to China under the auspices of the World Fundamental Baptist Missionary Fellowship. There is nothing to suggest that he hoped to attend a better established or more prestigious theology school or seminary, even if one would accept him after his role in the heresy scandal at Mercer. It seems his decision was driven by Norris's persuasive powers and the promise that he would be sent as a missionary to China.[35]

Birch saw Norris as a role model possessed of tremendous strength of will and purpose. Norris saw in Birch "a young minister of unusual powers and gifts—not only a student and teacher, but a preacher of remarkable ability," and invited him to preach at a large Sunday morning service at First Baptist Church, not long after his arrival.[36] Birch told the Fort Worth congregation, "One day I read about an old-fashioned, narrow-minded . . . Baptist preacher from Texas. I had heard a lot of talk about this man, and some of it was pretty bad." But he was mightily impressed when he heard Norris speak in Georgia. He went back to Mercer "resolved to stand for the Lord even if they expelled me and all my friends turned against me."[37]

Birch delivered a rousing sermon, asking what should be the place of the believer "in these dark and darkening times . . . in these days of distress and fear, and distrust and hatred among nations?" If there was hope, it was not to reform, improve, and "whitewash the present wicked world" but to "change it by living godly, honest lives," he declared. The Lord would take care of the Kingdom of God on earth. "We don't need to worry about that. . . . It is our mission to call men out of the world, to call men to repentance." There are those who say that fundamentalists are small-minded and old-fashioned, yet they admit something is missing in their own lives, said Birch. "We should count it all joy when we shall be persecuted for righteousness' sake."[38]

John Rawlings, one of the first sixteen students at the Bible Institute, remembers Birch as "very opinionated and very intelligent." Aside from classes, the students did some street preaching and attended revival meetings. Birch sometimes came over for meals with Rawlings and his wife to talk about Christianity and to debate issues in the Bible. "I never met a man more committed to his ministry. He was determined and patient and deeply moral." But Birch "didn't care much for preaching to cowboys and farmers and winos, and he didn't do much house-to-house evangelizing," Rawlings told me. Birch had no girlfriends, though he said to Rawlings, "I wish I could find a wife like yours."[39]

The Bible Institute's classes were taught at the First Baptist Church in the mornings and evenings, mainly by the president, Louis Entzminger, who had worked with Norris since 1913. He was the son of a country preacher from South Carolina, well known for his work with the Sunday school movement in Florida and Kentucky, which provided Bible study for children as well as adults, typically before or after church services on Sunday mornings. An efficient and effective organizer, the dour, bald-headed Entzminger was Norris's self-effacing right-hand man for thirty-four years. Norris called him "Entz," and he called Norris "chief." The students saw little of Norris, who traveled incessantly. Birch joked, "He seems in one respect to be a little like Elijah in that we don't know when to expect him."[40]

The Institute's first-year curriculum consisted of studying the scriptures from Genesis to Revelation. In addition to Bible study, preaching, and winning souls, Birch and his colleagues were educated about the business side of Norris's burgeoning empire. They learned about organizing Sunday school work and recruiting new members. Services in Fort Worth and Detroit were held in "practical and simple" auditoriums, not extravagant churches "where people feel ill at ease." Schedules and sermons were publicized on the radio and in a weekly newspaper. Men and women volunteered their time and labor. Everyone was instructed to be positive and enthusiastic. Underlying all of this activity was a "Bible only" philosophy; the Sunday school used no materials other than the King James Bible. "It was far better to study the Word of God than to study merely what someone had written about the Word of God," said Entzminger.[41]

With its limitless possibilities for saving souls and fulfilling prophecy, China was an irresistible cause for Frank Norris, who thrived on the adventure of foreign travel and was constantly working to boost his international profile. Norris, his wife Lillian, and G. Beauchamp Vick, superintendent of the Temple Baptist Church in Detroit, visited Shanghai in September 1939—just as Birch was starting his studies at the Bible Institute—and sent home enthusiastic reports about plans to build a "gigantic new tabernacle in the heart of Shanghai's millions."

(Nothing ever came of the idea.) They attended services that were "packed to standing room not only on Sunday but through the week." Norris baptized eighty converts one afternoon. Vick cabled Detroit and Fort Worth: "Conditions here in Shanghai terrible, but marvelous opportunity to proclaim Gospel and win souls."[42]

After visiting the bombed ruins of a sizable school run by Baptists on the outskirts of Shanghai, Norris callously concluded, "It looks like the judgment of God is on this mission that substituted education for evangelization." Christian missionaries had one purpose only, according to fundamentalists like Norris—Christ's command in the New Testament book of Matthew: "Go ye therefore, and teach all nations, baptizing them in the name of the Father, and of the Son, and of the Holy Ghost." This singular purpose was not to be confused with well-meaning charity. "There are so many things that are good things in themselves, but they are not in Jesus' Great Commission to preach the Gospel to all lands," said Norris. "It is not the business of the Church of Jesus Christ to go into the high school business. Imagine the Apostle Paul building gymnasiums and building high schools in Ephesus!"[43]

In June 1940, John Birch, Oscar Wells, and Ralph Van Nortwick were the first three graduates to receive their diplomas from the Bible Institute, one year after they had enrolled. Reinforcements were urgently needed for the small, struggling mission in China. It was later claimed that Birch completed a two-year course in half the time because he was so brilliant.[44] In reality, he never expected to stay in Fort Worth for more than ten months. It was clear from the beginning that the students would be sent out as soon as possible. Besides, the Bible Institute offered a limited number of courses, many of them already familiar to Birch from his studies at Mercer University, where he had studied the New Testament in Greek.

Led by Norris, about 150 members of the First Baptist Church gathered at the Fort Worth train station to send off Birch and Wells to the Far East, as East Asia was then known.[45] (Van Nortwick had been scheduled to join them but, with a wife and two-year-old child, decided against going because of the threat of war.) Norris opined, "The two heroic young men are undaunted by the war, and they go fully informed as to the dangers that await them, but they go like the Apostle Paul when he knew that it meant death at Jerusalem." When peace returned, Norris

Members of Temple Baptist Church, Detroit, Michigan, sending John Birch to China as a missionary in June 1940. From left to right in the front row are George, Douglas, John and Ethel Birch, and Louis Entzminger. Credit: Arlington Baptist College Heritage Collection.

added, new Chinese converts "will go back home throughout the country and kindle the fires of evangelism wherever they go." It would be "the greatest revival of all times."[46] It was not the first time that Birch would show tenacity in the face of adversity, nor would it be the last.

Before leaving for China, Birch visited his family in Macon and then drove with his parents and brother Douglas to Detroit, where Louis Entzminger joined them to sign up supporters for Birch's mission under the auspices of the World Fundamental Baptist Missionary Fellowship. In a photograph with members of Temple Baptist Church, Birch sits front and center, smiling and confident. The Birches visited Niagara Falls on the return trip to Georgia, where John bid farewell to his parents, siblings, and other relatives. He left saying, "Goodbye, folks. If we don't meet again on earth, we'll meet in heaven."[47]

Part Two

Waging War

LIKE SO MANY AMERICANS, John Birch would be remade in the crucible of war after Japan's December 1941 surprise attack on Pearl Harbor. He had written ten months earlier, "It does look as though Uncle Sam were about to go to war against the dictators; I'm for it, but let us not forget that ours is the bigger battle!"[1] Even as a college student, he was pessimistic about prospects for peace, telling his Aunt Marion in 1938 that the Munich Agreement "is not destined to be very permanent. We will continue to have international strife as long as we have national selfishness and . . . we will have individual selfishness everywhere except where it is replaced by individual self-surrender to Jesus Christ!"[2] For men like Birch, however, the "bigger battle" of winning China for Christ would have to wait until Japan was defeated.

The Chinese Nationalists (also known as the Kuomintang or KMT) had been fighting a war of attrition against Japan since 1937, trading territory for time, and victory was nowhere in sight. In spite of an increasingly desperate situation, Franklin Roosevelt confidently envisioned China as a strong, unified state and the essential anchor for peace, stability, and democracy in Asia after the war. The problem was that Roosevelt's high-minded rhetoric was never matched by American actions. Geography was the primary reason for this gap. By 1942, Japan controlled most of China's eastern seaboard as well as access through French Indochina (Vietnam, Laos, and Cambodia) to the southeast and Burma to the southwest. Supplies could only be transported by air from the Assam Valley in northeast India over the Hump—daunting mountain ranges the Chinese called the Camel Peak.

Time magazine correspondents Theodore White and Annalee Jacoby described the Hump as "the most dangerous, terrifying barbarous aerial transport run in the world. Unarmed cargo carriers crossed 500 miles of uncharted mountains and jungles at 20,000 feet in spite of the Japanese air force, tropical monsoons, and Tibetan ice."[3] During some months, the U.S. Air Transport Command lost more planes and personnel than the 14th Air Force in China, which it supplied. According to one source, more than six hundred planes went down, and 1,140 crewmen and passengers gave their lives. For two and a half years—until the Burma Road was reopened in early 1945—American transport planes ferried medicine, machinery, bombs, airplane parts, trucks, and jeeps into China. They also flew tons of Chinese bank notes printed in the United States to keep up with rampant inflation. On the return journey they brought out "wounded American soldiers as well as tungsten, tin and wolfram, pig bristles, and silk for parachutes."[4]

There were no American ground forces in China, only the relatively small U.S. Army Air Forces. Without adequate planes, pilots, spare parts, fuel, and ammunition during the early years of the war, even the best training, intelligence, and cooperation with the Chinese had little value. According to General Claire Chennault, commander of U.S. air forces in China, it took eighteen tons of materiel flown across the Hump for every ton of bombs dropped in China. It took six gallons of aviation fuel to deliver one gallon to forward bases in China. "The Fourteenth Air Force fought for the first six months of 1944 on supplies that could have been carried by six Liberty ships," complained Chennault.[5]

Chennault was sure that he could wipe out Japanese air power in China if the United States would earmark "even a small percentage" of its airplane production for his command.[6] More bombers were delivered by the fall of 1942, but the number of American personnel in China remained very low throughout the war compared to the U.S. presence in Europe and the Pacific. As of January 1945, U.S. forces in China numbered only thirty-three thousand, which increased to sixty-three thousand by August. As historian Warren Cohen writes, "it was important to give the Chinese enough aid to keep them fighting, but it was not necessary to give them enough to win."[7] Some critics would later conclude that America's relative neglect contributed to the Communists' rise to power, although it is doubtful that greater U.S. intervention would have made any difference in the outcome.

American war planners kept open the possibility of attacking Japan through China—which very likely would have meant cooperation with the Chinese Communists—but the United States opted instead for an island-hopping campaign across the vast reaches of the Pacific Ocean. The Nationalist government was simply too isolated, its military capabilities and politics too uncertain, and the Japanese presence too strong. Chinese factionalism and corruption as well as bitter feuds among American leaders produced rivalry, jealousy, confusion, and mistrust. The lack of a clear-cut strategy, bureaucratic infighting, and inefficient communication between Washington and Chungking ensured that China would remain a sideshow as far as the United States was concerned.

5

After Pearl Harbor

AS THE CLOUDS OF global war gathered, Birch decided to move his mission work into Free China, as the territory not occupied by the Japanese was called. In September 1941, one year to the day after arriving in Hangzhou, he struck out for Shangrao, a small city in Jiangxi Province, some two hundred miles to the southwest. The journey was not without risk, but in large swaths of occupied China it was said that Japanese control extended no farther than a rifle bullet travels. Japanese soldiers controlled points and lines—cities and towns and the railways, roads, and rivers connecting them—but lacked the manpower to rule the countryside. The enemy would send out patrols during the day; Chinese militia and guerrilla forces typically would operate at night.

Birch traveled with Wu Meng'en, a Chinese evangelist; a young guerrilla named Wang; and two baggage porters. Winding through the mountains with their bicycles, they hid from a Japanese patrol at one point along the way. While waiting in a bamboo and pine grove next to the trail, Birch later wrote to his parents, "I read the book of Ezekiel and ate a lot of Chinese persimmons." As they moved onward around sundown, several hundred Chinese converged along the path and Birch witnessed a strange assortment of "owners of small shops in inland towns, guerrilla officers, wives going to join their husbands in Free China, university students from Shanghai on their way to help a new China arise." There were "long lines of men with bulging loads swinging from the carrying-poles across their shoulders, hurriedly slipping along in the gathering dusk," smuggling goods from the coast to the interior.

Wang had come down with dengue fever and was too weak to walk, so he had to be carried on Birch's bicycle. After traveling several hours "by the light of a slender new moon," they reached a canal where they boarded boats and made their way across Japanese lines. Walking a few more miles, they slept in a small inn "in the very intimate company of several species of bugs." Enemy soldiers were not far away, and reportedly had killed seven of the Chinese behind them. That night Birch was awakened by the noise of a battle: "You could hear the Japanese cannon and the Chinese machine-guns and rifles talking back and forth like people quarrelling." Farther on they were fed a warm breakfast by a Christian Chinese officer and his wife, whom Birch had known in Hangzhou. At the next stop, they had the unusual experience of eating a meal with a captured Japanese officer. After spending the night in the town of Lanxi at a China Inland Mission compound, they boarded a train to Jinhua, the provisional capital of Zhejiang Province, where they had lunch with a Northern Baptist missionary couple from the United States before finally reaching Shangrao.[1]

Frank Norris eagerly published the details of Birch's harrowing journey in *The Fundamentalist* under the bold red-ink headline: "Thrilling Account of How John Birch Escaped from the Japanese." Norris said the story, which was broadcast over his radio stations in Detroit and Fort Worth, "should be read in every home, in every Sunday School class and every congregation."[2]

Northeast Jiangxi, where Birch was now located, produced rice, soybeans, sugar cane, millet, oranges, persimmons, and grapefruit. Cattle and water buffalo were common. But it was a poor and remote area and could be dangerous. During the warlord period of the 1920s, bandits regularly kidnapped foreigners for ransom. The Chinese Communists established a "Soviet" base in the area in 1931, targeting landlords as class enemies and missionaries as imperialist spies. The Red "bandits" were driven out by the Nationalists, but then Japanese bombing raids brought devastation from the air. "This town has been destroyed several times over," reported Birch, "but the Chinese build it back as fast as the Jap planes destroy."[3]

After getting settled in Shangrao, Birch and Wu preached to a local Fundamental Baptist congregation. "The people here use Mandarin and can easily understand me, and I can understand them better than the folks in Hangchow." He was eating rice and vegetables twice a day with Chinese workers. "On top of this, I'm taking a quart of milk a day from a Christian who has several cows." He weighed about 155 pounds. "Malaria and dengue knocked me down a little," he casually mentioned, "but I'm coming back up."[4] Since there was electricity, he unpacked his small radio and one evening heard messages from his family on KGEL, a short-wave broadcast from the States.

"I am having the time of my life," Birch wrote to his parents. During the previous month, he was making headway with attendance at Sunday services and had baptized nine new Christians in a local river—two women and seven men. "There were more candidates but they didn't come because the weather turned cold." In this area, "there are hundreds of thousands of souls who have not once heard the message of salvation." With the exception of Tibet and other parts of China's far west, he exclaimed, "this is the least evangelized place in all China!"

He was in good health and had a radio, telephone service, and enough Chinese to give a short sermon. In addition, he noted, being from the United States was a distinct advantage. "I am welcome anywhere because I am an American, and America is China's friend; the Chinese officials are more polite to me than they are to one another." On one occasion, Birch and two Chinese colleagues, Mr. Chen and Mr. Hu, rode their bicycles some eighteen miles into the countryside where they shared their message with a large number of people. In another town, the itinerant preachers were warmly welcomed by an audience of two or three hundred Chinese soldiers. "The Holy Spirit was present in a wonderful way; officers and men listened spellbound for over two hours." Some had read Generalissimo Chiang Kai-shek's booklet, "Why Should I Believe in Jesus Christ?" One officer had been a Roman Catholic, wrote Birch, until the three fervent Baptists brought him around to their point of view.[5]

"I want to join the army."

Soon after the United States declared war on Japan in December 1941, Birch contacted the U.S. Embassy in Chungking, China's wartime capital, to ask about his draft status. He was informed there was no requirement to register for the Selective Service since he was living overseas; if he wished he could volunteer with the American Military Mission. The situation in Shangrao was growing desperate. For six months, no money had reached him from the Fundamental Baptist Missionary office in Chicago, nor had he received any news from his family. Recently recovered from the debilitating sweats and chills of malaria, he found it increasingly difficult to survive on a diet of rough red rice and cabbage. One of the young Chinese evangelists working with him decided to leave for his home in the south. Motivated by patriotism as well as the need to survive, Birch decided to make a case for joining the U.S. Army:

> April 13, 1942
> The American Military Mission to China
>
> Gentlemen:
>
> I am writing to enquire as to the present opportunities for and the need of volunteer service in the United States armed forces in this part of the world.
>
> I am an American citizen (recently registered with the Consulate in Kunming), twenty-three years old, able bodied and single. I was first honor man, Mercer University (Ga.), '39, and an independent Baptist missionary in Jap-occupied Chekiang [Zhejiang] from July, 1940 to the outbreak of war on December 8, 1941. Since that time I have been preaching here in Free Kiangsi [Jiangxi], but am finding that increasingly hard to do on an empty stomach (no word or funds from home since November).
>
> To continue my self-glorification—I can preach and pray, both in English and Chinese, can speak enough Mandarin to get by, can build and operate radio transmitters and receivers, can stand physical hardship. I believe in God, his Son, in America, and in freedom; I hold them all more precious than peace and more precious than my earthly life. I have lived for more than a year behind the Jap front lines, and what I have seen strengthens my belief in the worth of freedom and the need of destroying the Japanese army.
>
> Why all this "I" stuff?—because I want to "jine the army." Why do I want to join the army?—There are two reasons: first, I want to do my patriotic bit in pushing back the gang that is swarming our boys in Bataan, P.I. [the Philippine Islands where U.S. and Filipino forces surrendered to the Japanese in March], and second,—the above-mentioned empty stomach.
>
> I should like to be a chaplain—I am an ordained Baptist minister (I think that's what they wrote in the minutes of the Georgia Baptist Convention (1937–39), but if there is no demand for chaplains I should cheerfully "tote" a rifle, run a short-wave set, or drive a truck, or be an interpreter, or whatever they tell me to do. What pay does a private draw a month? $21? That's more than

enough for me. Please write me what my chances would be if I were to go to Chungking to volunteer, even if you have to write "Nil."

Yours for victory,

John M. Birch[6]

Birch's decision to volunteer was inspired as much by idealism as the realization that his current path had run its course. The Japanese enemy was advancing, and he was without food or money. Leaving his small flock of believers was outweighed in his mind by the knowledge that war threatened not only his own survival but China's very existence. He was no pacifist after witnessing some of the horrors of war while in Hangzhou: "a humble Chinese brother who was beheaded because he preached Christ rather than the Emperor of Japan"; Chinese girls "after Japs machine-gunned them"; and a Japanese soldier who stole "the pitifully few grains of rice belonging to a large family of starving children."[7] Exactly what he would do in the army was unclear; he only knew that the time had come to reorder his priorities and give what he could to the war effort.

Birch thought that if the military did not want him, he would probably head for "virgin territory in West China" and start a new mission.[8] Though he could not yet admit it, he was growing disillusioned with the all-too-human flaws and failures of the mission enterprise. There were many selfless and inspired men and women serving the Christian cause in China, but bureaucrats bickering over money and grasping for control had soured him on organized religion. He had seen firsthand the wheeling and dealing of Frank Norris, and understood the compromises to be made. It all seemed too grasping, too worldly for his ever independent spirit.

His missionary colleagues back in Shanghai did not fare so well. Fred Donnelson remembered that John frequently urged him and Oscar Wells, Birch's partner from Fort Worth, to escape into Free China, but they stayed in Shanghai where their lives seemed more predictable. After the United States and Japan went to war, their status changed from untouchable neutrals to enemy aliens. First the banks closed and funds were frozen; then American businesses, churches, and schools were shut down. All foreigners soon were ordered to come to Japanese military police headquarters for fingerprinting. They were allowed small weekly withdrawals from their bank accounts, but food was scarce and prices skyrocketed. Gasoline was a banned commodity, and citizens of nations fighting Japan were "invited" to give up their cars. Next came the order to turn in all radios. Donnelson remembered that "blockades and blackouts were the order of the day and night and one never knew when he left his house whether he would return alive or not." Then came the chilling news that the Japanese arrested and beheaded Fu Lingben, a pastor who had worked for the Fundamental Baptists.[9]

Wells had fallen in love and married Myrtle Huizenga, an American nurse working in a tuberculosis hospital in Shanghai. Her father was a medical missionary. (Mother Sweet asked John Birch to marry Myrtle's sister, but according to Wells, Birch wanted "to take China for the Lord before getting married."[10]) It was not until February 25, 1943, after the U.S. government interned people of Japanese ancestry, that the Wells and their six-week-old daughter, Shannon, together with Fred and Effie Donnelson and their teenage daughter, boarded buses to be transported with other Westerners to an internment camp on the outskirts of Shanghai. (Shannon Wells Lucid would become an American astronaut who flew on several U.S. space shuttle missions and in 1996 spent six months aboard the Russian space station *Mir*.) On the campus of a former university, 1,500 American, British, and Dutch civilians lived for the next eighteen months in captivity. Food was limited; dysentery and scurvy were common.

Five hundred and thirty internees, the Wells and Donnelson families among them, were repatriated in exchange for Japanese prisoners in September 1944. Mother Sweet, who because of her age and poor health was not interned, decided to stay in Shanghai, where she died at the age of eighty-one in April 1945. In the neutral Portuguese colony of Goa on the west coast of India, the Western prisoners were transferred from the *Teia Maru* (originally a French ship seized by the Japanese in Saigon in 1942) to the MS *Gripsholm*, whose Swedish crew welcomed them with large Nestlé chocolate bars and fed them cheese, fresh fruit, and loaves of bread with butter. Frank Norris met the Wells and Donnelson families at the dock in New York City and took them straight to Temple Baptist Church at 14th and Marquette Streets in

Detroit, where they told the congregation how their faith had sustained them through the ordeal.[11]

Tokyo Raiders

A chance encounter deep in the countryside of Zhejiang Province added considerable luster to Birch's budding image as a hero. About one week after volunteering for the U.S. military, he happened to meet up with Lieutenant Colonel James H. Doolittle and his crew, a fortuitous experience for the young missionary. The American flier had just led an audacious air raid over Japan's main island of Honshu. It was an electrifying event. Four months after Pearl Harbor, it proved for the first time that the Japanese home islands were vulnerable to attack.

Volunteers for the mission to bomb Japan were trained on Wagner Field at Eglin Air Force Base in Florida, where for several weeks they practiced taking off from a very short runway. They then flew across the country to California; loaded their planes on the USS *Hornet*, an aircraft carrier docked at Alameda Naval Air Station in Oakland; and sailed under the Golden Gate Bridge and into the Pacific on April 2, 1942. There were eighty airmen in total, a crew of five for each of the sixteen B-25 Mitchell medium bombers.[12]

Steaming toward Japan early on the morning of April 18, the Americans sighted and sank two Japanese patrol boats. But because the Japanese sailors had time to send off radio reports about the U.S. task force, it was necessary to launch the bombers about ten hours earlier than planned, some six hundred nautical miles east of Tokyo. It was an unheard-of feat, since aircraft carriers were designed for small fighter planes, not large bombers. Doolittle piloted the first plane down the runway into heavy wind and rain. He was an excellent choice to lead the extraordinarily hazardous mission. The intrepid aviation pioneer, who stood only five feet four inches tall, held a doctorate in aeronautical engineering from MIT and had set several records, including a flight across the United States in less than twenty-four hours. He was the first airman to take off, fly, and land an airplane solely by instruments.

The early Saturday afternoon attack on the cities of Tokyo, Yokohama, Nagoya, Kobe, and Osaka caught the Japanese completely by surprise. Several of the bombers sustained damage from anti-aircraft guns, but none was shot down. It was impossible to return to the *Hornet*, which turned around and headed back to Honolulu with its task force immediately after launching the planes. Doolittle's plan was to keep flying west and south to airfields in unoccupied China, where they could land, refuel, and continue on to Chungking in Sichuan Province. But in order to maintain total secrecy, the Americans had not informed the Chinese of their impending arrival. Even Chiang Kai-shek and Claire Chennault, in charge of U.S. Army Air Forces in China, had no idea that the B-25s would come from the east, rather than flying from India to bomb Japan from bases in China. Chennault wrote in his memoirs, "If I had been notified, a single A.V.G. [American Volunteer Group] Command ground radio station plugged into the East China net could have talked most of the raiders into a friendly field. . . . My bitterness over that bit of bungling has not eased over the passing years."[13]

Because of the early launch and with the push of a strong tailwind, all but one of the aircraft reached China's southeastern coast around dusk instead of dawn. The pilots were forced to look for strange airfields in the dark, and there were no homing devices—a plane from Chungking carrying the radio beacons had crashed in bad weather a day or two before—nor were there light beacons or landing flares at any of the five designated fields. "To the contrary," remembered Doolittle, "when our planes were heard overhead an air raid warning alarm was sounded and lights were turned off." All the pilots could do was "set a dead-reckoning course in the direction of Chuchow [Quzhou], abandon ship in midair, and hope that we came down in Chinese-held territory."[14]

Flying low on gas through dense clouds and heavy rain, the Americans had covered 2,250 miles during some thirteen hours at a low altitude and low speed to conserve fuel. Doolittle, the last to bail out of his plane, was the only one of the airmen with any parachute training. He had broken his ankles fifteen years earlier when he fell out of a window in Chile, but this time landed softly in a recently fertilized rice paddy where the stench of manure was overwhelming. He knocked on the door of a nearby house, calling out in halting Chinese, "I am an American." The people inside promptly bolted the door and turned off their lantern. Soaked to the bone, he found shelter in a mill and spent most of the night doing light calisthenics to stave off the cold. Fortunately, he had come down in unoccupied China, about seventy miles north of the intended landing site. Other men from his and several other planes were scattered across the surrounding valleys and mountains; some wrapped themselves in their silk parachutes to keep warm.

There was wind and torrential rain in the area of Tianmu Mountain on the night of April 18, recalled He Yangling, the young Nationalist Chinese governor of western Zhejiang Province. Hearing the roar of a plane overhead, he issued orders for a blackout and twenty minutes later heard a tremendous crash. The next morning, the governor was informed that German and Italian paratroopers had landed in the area, a report that sounded strange to him.

Doolittle awoke to a clear sky and found a farmer who took him to a Chinese military garrison where there was a young major who spoke some English. "I still had my .45 automatic and the first thing he asked for was my weapon," recalled Doolittle. "I refused and told him that we were allies, that we were fighting a common cause and that neither one of us was supposed to take anything from the other. He was very firm, but I was also very firm." Only after his parachute was discovered was his story confirmed, and from then on "everything went very smoothly."[15]

Not long afterward, Governor He was informed about two foreigners in military uniforms who had been hiding themselves in an ox cart. They were brought to him and proved to be Americans. One was Doolittle (described by the governor as "short and strong"), and the other was Lieutenant Richard Cole, his co-pilot ("taller and bigger"). They arrived at the governor's residence and his wife gave them breakfast. Doolittle washed and put on fresh clothes and cloth shoes; his uniform stank from the paddy field. He then sent a telegram to General Henry "Hap" Arnold in Washington, commander of U.S. Army Air Forces, via the U.S. Embassy in Chungking: "Tokyo successfully bombed. Due bad weather on China coast believe all airplanes wrecked. Five crews found safe in China so far."[16]

By early afternoon, Chinese search parties located the other three members of Doolittle's crew, Lieutenant Henry Potter and Sergeants Fred Braemer and Paul Leonard. On the following day, he and his crew went to investigate their plane's crash site. The wreckage of the

B-25, strewn across the mountainside, had been ransacked. Clothing, food, machine guns, and metal pieces of the fuselage had disappeared, but some documents and maps eventually were recovered from local people.

Word of the U.S. attack on Japan spread like wildfire, and the crew received a hero's welcome when they returned to Tianmu Mountain. Little girls presented them with flowers. Farmers offered them hens, eggs, peanuts, and shoes. A young Buddhist monk gave Doolittle a basket of tea and dry bamboo shoots.[17] Another crew member, who had hidden from the Japanese in a Buddhist temple, reported, "Everywhere the magistrates or high officials of the cities paid honor to us and gave us banquets, provided lodging for the night, and we always had

Jimmy Doolittle (center) and his crew with Governor He Yangling (third from left) and his staff in Zhejiang Province after they bombed Tokyo in April 1942. Credit: Jimmy Doolittle Collection, History of Aviation Collection, Special Collections Department, McDermott Library, University of Texas at Dallas.

a military guard accompany us to the next large city. Wherever we went we got the best of everything. Two Chinese doctors took care of the boys and refused any charge whatever for board, room or medicine."[18] Two women missionaries from England and America helped other airmen.

Because all sixteen planes were lost—even though they had successfully dropped their bombs over Japan—Doolittle was convinced that the mission was only half successful. He even believed that he might be court-martialed or would "sit out the war flying a desk."[19] To the contrary, even though the B-25s inflicted relatively little damage—each plane could carry only four five-hundred-pound demolition and incendiary bombs—the psychological impact was huge, both for Japan and the United States. The daring raid gave an enormous boost to American morale. Spencer Tracy played Doolittle in the 1944 Hollywood movie *Thirty Seconds Over Tokyo*. Rather than receiving a reprimand, Doolittle received the Congressional Medal of Honor from President Roosevelt at the White House on May 18, 1942.[20] All of the airmen on the mission received the Distinguished Flying Cross, and those who reached Chungking were honored with official Chinese decorations from Madame Chiang Kai-shek. It would be more than two years before American bombers appeared over Japan again.

"The first white man they had seen"

The American airmen made their way to a designated meeting area in Quzhou by foot, boat, train, car, pony, and sedan chair. Doolittle and his four men were accompanied by Governor He's secretary, Mr. Chao, who noted, "In every town we passed, in addition to being greeted by county chiefs, there were countless welcome gestures of the local people."[21] When they boarded a small boat, however, they hid in its cabin, fearing that Japanese informants might report their whereabouts. On April 19, they stopped at the town of Yandongguan on the Lan River in an area where John Birch happened to be visiting small churches. He remembered,

> I was eating in a small Chinese restaurant which overlooked the river and a Chinese officer came in who saw in me an opportunity to

practice some English, so started a conversation and soon remarked
that some Americans were in a boat anchored below the restaurant.
I knew there were no Americans in that area and told him he was
mistaken, but he said they were on a General's [Governor He's]
boat and had a policeman in a black uniform standing guard on
the boat. I went down there and said to the policeman, "Have you
any Americans on this boat?" He answered, "Mei Yu La" ("No"). So
I shouted: "Are there any Americans in there?" The doors broke open
and a lot of bearded faces said: "Come in here!"[22]

Doolittle said the voice was so convincing that they opened the door.
They saw a gaunt Western man with several days' growth of beard,
and one of the airmen exclaimed, "Well, Jesus Christ!" Birch replied,
"That's an awfully good name, but I am not he."[23]

According to Birch, Doolittle and his crew were very pleased to
see him because "they had an interpreter whose heart was in the right
place, but he didn't understand much English. They asked me to go
up the river with them as far as I could. . . . They didn't know what
the score was, [and] whether they had bailed out in occupied or unoccupied territory." He wrote to his parents, "They insisted that I leave
my boat and accompany them up the river—I was the first white man
they had seen in China." He was glad to help out; it was "the first time
I'd associated with celebrities."[24] Coming upon the Tokyo Raiders was
an extraordinary introduction to the U.S. military for Birch, a lucky
break for a starving missionary faced with limited options. Doolittle
recalled that "Birch was as delighted to see us as we were to see him. He
obviously knew his way around and could speak the language. I briefed
him on our predicament and he agreed to join us, translate for us, and
help us get on our way to Chuchow [Quzhou]."[25] As they traveled,
Birch talked about his missionary work and his willingness to assist the
war effort by joining the military. Doolittle promised to put in a good
word for him when he reached Chungking.

On the river that evening, Birch expounded on Chinese social and
cultural norms. Mr. Chao decided to refute the American preacher's
statements one by one. Birch claimed, for example, that the Chinese
understood the concept of home but not country. Chao replied, "In
the past, the Chinese were more loyal to the emperor than to their

homes, and the emperor was the symbolic head of a country. In recent years people love their country more than their homes, especially the younger generation." Staff Sergeant Fred Braemer asked, "Besides one's life, what do the Chinese hold most precious?" Birch said that material life was most important. Chao disagreed, quoting the philosopher Mencius who said it was not a source of regret to sacrifice oneself for the sake of justice.[26] When they reached the town of Lanxi the next morning, Birch returned to Shangrao by train. He never saw Doolittle again. After returning to the States a few weeks later, Doolittle wrote to Frank Norris to tell him that missionaries in China had been "most helpful to my men and me." But they were "all in a very bad way, eating inadequately and irregularly. Their condition is critical."[27]

"It never rains but it pours," Birch wrote home after finding two telegrams awaiting him in Shangrao. The first conveyed money from the Fundamental Baptist's Chicago office, and the second was from General Clayton Bissell, the principal aviation officer on General Joseph Stilwell's staff, "asking me to go to Chuhsien [Quxian, also known as Quzhou], find as many Tokyo raiders as possible, ship them out, bury the dead, and get hospitalization for the wounded. . . . How temporary this job is I do not know but I believe that Chen, Tu and Hu can carry on the church work around Shangjao until I return."[28] Doolittle had wasted no time in recommending Birch to his colleagues in Chungking.

Birch arrived in Quzhou on April 28, where he found Captain David M. Jones and about twenty B-25 pilots and crewmen at the airfield hostel. Doolittle already had left to speak with a Chinese general about either military action or a ransom to recover the airmen captured by the Japanese, neither of which proved possible. A majority of the Americans had set off for Chungking by this time, and "when the dead and wounded shall have been cared for, I shall go on, too," said Birch.[29] During daily Japanese bombing raids, the men found shelter in a nearby cave carved from a limestone cliff. Chinese workers would fill craters in the runway every evening.

Considering the enormous odds they faced, the Doolittle Raiders sustained remarkably few losses. The crew of one plane flew north and landed safely near Vladivostok, where they were interned by the Russians—who wanted to avoid war with Japan while they were fighting Germany for their survival—and were held until they escaped into Iran one year later. The Japanese captured eight fliers in China; three were executed by firing squad, one died of malnutrition in prison, and the other four were discovered in a prison camp in Beijing a few days after Japan announced its surrender.

Two men drowned after ditching in the sea close to the shore, and Corporal Leland Faktor, a twenty-one-year-old engineer-gunner from Plymouth, Iowa, was killed when he parachuted from his plane. Doolittle told a journalist that when Faktor's body was brought to the Americans, "they had taken his clothes away and he was being carried on the [bamboo] pole with his arms and legs lashed around the pole."[30] Doolittle left money with a Canadian missionary with instructions for Birch to locate a burial plot for Faktor. Since the outright purchase of property by foreigners was not allowed, the Chinese Air Commission offered the Americans free use of the land. "Shall accept unless otherwise instructed," Birch reported to Chungking. "The funds I received . . . are untouched." When the grave and headstone for Faktor were finally ready on May 19, Birch led a burial service for him with military honors, including a gun salute.[31] His remains would be exhumed and sent back to his home in Iowa sometime in 1947.

Shocked by the American air raid on Tokyo and other cities, the Japanese worried that airbases in southeast China might be used for future bombing raids on the home islands. Determined to prevent this, they exacted terrible revenge on the Chinese. In mid-May, they launched a military campaign with over one hundred thousand troops. Thirty-four Nationalist Chinese divisions opposed them, sustaining more than thirty thousand casualties. As Japanese troops drew close to Quzhou, authorities ordered the city's forty thousand inhabitants to evacuate, just as huge floods inundated the area. The Chinese pursued a scorched-earth policy, burning those homes not already destroyed by residents themselves so that nothing of value would fall into the hands of the "Japanese devils," as they were called. The enemy bombed the area, fired artillery, and released poison gas. A Tokyo news agency reported more than one hundred attacks and thirty machine-gun and bombing assaults against retreating Chinese forces. Five airbases in the provinces of Zhejiang, Jiangxi, and Guangxi were destroyed.[32]

Birch waited until May 25 to leave—after all of the American air-men had departed—by which time the Japanese were just outside the city. "You could hear their guns," he reported. Before leaving Quzhou that night, the Chinese gave him some equipment, maps, weapons, and personal articles salvaged from the B-25s. Two days after he left, the officers' training school where he had been staying was bombed and four men were killed. He spent the next three weeks making his way westward along narrow, winding, hilly roads by truck, train, and foot. "Coming through Kiangsi [Jiangxi] Province, we were greatly delayed by floods, washed-out bridges, impassable ferry crossings, and the like, time and again." After reaching the U.S. airbase at Guilin, he experi-enced the first airplane ride of his life. It was then, on June 17, that he coincidentally met Colonel Claire Chennault (soon to be promoted to General) and hitched a ride with him to Beishiyi Air Field, about thirty miles outside Chungking.[33]

In the parlor game of telephone—or Chinese whispers, as the British call it—a story changes slightly as it is relayed from person to person until the final version bears almost no resemblance to the original. So it was with Birch's useful but limited role in assisting the Doolittle Raiders. He never claimed that he had single-handedly rescued Doolittle and his men, but others came to believe that he did. Frank Norris quickly and happily embellished the story, placing Birch at the center of the action. By the time Robert Welch wrote his biography of Birch in 1954, he stated that Birch had rescued Colonel Doolittle and had been "instrumental" in locating and saving many of the Americans from other planes. Welch grandly, but wrongly, concluded that without Birch, few if any of the fliers would have survived capture and torture by the enemy.[34]

Doolittle later described Birch as a "courageous, dedicated, intel-ligent and resourceful young man who made himself extremely use-ful."[35] Yet there was never any doubt that the Tokyo Raiders owed their lives to the courageous Chinese farmers, soldiers, and officials who faced so much danger in guiding them to safety. Mostly nameless, they paid a horrific price for their good deeds. Chennault said in his mem-oirs about the enemy's retribution, "In a three-month campaign, the Japanese drove their bloody spear two hundred miles through the heart of East China, devastating twenty thousand square miles, ploughing up landing fields, and exterminating everybody remotely suspected of aiding the Doolittle raiders." Historian Keith Schoppa writes that the Japanese occupation of the area that summer "was remembered for its rapes, arson, pillage, and murders." Chiang Kai-shek reported to General George Marshall that the Japanese troops "slaughtered every man, woman, and child in these areas—let me repeat—every man woman and child."[36]

6

Becoming a Soldier

WHEN NEWS CAME THAT Birch's church in Shangrao had been destroyed, he was "both angry and discouraged." He later told an Army Air Forces historian, "I didn't feel like doing much more mission work. I asked the Mission Board to release me; they did, and I joined up." He had no military training; he had only witnessed some guerilla fighting "from a safe distance." Yet the transition to a soldier's life occurred with remarkable ease. In his mind there was no contradiction between his former life as an evangelist and joining the army, no need to reject or deny his past. He had substituted one all-consuming passion for another, a battle against a different form of evil, a tyranny that happened to be temporal instead of spiritual. He quite naturally expected to become a chaplain, which would afford "the double opportunity to serve God and country."[1] Little did he imagine he was about to assume an entirely new identity, not as a preacher but as an intelligence officer.

The start to his changed role was marked by a gathering in Chungking where Madame Chiang Kai-shek (Soong Mei-ling) hosted General Claire Chennault and the American Flying Tigers for a barbecue party to celebrate the U.S. Independence Day. Birch, who had just arrived, was included among the guests. Because of rain, the group had to move indoors where the "incomparable Madame Chiang," as Birch described her, "turned it into a real old-fashioned American get-together." They played a game of musical chairs, drank non-alcoholic punch, and Chennault received an oil painting of himself with Madame and

Generalissimo Chiang. It is not known if Birch was able to tell Mei-ling and her sister, Ching-ling, who was also at the party, that he was from Macon, Georgia, where both women had attended Wesleyan College.[2]

That same July 4th also marked the formal end of the Flying Tigers—officially named the American Volunteer Group (AVG)— although U.S. airmen in China would continue to be known by the more colorful name of *Fei Hu*. Now that the United States was formally at war, Chennault was recalled to active service as a brigadier general and made commander of the newly formed China Air Task Force, which became the 14th Air Force in March 1943.

On a hot, humid morning a few days later, Birch climbed the stairs of the headquarters building at Beishiyi Air Field, his shirt soaked in perspiration. He was looking for the office of Colonel Merian C. Cooper, Chennault's chief of staff. Thomas Trumble, Chennault's personal secretary, recalled that Birch entered the office as a missionary and came out as a second lieutenant. "He returned to our table and we welcomed him with coffee and toast and discreet questions." Trumble took an immediate liking to Birch, who asked for help in learning how to shoot a Colt .45 sidearm. The newly minted officer had never fired a gun in his life, and Trumble was happy to instruct him.

> I sketched out some paper targets and we walked into the countryside to find a place to practice. I pinned a target onto the face of a crumbling gravestone and showed him how to load and fire. The shots from his first clip were absolute misses. I showed him on a sketch how the sights should appear when they were lined up and his second try would have done credit to a practiced marksman. He fired a third clip and I was well satisfied.[3]

Trumble, Birch, and Arthur Hopkins, a Yale graduate who taught with the Yale-in-China program in Changsha before volunteering for the army, roamed the hills overlooking Beishiyi on nights when the summer heat made it too uncomfortable to sleep. Trumble, who had spent several years with the U.S. Navy before joining the Flying Tigers, said that he learned from them "about a China which I had never known existed." He was impressed that they liked and respected the Chinese, unlike most American soldiers.[4]

When asked what he could do, Birch replied that he was a missionary. He was told, " 'We have got one padre named [Paul] Frillmann and he's down in Kunming. He does a lot of things besides being a padre. He's the Mess Officer, Chinese Relations Officer, Special Services Officer and all kinds of things. You do the same thing here that he is doing down there and we'll call you the Assistant Chaplain.' So they took me on that way." Birch recalled someone saying tongue-in-cheek, "You don't know enough to be a private, [so] we will make you a Second Lieutenant."[5]

He quickly learned that the U.S. Army was a melting pot of men and women from all parts of the country and all walks of life—although racial segregation would not end until 1948. Stepping outside his more limited Baptist missionary experience, he had entered a world where differences mattered far less than comrade and cause. Money and class, even religious and political beliefs, were not the determining factors they had been for civilians. Everyone was united by a single goal of winning the war, and hierarchy was defined only by rank. The straight-and-narrow Birch got along surprisingly well with his hard-drinking, profane companions. The camaraderie of being with other Americans must have been exciting. Aside from meeting the Tokyo Raiders, his only interaction with foreigners in previous weeks and months had been periodic encounters with other missionaries.

He still expected to be made an Army chaplain "after certain regulations are waived from Washington," although ministering to men from a variety of Protestant denominations would have been a concession for the resolute fundamentalist. For the time being, however, he was learning about intelligence operations and finding the work "immensely interesting." After sharing the deprevations of the Chinese in the countryside, he relished the luxury of American-style food, including ice cream, cookies, and candy. "Imagine eating cookies that have been flown half-way around the world!" he exclaimed.[6] Hopkins—who was six-feet tall and no slight eater himself—remarked, "I never saw a man who could eat as much as John. . . . I would eat a large dinner with John and be filled up, but then he would eat a second dinner just like the first, starting with soup right on through dessert." Following dinner, Birch enjoyed playing chess with Tom Trumble.[7]

After a few weeks, however, Birch was informed that he could not be appointed as a chaplain "because of insufficient training." His degree from the Fort Worth Bible Institute was not equivalent to one from a fully accredited seminary. It seems he was not especially disappointed with the decision. And even if he had been approved to pin a cross on his collar, Chennault had other plans for him.[8]

"More valuable than any pilot"

Claire Lee Chennault was a hard-driving, chain-smoking, outspoken man from Louisiana who loved airplanes. With the men of the Flying Tigers, according to one account, he drank bourbon; hunted for ducks and doves in season; and played bridge, dominoes, mahjong, cribbage, and poker. He regularly sought out female companionship.[9] He attended Louisiana State University, briefly taught high school, and joined the army to become a pilot. After retiring from the Army Air Corps with the rank of captain at age forty-three, he was hired by Chiang Kai-shek in 1937 to advise the Chinese air force, just as war was breaking out between China and Japan. His health was poor and he was deaf in one ear from years of open-cockpit flying, but the pay was good and he had to support a wife and eight children. China offered the chance for a new start and possibly the right place to test his theories of air warfare, which stressed the advantages of fighter planes over bombers.[10] After the war, Chennault divorced his wife and married Chen Xiangmei, a Chinese journalist thirty-two years younger than he. Known in America as Anna Chennault, she was active in business and politics for many years after her husband's death in 1958.

At Chiang's request, and with President Roosevelt's approval, Chennault recruited three hundred men from the U.S. Army, Navy, and Marine Corps. They went on leave, held no rank, and were paid by the Chinese government in American dollars. According to Paul Frillmann, Chennault's chaplain and a former Lutheran missionary in Hankou, China, most of them had problems and were escaping something. Ranging in age from nineteen to forty-three, "they were all feeling their oats for the first time in a long time; they were making more money than they had ever made before or would be making in the armed forces, and they were all raring to go." Sailing from San

Francisco to Hawaii, Manila, Hong Kong, and Singapore, they drank Bols gin morning, noon, and night. Chennault met them on the dock in Rangoon, Burma, in the summer of 1941.[11]

Earlier Chinese air force training programs, first with Americans and then Italians, were failures. Starting in 1939, the Soviet Union supplied a number of airplanes flown by Chinese and Russian pilots, but the Russians pulled out after Germany invaded the USSR in June 1941. Chennault's fliers filled the gap while China trained new pilots and acquired new aircraft. Equipped with one hundred P-40B Tomahawk fighter planes—painted with a menacing shark's mouth and teeth on the front—the Flying Tigers fought alongside Britain's Royal Air Force in the skies over Burma before coming to China. Although there were only a few dozen serviceable planes at any one time, their exploits were legendary. The American public was captivated by these swashbuckling heroes who had volunteered to rescue the Chinese people. John Wayne starred as a pilot in the popular 1942 Hollywood film *Flying Tigers*. Chennault's chiseled face was featured on the covers of *Time* and *Life*.

Birch and Chennault developed a strong bond, despite their obvious differences in rank and age. Both men were fearless, strong-willed, and adventure loving. Both were mavericks who could be loyal to a fault, to other people and causes they deemed worthy. Both respected the Chinese as partners and allies. Colonel Jesse Williams said Birch was "particularly and thoroughly sold on General Chennault and rendered him, at all times, the most complete loyalty." Frillmann said Birch "was almost fanatical in his admiration of Chennault."[12] Chennault had similar appreciation for Birch. Upon learning of his death in 1945, he wrote in sympathy to his parents, "I have always felt that John was more than just a very good officer in my command, in fact I have always felt towards him as a father might feel toward a son. . . . His loyalty to me personally and his devotion to duty was beyond anything that was expected of him. I cannot praise his work sufficiently."[13]

At the outset of the war, American air power in China was badly hampered by a lack of timely, accurate information on the Japanese enemy. An official postwar evaluation bluntly stated, "As of [the] end of 1942, organized military intelligence gathering facilities as such, did not exist." China was the least known and probably the most difficult theater of air operations.

Maps and charts were inadequate and incorrect; different names are in use for [the] same cities and towns; many difficult Chinese dialects are current in different areas and provinces; provincial Government and military organizations make the friendly ground situation most confusing, and extremely difficult weather conditions combine to offer more natural opposition to successful air operations than is found in other theaters, not to mention the extreme difficulty of obtaining sufficient basic supply for essential operations.[14]

Birch stated in an interview with the 14th Air Force Historical Office staff, "There was no photo intelligence. We had to get what information we could from Chinese intelligence reports, mostly coming from Chungking; Chinese red tape is worse than ours. There was no rating of information [to determine reliability]—Chinese rumors and accurate intelligence were all mixed up together." Reports were often outdated by the time they reached headquarters. It was difficult to have Chinese documents translated because very few interpreters were available. "We practically had to start from scratch."[15]

One of the greatest intelligence needs was an early warning procedure to give fighter planes enough time to intercept enemy bombers before they reached their targets. The existing Chinese air-raid warning network was called the *jingbao* (alert) system, which used bells, sirens, or large colorful balls hoisted on a pole or a building. One ball warned people that enemy planes had been launched; two meant planes were heading for their area; and three signaled that an attack was imminent and everyone should take cover. Chennault added teams of people to the *jingbao* system to report by telephone and radio on the location, altitude, number, and type of Japanese planes. That information was then plotted on a map to determine the course and speed of incoming aircraft.[16]

Birch had some knowledge of China's geography and could locate place names, so he stayed busy helping Colonel Cooper and Lieutenant Martin Hubler with combat intelligence and target information. His ability to read Chinese characters was "invaluable," recalled one officer.[17] He also served as transportation officer at the Beishiyi base. But after Chennault's headquarters relocated to Kunming in November 1942, the office grew crowded with higher-ranking officers freshly arrived from the States. Birch began to feel he could be more useful in the field.

Early in 1943, Colonel Jesse Williams agreed to send him to investigate the condition of airfields in the southeast provinces of Fujian, Jiangxi, Zhejiang, and Guangdong. He traveled for forty days by plane, train, charcoal-burning and diesel bus, gas-burning and alcohol-burning truck, bicycle, sampan, and foot. The Japanese had done a thorough job of destroying bases after the Doolittle raid; Chinese workers had been conscripted to dig deep ditches across the landing strips at Quzhou and Lishui. Birch discovered one bright spot. Hidden in the hills near one airbase were thousands of fifty-five-gallon drums of 100-octane aviation gas.[18] The perilous but successful mission gave the former missionary the opportunity to prove his mettle.

Upon returning to Kunming, Birch learned that General Chennault was setting up a network of combat intelligence agents to coordinate with Chinese ground forces and relay information back to U.S. airbases. "Most of our field intelligence officers were old China hands," Chennault explained in his memoirs. "I tried to pick men who had lived in China before the war, spoke the language, knew the customs, and could live in the field on Chinese food." John Birch, Paul Frillmann, and Robert Lynn were former missionaries; Wilfred Smith and Sven Liljestrand were missionary sons; Malcolm Rosholt had been a journalist; and Sam West was a businessman.[19] Birch proved to be an excellent choice as the first American intelligence officer to live and work with Chinese troops in the field. He had done farm and crop surveys with aerial maps during his college years, knew how to operate and repair radios, and could survive harsh conditions. He was tough-minded and resolute about doing whatever it took to win the war.

Although Birch enjoyed intelligence work and was very good at it, he had become enthralled with the idea of flying airplanes. Hopkins remembered John's "greatest hope was to return home and become a fighter pilot. He did not feel that he was doing enough walking around behind enemy lines, but wanted to be in there shooting." Birch told his parents that men with wives and babies back home "are risking their lives while I work in comparative safety on the ground."[20] In the spring of 1943, he applied for training as a pilot, passed the physical exams, and was eager to return to the States for flight school, which would also give him the opportunity to see his family in Georgia. He repeatedly asked Chennault for permission to become a pilot, but the opportunity never came.

"Chances of transfer home for flight training diminishing as importance of job here increasing," he told his mother in a V-mail letter in December.[21] Chennault later explained to his parents, "John wanted flight training, but I persuaded him to stay on because he was most valuable to the 14th Air Force and his country as a liaison intelligence officer, more valuable than any pilot I had in my entire force."[22] After Birch's application was definitively rejected in early 1944, he vowed, "I'll learn to fly, someday, anyway; I believe planes will be useful after the war, in serving mission stations across the wastes of Central Asia and West China."[23]

Even while wearing a military uniform and operating as an intelligence officer, religion was never far from Birch's mind. James E. Tull, the son of a Southern Baptist minister from Arkansas, was the only Army Air Forces Protestant chaplain in China after the Flying Tigers were disbanded in July 1942. Itinerating from base to base, he was hard-pressed to hold services at several different locations. "Learning that Lieutenant Birch had been a Baptist missionary in China, I invited him to preach at one of our services. He accepted, and deeply impressed the men who heard him with a challenging, fearless gospel message. Thereafter, I asked Lieutenant Birch to speak whenever he had time to do so." From Tull's perspective, as he told John's father, Birch was "self-reliant, friendly, shrewd, and consecrated.... Others of us grew tired of China, tired of our tasks, and weary in spirit. He seemed to maintain a buoyant interest and vitality." Tull was convinced that Birch would return to his calling in due time. While the war had interrupted his evangelizing work, "his great ambition still is to settle down as a missionary of peace."[24]

Back in Texas, Frank Norris regularly featured Birch's exploits in the pages of *The Fundamentalist*, long before Robert Welch knew the name. When Birch became an army officer, Norris lionized him as the perfect fusion of evangelism and patriotism. This melding of religion and nationalism was meant to show that Norris and the Independent Baptists were on the right side of history.[25] He did not hesitate to inflate Birch's biography. A front-page headline in *The Fundamentalist* read, "John Birch Promoted to Three High Honors and Positions of Trust."

The Fundamentalist newspaper, published by the Texas preacher Frank Norris, regularly featured John Birch's exploits in China. Credit: Arlington Baptist College Heritage Collection.

It was stated that General James Doolittle and Madame Chiang Kai-shek ("no doubt the greatest woman of this age") both had praised Birch as "one of the greatest characters I ever met."[26] None of this was accurate, but John's parents must have been bursting with pride.

Dog Sugar Eight

Birch was assigned to Changsha, Hunan's provincial capital, in March 1943. Famous for its spicy food, Changsha is situated in a fertile, rice-producing region with a large river and a major north-south railway. Because of its location as a gateway to the south, the Japanese invaded the city four times between 1938 and 1944, finally occupying it until the end of the war in 1945.

Leading a small contingent of Americans, Birch's job was to serve as a liaison to General Xue Yue, commander of the Nationalists' Ninth War Area, where most of the American airbases in eastern China were located. "The Chinese received my party very well," recalled Birch. "From the very first day we had very happy relations."[27] The American team set up their radio equipment in a brick building on Yuelushan, a mountain opposite Changsha on the west side of the Xiang River, where their radio call sign was Dog Sugar Eight (DS8).[28] Paul Frillmann, who met Birch there after returning from the United States, discovered "a very lean, hearty, enthusiastic, strongly anti-Japanese American who gave me the impression that his only job in life was really to win this war against the Japanese." Birch was "a very religious man who daily invoked the help of God to help him kill Japanese," remembered Frillmann.[29]

General Xue, known as the "Little Tiger," was small in stature but a fierce fighter who led a successful defense of Changsha in 1941. Lulu Birkel, an American Presbyterian missionary, described "awful days of danger and destruction" during that battle. With daily bombings from the air, she recounted, people were getting jittery and many were leaving the city. There was widespread looting, and a number of women were assaulted when the enemy suddenly entered the city at dusk on September 27, only to be driven out by Chinese forces three days later. "The bodies of soldiers, policemen, and civilians are still lying dead in the streets. Many thousands of people sleep out in the open on the ground in three refugee camps set up by various mission groups. Their one meal per day is served in their laps since there are not enough bowls and chopsticks to go around." Her husband, A. H. Birkel, wrote, "The whole experience has been like a terrible and prolonged nightmare; but alas, there is no sudden awaking with a sense of unreality. The stark reality of death, destruction, cruelty and intense suffering is all about us."[30] Much of the city was devastated and under constant threat from bombing. Marjorie Tooker, an American nurse with Yale-in-China's Hsiangya Hospital, was "astounded by the resistance of victims who could survive for days on end with a bullet hole through neck or chest, or with broken bones or organs hanging out of their bodies."[31] Never was there enough hospital staff, supplies were touch and go, and inflation was an endless worry. The battle against bed bugs was perpetual.

The small enclave of foreigners in Changsha included English, German, Norwegian, and American missionaries—Methodists, Lutherans, Northern Presbyterians, and members of the China Inland

Mission. All of them spent much of their time doing either medical and relief work or education and training. The German mission ran a school for the blind where women and girls learned to knit sweaters. The American Presbyterians sponsored a spinning and weaving program for women. It was not a life of unremitting anxiety and discomfort, however, and at times the war seemed distant. There was an international glee club, led by a Chinese doctor. Maude Pettus, another Yale-in-China nurse, remembers Marjorie Tooker often would have a musical hour for Chinese and foreign staff at her home in the evenings. In this community, recalled Tooker, "I found many wonderful people, full of life and humor, dedicated and inspiring. They had one clear, common purpose in life, to serve the Lord and their fellow men."[32]

The Changsha missionaries also found time for evangelism. Lulu Birkel wrote to her board in New York that "disturbed conditions afforded an excellent opportunity for preaching the gospel.... Every evening when it was possible, and the weather was fit, a group of workers left our compound with hymn sheets, a bright lantern, an accordion, and a box for the speaker to stand on. The crowds listened with rapt attention, and eagerly reached out for the tracts which were distributed after the meetings."[33] Birch was pleased when Reverend Sunberg of the Evangelical Mission asked him to preach in Chinese at a young people's service. On another occasion he proudly told his parents about leading a Christmas service on one airbase and then flying to another base for one more service that same night.[34]

Later in the war, Frank Norris asked Birch about the prospects for expanding the Fundamental (Independent) Baptists' work into China's heartland. Birch recommended Changsha—which he called the cultural, political, economic, and military center of Hunan Province. He suggested that Norris approach the Bible Institute of Los Angeles about purchasing the Hunan Bible Institute, which included eight brick buildings on lovely grounds with "lawns, shade trees, and restful to the eye." But he politely declined the idea of leading such an enterprise himself. "I think an older man, one more experienced than I in matters of administration and whose recent life has been more wholly and fruitfully spent in the vineyard of the Lord, should be in charge. How wonderful if Fred Donnelson were there!"[35]

"Exceptionally meritorious conduct"

The first test of the new air–ground liaison system came in May and June of 1943 when the Japanese sent their troops into an area west of the large Dongting Lake in northern Hunan. Birch and his men gave real-time reports on the battle to American and Chinese airmen in fighter planes and bombers, who in turn coordinated with General Xue Yue's troops on the ground. "We were able at that time, simply by radioing information directly to Kunming, to give the air force faster and more accurate intelligence than any other American outfit was getting in China," said Birch. He was on the radio constantly communicating with fliers as they attacked. "The pilots used to talk about how much help it was and often said it was like being led by the hand to the target," recalled one American officer. "We called him the eyes of the 14th Air Force."[36]

Cooperation with the Chinese improved, and the information sent to 14th Air Force headquarters in Kunming became more detailed and reliable after the success of the first Dongting Lake campaign. Liaison

American and Chinese members of a radio and field liaison team led by John Birch, who is second from the left in the front row. Courtesy of Robert G. Birch.

teams were organized and sent to other war zones, and General Xue decided to set up a communications school in Changsha to train additional Chinese radio operators. The students, instructed in International Morse code, learned about the operation and maintenance of radios, studied the identification of enemy aircraft and ships and order of battle (information on the strength and disposition of military units), and were taught how to use panels—large pieces of cloth laid on the ground to signal information to pilots. Unfortunately, this well-meaning venture left much to be desired. Captain Thomas West of the Army Signal Corps reported that sixty-two students had only four STR-1 radios, "of which one set and battery were beyond repair, and the other three batteries required 48 hours to re-charge with our hand generators; twelve head sets; three keys; one PE [portable electric] generator which had been in service two years; and a makeshift switchboard made from old wire and nails obtained from the Chinese shops in Changsha."[37]

Radio field intelligence teams typically traveled with ninety-pound V-100 radios powered by a small hand-cranked generator. (Larger radio transmitters and receivers with Onan gas generators could send messages one thousand miles or more.) Messages were encoded and decoded upon receipt with the M-209, a small machine that cryptographers sometimes called "Little Jesus"—presumably because it could "speak in tongues." Based on a prearranged schedule, the numbers on disks inside the M-209 were set with four digits to represent specific Chinese characters according to the Chinese telegraph code, a standardized system which is still in use today. On Monday, for example, the schedule might add six to each digit; on Tuesday it would subtract fourteen, and so forth. The text of a message emerged on a piece of yellow tape paper. An operator would decipher the numbers as characters and translate them into English.

In August, Birch traveled north from Changsha with a group of men to survey conditions along the Yangtze River. His parting words to Arthur Hopkins were, "If anything should happen to me please tell my family I am deeply grateful for my Christian home and upbringing." He carried a Thompson submachine gun (a Tommy gun) and a .45 pistol. In addition to three Chinese radio operators whom Birch recruited in Kunming, there were "half a dozen Chinese coolies to carry the radios and their scant bedding," remembered Hopkins. Dressed like the local

Chinese, Birch and his companions walked for the entire trip because the roads were in such bad condition. The men ate poor-quality red rice and D rations—concentrated chocolate bars made by the Hershey Company. Along the way, they learned about a large iron ore smelting plant operated by the Japanese at Shiweiyao and relayed that information back to a U.S. airbase by radio. "I had the satisfaction of watching the first B-25 bombing of this target," said Birch.[38]

Birch told Colonel Wilfred Smith, his commanding officer, how thrilling it was when "he stooped down and scooped up some of the Yangtze River." His team rendezvoused with guerrillas in the area and set up a radio station on a hill overlooking the mighty river. Japanese artillery shelled them from the other side on one occasion. "They were pretty poor shots, but we wasted no time in taking cover." He later mentioned to his parents, "I came rather close to death a few weeks ago, but I have never felt more safe or secure."[39] Birch headed back to Changsha after about eight days. During the roundtrip he wore out two pairs of shoes while covering three hundred miles. He returned "lean, deeply sunburned but in splendid condition and greatly inspired with the success of his mission," wrote Hopkins.[40] It was gratifying when the Chinese spotters reported information on enemy ships passing through the Yangtze during the next twelve months.[41]

Birch traveled on to Hengyang, due south of Changsha, where Colonel Taber, head of the 11th Bomb Squadron, wanted to know if he had seen any good targets. He described a village near Hankou, a city on the north bank of the Yangtze, that was full of Japanese soldiers. "Can you show us where this place is?" asked Taber. Before long, Birch was riding in the nose of a B-25 in the bombardier's compartment to help locate the village. "The next day," he remembered, "my Chinese radio operators watching the road north . . . counted 30 Jap trucks piled high with bodies, leaving the village." He added, "That is about the only direct contribution I ever made to the war effort."[42] Birch was self-effacing about his accomplishments; he was just doing his job. But his feats were adding to a larger-than-life image that would be magnified many times over in the years to come.

The Japanese mounted a second, more ambitious campaign in the Dongting Lake region in the fall of 1943. The first news of the offensive came from Birch's intelligence network, which reported one thousand enemy soldiers crossing the Yangtze and one thousand more follow-ing, with another forty thousand concentrated in the general area. On the same day, Birch sent a request for planes to strafe Japanese cavalry along the road.

Captain Paul Frillmann and Corporal Sven Liljestrand were with Chinese forces in the city of Changde as the Japanese advanced west of Dongting Lake. They broadcast a steady stream of radio messages back to Birch in Changsha, which he pieced together and relayed to airbases in Hengyang and Guilin. During a critical phase of the fighting when the situation was changing rapidly, he asked for permission to transmit radio reports in the clear, without coding. This request was approved, except that place names were given female names such as Rose, Lily, and Louise, to keep the enemy from knowing their locations. The code name for Changsha was Marjorie—which happened to be the name of an American nurse whom Birch had met there.[43]

As the enemy surrounded Chinese troops from the 57th Division, Frillmann and Liljestrand's radio went silent. It was four long days before they came back on air to say they had escaped and were safe. At the height of the battle, Birch had urgently requested that planes be sent to bomb east of Changde, but this was denied with the explana-tion that "no city occupied in whole or part by Chinese troops will be bombed by our planes except by direct order of the Generalissimo." Birch asked General Xue Yue to rush a message to Chungking, which he did, and permission to bomb finally was received about thirty-six hours later. In the meantime, the Japanese pounded Changde with dive bombers and artillery. "The Japanese were not tied down by Chungking red tape," Birch later said resentfully. The Chinese troops fell back to a nearby mountain, but because of the delay only four hun-dred out of eight thousand men escaped, all of them starving. "I was never so mad at vested authority in my life. Definitely good training for anarchistic feeling," he added ruefully.[44] Birch also reported that forty Chinese-made portable radios had failed during the battle. "Because of poor construction the sets were worthless," he told Chennault. As a consequence, General Xue wished to purchase American-built radios.[45]

Chinese reinforcements retook Changde on December 9, 1943, pre-cipitating a hasty retreat by the Japanese. The Chinese persistence, aided by attacks from the air, threw the enemy into confusion. The 14th Air

Force had flown at least 1,276 sorties. "Our planes were definitely the deciding factor; it would have been a Japanese victory if our planes had not been in there," said Birch, although he acknowledged that most of the casualties were inflicted by Chinese infantry. "Those Chinese boys had been underfed, indifferently led, and were up against people whose equipment was new and a lot better than theirs.... I do not think you can praise them too highly." Instead of congratulating himself for contributing to the victory, he credited Frillmann and Liljestrand with the success of the first direct air–ground combat liaison operation in China.[46]

After the battle of Changde, Birch constantly traveled from place to place as Japan's military strength ebbed and flowed. He and his men relayed information about weather, the disposition of the Chinese soldiers, and Japanese shipping and troop movements; helped guide air attacks and reported on the results; and assisted in the rescue of downed

John Birch received the Legion of Merit from General Claire Chennault in July 1944 for "exceptional conduct and outstanding achievements." Credit: U.S. Army Air Forces.

American pilots. He was authorized to travel "by military or commercial aircraft, rail, motor vehicle or other available means of transportation." The items requisitioned for one of his missions included radios, weapons, demolitions, a significant amount of Chinese currency, and some small gifts—lipsticks, watches, fountain pens, cigarettes (Camels preferred), and lighters.[47] Between assignments, he spent time at the rear bases in Chungking, Kunming, and Guilin, where he gathered supplies, received instructions on new assignments, and recuperated from being in the field.

On July 17, 1944, General Chennault presented Birch with the Legion of Merit for his actions in the two Dongting Lake campaigns, citing his "exceptionally meritorious conduct in the performance of outstanding services and achievements." Birch called it "a rather ordinary job" and told his brother George Stanley, "I hate to see Uncle Sam's medals bestowed so commonly, but since they gave me one, I am happy for Mother's sake."[48] Regardless of his response, the award added to his growing reputation as a legend in his own time.

7

Searching for Love

JOHN BIRCH HAD NO time for romance at Mercer University or the Bible Institute in Fort Worth. But in China, despite being frequently in the field, he fell in love with three women, each of them lively, attractive, and intelligent. It was more than charm that drew them to John. Never had they met someone so focused and intense, a man with such clarity and purpose.

Two of the women grew up in China as the daughters of missionaries, which gave them a natural affinity with Birch. Marjorie Tooker was a nurse with Yale-in-China, and Audrey Mair was a Scottish nurse with the British Red Cross, both in the city of Changsha. The third woman, Dorothy Yuen, was a Chinese American from New York City who worked for the 14th Air Force at various bases in China. His letters to each of them reveal a tender, impulsive, romantic side of Birch, different from the dour image of a prudish missionary or a straight-laced soldier. His rough edges were sanded down as he shared his hopes and dreams with these women.

When a British Red Cross contingent of seventeen nurses and several doctors arrived in Changsha in September 1942, "the newcomers added considerably to our bridge and dance sessions," noted Tooker.[1] With the help of the Chinese Red Cross, the British unit found quarters and set up a small hospital and nursing school in a large building abandoned by the Bible Institute of Los Angeles (the same complex that Birch recommended to Frank Norris). Medical supplies were always inadequate, so the staff resorted to improvisation: "Many operations were successfully performed with a knife, a pair of forceps and a few borrowed instruments made of bone. Knitting needles belonging to one of the Red Cross workers proved an efficient substitute for the metal pins used in setting fractures," wrote one of the British surgeons.[2] A number of patients were poorly fed, badly clothed, generally wretched Chinese soldiers. From time to time the British also cared for downed American pilots, some of them terribly wounded.

Among the British Red Cross staff was Audrey Mary Mair. She was born in China in 1913 in the east-central city of Anqing where her parents served with the China Inland Mission, a large nondenominational evangelical organization. At the age of three, she returned with her older brother and mother to Scotland, while their father worked with Chinese laborers who had the grim job of clearing battlefields in France after World War I. The Mair family sailed back to China in 1923, and Audrey attended the Chefoo School, a British-style boarding school for missionary children on the north coast of the Shandong peninsula. (The publisher Henry Luce and writer Thornton Wilder were Chefoo students in earlier years.) After training as a nurse at the Sick Children's Hospital in Aberdeen and the Royal Infirmary in Edinburgh, she joined the Red Cross and was sent to Changsha, where Birch met her.[3] A trove of letters shows how smitten he was:

> I try in vain to concentrate on my work these days; coherent ideas slide away and I see your dark eyes gazing into mine with a kindness that belies your brisk Scots tongue. For many hours in the night, I cannot fall asleep, and when dreams finally come, bringing you with them, I no sooner recall your lips with mine than I awake trembling, to find you gone, and I am left with a lost and lonely feeling. . . . You see, my heart is in your hands now.[4]

He wrote her a poem, which read in part,

> A glimpse of thee, bonnie Scottish flower,
> In this darkened land and time,
> Has roused my soul, not for this hour,
> But forever, to love and cherish thee and thine.

Too short have been the days I've known thee;
If now we part, despite our wills,
Yet will time come when home I'll take thee
And we will roam the Highland hills.[5]

When Mair left Changsha in March 1944, Birch wrote her a series of letters burning with passionate longing. "Oh, Audrey! I never before knew what loneliness was! Darling, I need you. . . . If you can think of anything I can do to serve or please you, you will tell me, won't you? Please forgive this confused and incoherent note; my only excuse is, I'm a little mad from longing for you." He told his sister, "Frankly, I lose what little sense God gave me when I am near her."[6]

Birch asked for two copies of her photograph, one for him and one for his mother back in the States. "I wrote Mother of a Scots angel who

Audrey Mair was a nurse with the British Red Cross in Changsha. This photo was taken in Bombay, India after she left China in 1944. Courtesy of Michael Mair.

had fallen just low enough to notice her son and steal his heart and mind away." He wrote to Audrey that his mother "should have been a queen, but was born several hundred years too late, and in a land so free that too few may recognize and render the homage due to souls so rare and noble as hers." He then told her about himself:

> I am something of a farmer, something of a minister, something of a roving soldier; I expect after this war to pioneer missionary (mostly evangelistic—a little agricultural) work unless I shall have lost my hearing and vision spiritually, in which case I shall return to my moderately fertile land in Georgia, to be a poor farmer-philosopher. I shall always be poor, but with enough to eat and wear and read. Is this life repugnant to you, or unsatisfactory? Please answer me freely and frankly, Audrey, without sparing my feelings. If it lies beyond my power to make you happy, the earlier I know it the better! I love you more than life!
>
> Money cannot buy (but may destroy) the joy of a crimson sunset, a long look between lovers' eyes, the song of a bird at dewy sunrise in the mountains, the feel of prayer "going thru" to our God, the crash of the sea on rocky shores, the surge of strength when one rises in health on a cool morning, the peace and calm in a heart that has heard the promises of endless life from Christ, the stately beauty of still lakes surrounded by wooded hills, the look in the eyes of an unfortunate fellowman whom one has been able to help at a critical time, the babble of healthy little children, tired muscles stretched on a smooth bed at night,—this Audrey, is life as I like it, and in large measure, have found it, in the pilgrimage through this world![7]

Birch was concerned that "real and satisfying as these [things] are to me, they may prove insufficient for you; I will not drag you into a life which cannot offer you lasting joy, even tho', God knows, life without you has become torment for me." If she could not accept him, Birch told his father, "I will go my way alone, even tho' I love her so much that all other women (except Mother) no longer exist for me."[8]

Birch spent several days in Kunming in mid-March, longing to see Audrey again before she left for India. He borrowed a car and met every transport plane flying into the airbase. "Not one decent night's sleep has been mine since that night [in Changsha] when I discovered I loved you," he told her. "You entered my blood like a fever, and I'm afraid the fever is incurable!"9 When she finally appeared, Birch asked her to be his wife. It was on a moonlit, wind-swept hilltop that he proposed to her, on the eve of her departure for India. Allaying his fears about the trials of being a missionary wife in a remote area of China, she told him, "I'd rather be poor with you than to have a million dollars with anyone else in the world." Birch recalled, "Then we knelt down and asked God to forgive our wandering, to direct and bless our lives; after that I took her to the British Consulate where she is staying until she flies to India day after tomorrow." He told his parents, "I hope to get leave and see her in Simla. Wouldn't it be strange if I marry Audrey within a few miles of my birthplace!"10

Almost immediately he had second thoughts. "Never in my life have I been beset with so many devils of doubt and misgiving and fear." He was concerned about the "dark and confused state of our time," and worried that he did not know Audrey well enough. He asked her age, not realizing she was five years older than he. He confessed to his parents a "selfish desire for freedom from the bonds (even tho' they be of love) of any woman."11 He still worried that she could not adapt to being a missionary's wife in China's isolated far west. In spite of these anxieties, he was looking for a diamond ring.

Less than two months later, Birch decided to call off the engagement. "I feel called to do some pioneer work in Central Asia after the war, and it will be no place for a woman, unless she be more consecrated than Audrey ever will be. Her very traits which decided me against our marriage would make her a social success." He was "disappointed with both Audrey and myself," but found himself unable to accept her "without surrendering too much of one's principles and plans." His father could rest assured that "there will be preserved the Birch tradition that a virgin groom will take a virgin bride." Still, he lamented, "it seems now that she has entered so deeply into my heart, that I'll never be able to care for another woman."12 Finding the right balance between his moral rectitude and the realities of life proved to be painful experience.

After working as a private nurse in Simla, Audrey found a post at the Royal Indian Naval Hospital near Bombay [Mumbai] where she met up with her father, stepmother, and brother. She continued to write to John from time to time. After the war, she was a nurse in London and then moved to Glasgow, where she became a community health nurse, or "brown lady" as they were named after the uniform they wore. She was completely dedicated to the people she served, many of them living in slum conditions.

Her nephew Michael Mair remembers Audrey as "a wonderfully affectionate and explosively funny woman." She was not prudish. "She enjoyed a drink, smoked Du Maurier cigarettes, and loved company." Yet, he told me, she could not forget her short engagement with Birch: "Clearly she had decided not to seek another partner in life, although she was a very attractive woman." Some years later, John's aunt, Margaret Birch Taylor, met Audrey in Scotland and invited her to visit Georgia, which she did on one or two occasions.[13]

"A swift, clear river"

"I have been on this boat four days already and shall probably have two more,—plenty of swimming and sunbathing," Birch wrote to his sister.

> Wish I had someone besides these Chinese boatmen to share it with me! It's lots of fun, if you don't mind a few fleas and eating and sleeping with these rough-and-ready Chinese rivermen. . . . I have an air-mattress, a luxury unknown when I used to make trips like this as a missionary,—which I inflate, then stretch out on the deck of the boat and revel in the feel of wind and sun, the sight of the changing shore, the sounds of water and creaking oars, and the goodness of God.

The natural beauty of his remote surroundings was a welcome respite from the stress and tedium of war.

> A swift, clear river winding through towering green mountains, of which some still have snow on the peaks; sheer sandstone cliffs hang over us, with flocks of little white goats high up on the rocks looking as tho any minute they might topple over and come crashing down into the water; mountaineers' huts, made of grey stone, perched on

the hill sides; small groves of bamboo and other trees that look like Lombardy poplars, waving in the winds that sweep the mountainsides; great grey rocks that look like elephants out in the river, splitting the stream into several roaring channels, forming rapids that are miniature reproductions of the Yangtze gorges.[14]

He sounded like the American transcendentalists Emerson and Thoreau in his devotion to the natural world. He wrote to his father, "I think it would be easier to bring men to Christ and His peace, if all men lived closer to fields and flocks, winds and rain."[15]

In the spring of 1944, Birch, Lieutenant William Drummond, and Sergeant L. I. Eikenberry made their way north of the Yangtze River to Henan Province, which was new territory for an American intelligence team. Birch remarked that he and Drummond made an odd couple—an ex-Baptist missionary from Georgia and a former curio exporter from Beijing who had been a graduate student in political science at Columbia University.[16] During their two-week journey, they provided the first reports about large numbers of Japanese troops moving south along the Ping-han railway: more than twenty thousand troops with cavalry units, several hundred trucks, and a few light field guns.[17]

They arrived in Shenqiu on the Yinghe River in early June, and made contact with He Jiuguo, commanding general of the 15th Army Group, who had previously served under the "Young Marshal" Zhang Xueliang in northeast China. General He's ability to fight the Japanese, remarked Birch, "has been limited by [an] inefficient, unsteady supply of ammunition, funds, etc. from Chungking." The single greatest handicap for the Chinese, however, was their lack of communications equipment. "The reports of their agents are accurate, important and well evaluated but usually too late to be of much tactical use." From their Shenqiu base, the Americans relayed information on bombing targets, provided weather reports, forwarded Japanese documents, made contact with guerrillas, and sent Chinese agents into Japanese-held territories with portable radios. These agents and their contacts "would be loyal to the Kuomintang, rather than to the Communists, in this area where the political dividing line is drawn sharply and bitterly," noted Birch. His team would be able to carry out sabotage and demolition projects on railway bridges, camouflaged ammunition dumps, and other targets "if given the necessary supplies and equipment and if such sabotage is desired by the Commanding General."[18]

Birch recommended the construction of two airfields about fifty miles away to the south, an area "almost under the nose of the Japanese" but protected on all sides by hilly terrain. This would allow B-25s to deliver radios, money, and other supplies; fighter planes would be able to stop and refuel as they flew missions deep into enemy territory. Chinese soldiers and farmers worked to construct the fields, which heavy rains soon washed out, but the landing strips were completed in the fall. In the meantime, Eikenberry, their radio operator, came down with cholera and recovered, but then had to be evacuated after contracting another, undetermined illness.[19]

Chennault praised men like Birch who "served for long months of combat with Chinese armies under the most primitive field conditions and came out of their experience with the greatest respect for the Chinese as fighting men." It was, said Chennault, "a very rugged and dangerous sort of life," and their attitude was "in marked contrast to the cynical sneering over the Chinese war effort, then the fashion among rear-echelon staff officers."[20] Birch relished being with Chinese troops because "he felt he was doing something positive in fighting the enemy." He also liked having a job with considerable independence and appreciated having a boss like Chennault, who was more concerned with results than military discipline. As he learned to organize and lead men, Birch mused that "these years of violence are not entirely wasted."[21]

He was well and fit, "having survived the hottest summer of my life." He left Shenqiu for Kunming on September 20 before returning north. As the seasons changed, it was, he said, "my coldest winter so far in Cathay: the river beside this house is frozen over except in spots where the turbulence of the current prevents it." He wore a padded Chinese cotton jacket and a "dandy" pair of wool socks that Marjorie Tooker sent him. They would be "mighty welcome for at least six more weeks."[22]

Earnie Johnson, a B-25 tail gunner, met Birch in December on a small airbase near Laohekou, a town on the Han River in northwest Hubei Province. Johnson first saw him with two Chinese officers who were escorting two American airmen. One of them was Danny Lewis, a P-40 fighter pilot shot down by antiaircraft guns over Hankou a month before. Wearing a happy grin on his face, he carried a captured Japanese pistol in one pocket and a bottle of beer in the other. The second flier was a quiet B-29 gunner who had bailed out over Manchuria several months earlier. Johnson was impressed with Birch. "There was a charisma about him and a twinkle in his eye that made me like him at once."[23]

They walked to the nearby home of a Norwegian missionary couple named Jorgensen, who "greeted John Birch with much affection," recalled Johnson. While the group was having tea, another man arrived at the house. He had a British accent and treated Birch like a brother. "They discussed the urgent need to evacuate fellow missionaries from an area then being threatened by both the Japanese and the Communists."[24] Birch said he would try to arrange for a U.S. transport plane to fly them out.

Johnson also witnessed Birch's compassion for the Chinese. A report came in one day that a Chinese P-40 fighter pilot had crashed close to the front lines. His leg was broken, and he needed to be rescued as soon as possible. Birch asked an American flight surgeon to go with him to treat the pilot's injury, but "the doctor refused, saying he did not make house calls." His attitude so enraged Birch that he prepared to make the trip alone, and Johnson volunteered to go with him. As they were about to leave, another message informed them that the pilot had been "saved by local Chinese so we weren't needed."[25]

"It was April, soft and sweet."

Despairing over his failed engagement with Audrey, Birch returned to Changsha, where he fell into a less tempestuous, more durable romance with Marjorie Kendrick Tooker. She was quite taken with Birch. "I was much attracted to this handsome young man with his devotion to China and his burning missionary zeal, to say nothing of his charm and appealing southern courtesy." He was "sincere and dedicated," she wrote in her memoirs, "ardently devoted to serving God, his country, and his family, and burning with determination to secure peace in China so he could preach the Gospel of Christ to those who had not heard it."[26]

Her parents had both been China medical missionaries, posted in Jiangxi Province in Kuling by the Presbyterian Church. One of six children, Tooker was born in Shanghai in 1912. She attended Wellesley

Marjorie Tooker served with Yale-in-China's Xiangya Hospital in Changsha. After Japanese troops occupied the city, she became a lieutenant in the U.S. Army Nurse Corps, as shown in this photo. Courtesy of Jean Whittlesey.

College (alma mater of Soong Mei-ling, Madeline Albright, and Hillary Clinton) and studied in Germany at the University of Munich during her junior year. The day after college graduation in 1933, she left for China to teach English and music at a girls' school in Changsha for two years. She then returned to the United States for training as a nurse at Western Reserve University in Cleveland, Ohio, and went back to Changsha in 1939 to take charge of the nursing program at Yale-in-China's Xiangya Hospital, the chief medical center for Hunan Province. Within a year, she "impetuously became engaged" to a Yale graduate who taught English, and was "heartbroken when he returned to the United States."[27]

Marjorie sometimes hosted American servicemen passing through the city, most of them "overjoyed to find an American home, a bit of home cooking, and a welcome after months or years of separation from wives and families." They were surprised and delighted to sit down to a table "graced by a tablecloth and flowers." The American boys were especially fond of waffles, cornbread, and cake. "They reciprocated with such exotic gifts as chocolate bars or marshmallows. Very choice gifts were American magazines."[28]

After Birch and his men arrived in early 1943, she invited them for a meal, or perhaps it was an Easter church service at which she played the organ and he preached that they first met. He was not easily overlooked, recalled Marjorie. He was handsome in his uniform and "stood very straight and strong." She felt an immediate connection with him when they were introduced: "Shock waves of recognition passed between us, as though we had known each other forever, or in a previous existence." John later wrote that he had a "keen awareness of her presence" and sensed that she would have understood any of his thoughts "with the exchange of very few spoken words."[29] She was more worldly than John, having attended an elite women's college and studied in Europe, but they shared an abiding commitment to China and its people.

About one year after their initial meeting, Birch was delivering medical supplies for the Xiangya Hospital and came to say goodbye to Tooker before returning to 14th Air Force headquarters in Kunming. "It was April, soft and sweet," she recalled. "The perfume of tropical flowers, the songs of night-birds and a full moon were intoxicating, irresistible."

> As he was leaving, I walked with him toward the gate of the compound. It was late evening; the school grounds and ruined buildings were deserted. We could smell the gardenias that bloomed around my house and hear the bamboo bird whistling his four notes in monotonous, enchanting repetition. At the last bend in the walk before the gatehouse, where we would have to waken the gateman to let my visitor out, John turned and kissed me goodbye. That moment, that spot, and that kiss haunted many of John's letters to me and had to last us both through the rest of the war and the rest of John's life. I never saw him again.[30]

Lonely and depressed in his north China outpost, Birch poured his heart out in his letters to Marjorie. He felt wonderfully open, relaxed, and uncensored with her, able to reveal his innermost thoughts: "I find joy in realizing and trying to share the love of Christ (although my life had been drying up somewhat in this field during the last year); in the glory of Nature as opposed to art (a beautiful dawn makes me happy for hours); I feel exalted when hiking over the hills and along the clear rivers of Chekiang and Fukien." He took pleasure in simple pastimes—sitting with his father on the porch on a Sunday afternoon watching the river flowing past down below and "listening to his philosophical remarks that slip out about one to the hour; the cows grazing on the hills across the valley; listening to classical music from Radio Berlin." He liked movies, double-thick malted milks, streamlined air-conditioned trains, and football games. "I have never found joy in my brief nibbles at smoking, drinking, or dancing; this might be due to prejudices built by discipline back home, or maybe these pleasures really aren't good for me,—I don't know."[31]

Birch confessed to Marjorie that "a quite lovely Chinese girl" whom he met in her "dignified Confucian home" in Anhui had said she loved him. "She is the first woman I have kissed since I bade you good-bye a thousand years ago. Why am I telling you this? Perhaps I feel, in some vague way, that I belong to you, and that I have been disloyal." He worried that Marjorie deserved "a better, bigger man," but ended his ruminations on an exuberant note about a song from the musical *Oklahoma*. "Yes, I do know 'Oh, What a Beautiful Morning'! A sergeant who bailed out of a B-29 in December taught it to me then! That's the way I felt this noon, when your two letters came.... God speed the day when we can resume our own lives at home! Always your admirer, John."[32]

———

When Changsha was evacuated for the last time in June 1944, it was an emergency that came "much more suddenly than any previous one," wrote Tooker. She escaped on a small boat with over fifty people, heading south on the Xiang River. When John finally received this news in August, he wrote, "I thank God you're safely out of Changsha, Marjorie dear! For a while, the frequent thoughts I had of you were sheer torture; as far as I could follow the campaign from the news we get up here, the

Jap advance on Changsha was very fast, and I didn't know whether you had gotten out."[33]

Birch was still very much a fundamentalist who believed that evangelism must take precedence over good works. "You mention having never wanted the kind of life I want," he told Marjorie. "You also speak of wanting to make people well and happy rather than to change their faith." He was grateful to her for her honesty. "It blasts some fond hopes I just realized I had, but it lets me know on what basis we can build our future relationship." Struggling to match his expectations with hers, he reasoned, "I can't escape the conviction that individual salvation by the power of the Gospel is the beginning of life; that a prayerful Christian life is the root of a tree whose fruits are schools, hospitals, cleaner homes, happy families, capable and eager youths, etc., etc."

He wrote, as he had to Audrey, that the prospect of his living in far western China after the war would be too hard and too insecure for a woman, "even one so strong as yourself! So, fool that I am, I am torn between two desires: a hunger for your nearness, and a conviction that the only right thing is to stay out of your life entirely." Just now, Uncle Sam was deciding in favor of separation. But neither had he given up on their relationship: "I intend to find you once more this side of Heaven and have one more talk before abandoning finally the dream that was born on the path at Changsha. God guard you, dear! I love you."[34]

In his final letter to Marjorie, two weeks before his death, he shared a terrible premonition: "The other nite a dream of mine was giving me a visit with you (I think it was in your living room in Changsha) when something external, a loud voice, perhaps, woke me up. The sense of loss, even of just your ghost, was a painful and disturbing experience."[35]

"I'm afraid I'm falling in love."

Birch met Edith Dorothy Lillian Yuen in January 1944 at Kukong, an airbase in northern Guangdong Province, which was the headquarters of China's Seventh War Zone. Dorothy was born in 1922 in New York City, where her Chinese father, when he was a graduate student at Columbia University, met and married her Swedish-American mother. At age thirteen, Yuen moved with her parents, two sisters, and brother to Shanghai. They evacuated to the Philippines two years later when the Japanese took over her father's factory. When they returned to China the following year, her father joined the Nationalist army as an engineer. After the Americans entered the war, Yuen was employed as a civilian by the U.S. military and had assignments at several bases doing administrative work. At Kukong, she translated into English the mapped locations of enemy aircraft. When the war ended, she worked with Chennault while he was setting up China Air Transport in Shanghai, an airline under contract with the Nationalist government. She returned to the United States in 1947 after contracting tuberculosis.

Dorothy and John Birch were introduced to one another at a big Chinese dinner party—they were the only foreigners there—and afterward he walked her home and met her parents. She was impressed with his ability to speak Chinese and liked his self-deprecating sense of humor. He told her, "If you don't care to give me the pleasure of keeping your picture, feel free to keep mine, anyway, to scare the rats away."[36] Vivacious and attractive, Yuen was one of very few young women in a sea of homesick American soldiers. Men away from home and at war

Dorothy Yuen was a civilian with the 14th Air Force in China. This photo was taken after she returned to the United States in 1947. Courtesy of Edna Chiang.

are often careless and take people for granted, she observed, but John was different—kind, considerate, and deeply interested in China. She remembered him as "very much of a gentleman." While not an evangelical or fundamentalist herself, Yuen admired his faith. He had "such a profound belief in God that he was fearless."[37] She was especially grateful when he arranged for two of his men to rescue her Chinese grandmother and her aunt from behind Japanese lines in Zhejiang Province.

For his part, John was captivated by Yuen's charm and poise. "Dorothy," he wrote, not long before proposing marriage to Audrey Mair, "you have not left my thoughts since the first night I saw you . . . I am horribly jealous of those fellows who have opportunities to see you. . . . I dare not hope for more than our friendship, but still I want to be yours, as much as you will have of me."[38]

Yuen and Birch did not see each other again until March 1945 in Kunming. (Both Mair and Tooker had left China in the previous year.) "You never knew when John was coming or where he was going in his covert work. . . . He was always half-starved, and made up for it when he showed up. He had a voracious appetite," Yuen remembered. Later that spring, Birch was being treated for a recurrence of malaria when the two met again at Beishiyi Air Field outside Chungking. She visited him in the hospital every night for two weeks, and when he was well enough they attended movies together. "I knew my visits meant a great deal to him but they also meant a great deal to me, however, I'm afraid they made him grow very fond of me."[39]

"I'm afraid I'm falling in love with you," John said to Dorothy. But he feared it would be a mistake. "You want a life of city lights, gay parties, many friends, and much excitement. I want to find my pleasures where sunlight dances on grassy meadows, where blue mountains tower into the sky, or where ocean waves break on moonlit beaches."[40] Yuen later wrote to John's mother, "I was sorry he thought I was so different from him for I'm not. I felt the same way he did about friends and parties. Because I am a gay person and I can always smile, people don't realize that I'm living up to what is expected of me."[41]

During their last few hours together, they took a walk in the same hills Birch had explored with Tom Trumble and Arthur Hopkins nearly three years earlier when he first entered the army. He and Dorothy sat down under a big tree. "It was here that John became overwhelmed with devotion for me.... Altho I was extremely fond of John I was not in love with him and neither with anyone else."[42] Given the uncertainty of war, she knew she was not ready for love and marriage. After returning to Anhui, he wrote a last letter, twelve days before he was killed, telling her, "I am in excellent health, a little thin, and very sunburned from swimming in a river that flows by my station.... It really begins to look as tho this long terrible war will soon be over. Yesterday, Sunday morning, I held a church service here, thanking God for bringing us to the eve of victory.... Please write me whenever you can. Affectionately, John."[43] When news of his death came two weeks later, Dorothy couldn't speak: "I felt as if every drop of blood had left me."[44]

Sadly, forces beyond Birch's control intervened before he was able to find the partner in life he so longed for. He had become more questioning and vulnerable as he tried to reconcile his spiritual vows with earthly desires, but his search for love would be unfulfilled. Much like America's larger hopes for China, his personal dreams would go unrealized.

8

The China Theater

BY MID-1944, JAPAN WAS losing the war and Birch was optimistic about the future. "I believe most profoundly that the Far East will play a rising part in the affairs of the post-war world—a world that should be more ripe for the Gospel than ever before," he wrote to Frank Norris.[1] His confidence was misplaced. China was on the verge of an immense revolution that would brand Western religious emissaries as "cultural imperialists" and enemies of the state. It would not be until the 1980s, after the radicalism of Mao's Cultural Revolution was discredited, that scholars in China as well as the United States would begin to re-evaluate the pros and cons of the missionary legacy.

A more immediate event for Americans in China was the arrival of Albert Coady Wedemeyer, who took over from Joseph ("Vinegar Joe") Stilwell as commanding general of U.S. forces and chief of staff to Generalissimo Chiang Kai-shek in October 1944. He and Stilwell were opposite personalities. Stilwell was a down-to-earth, outspoken, rough-and-ready infantryman who was relieved of his command by President Roosevelt after demanding control of the Chinese army. Wedemeyer was a cautious, diplomatic man who had worked his way up through the ranks as a staff officer with no combat experience.

Stilwell had nothing but contempt for Chiang Kai-shek, telling Roosevelt he was "a vacillating, tricky, undependable old scoundrel, who never keeps his word."[2] Wedemeyer, on the other hand, was respectful of "this small, fine-boned man with black piercing eyes and an engaging smile." He judged Chiang to be "an unfailingly honorable soldier and a staunch ally" and was impressed with the Generalissimo's "obvious depth and sincerity of his love for the Chinese people, and his hopes for their future," an opinion shared by U.S. ambassador Patrick Hurley. Stilwell believed the Chinese Reds offered a welcome alternative to the greed, corruption, and repression of the Chinese Nationalists. Wedemeyer was not blind to their failures but was skeptical about cooperating with the Communists. He later avowed that Mao and Zhou Enlai struck him as "scheming and determined leaders," interested only in power.[3] He would try his best to keep out of the morass of Chinese politics, but that would prove impossible.

Albert Wedemeyer was a tall, slim West Point graduate from Omaha, Nebraska, who spent two years in the Philippines—then an American colony—and served with an infantry regiment in Tianjin in north China at a time when Chinese warlords were vying for control. That tour was followed by three more years in the Philippines and two years in Berlin during the mid-1930s at the German War College, on a military exchange program. After an assignment in Washington where he drafted plans for the Allied invasion of Europe, he joined the staff of the new Southeast Asia Command in New Delhi under British admiral Lord Louis Mountbatten, who would preside over the dissolution of British rule and the partition of India a few years later.[4]

Wedemeyer had considerable trepidation about taking over from Stilwell, writing in his memoirs, "I had heard many times over that China was a graveyard for American officials, military and diplomatic. . . . Many a good officer had had his career ruined in China."[5] He arrived in Chungking to find that China was at the end of the pipeline, "remote from sources of supply and with the lowest priority of all theaters of war."[6] The situation was desperate. When he visited a Chinese army hospital in Kunming soon after his arrival, he was "unable to tell the living from the rows of dead."[7] He refrained from criticizing his predecessor in public but wrote privately that Stillwell "made a botch of the job," spending too much time fighting in the jungles of Burma and neglecting his job in China. Even basic information about where American troops were and what they were doing in China was "a jumbled mess."[8]

Albert Wedemeyer, Chiang Kai-shek, and U.S. ambassador Patrick Hurley in Chungking during a radio broadcast in 1944 or early 1945. Credit: Hoover Institution Library and Archives, Stanford University.

Chinese and American air units did become more effective over time. They bombed Japanese ships on the Yangtze River and off China's southeast coast, attacked military installations on Formosa (Taiwan) and in Hong Kong, and mined Haiphong harbor in Vietnam. Their planes shot up power plants, supply dumps, and warehouses. They strafed and bombed bridges, barges, ships, tunnels, rail yards, locomotives, and freight cars. But when the weather turned bad or critical supplies were unavailable, the air war was suspended, sometimes for weeks at a time.

Another glaring problem was the cultural gap between Americans and Chinese. Most of the American soldiers were ill-prepared to deal with the country's poverty, disease, and lack of sanitation—conditions only made worse by Japan's blockade of China's coast. Americans saw an economy in shambles, an increasingly ineffective government riddled with corruption, and a desperate population saddled with inflation and made miserable by conscription and taxation. Instead of heroic allies, the average U.S. soldier found grasping officials, conniving prostitutes, and black-marketeers peddling American supplies. In frustration, the American GIs used racist epithets like "chink," "slope head," and "Chinaman." This yawning racist chasm defined the war effort as much as questions of military strategy or how many tons of supplies could be flown over the mountains from India, observed journalists Theodore White and Annalee Jacoby. "The uneducated American attitude was a major tragedy in a land of many tragedies. No one attempted to explain the war to the American soldier, to teach him how and why the Chinese people were as they were."[9]

"China hands" who understood something about the country were the exception not the rule in the U.S. Army. Many of them took the time to learn the language and culture, even though they believed in the inherent superiority of Western culture. Arthur Hopkins observed that John Birch showed it was possible for Americans to "get along on just the same as a Chinese soldier," living and working together for a common goal.[10] Toward the end of the war, Birch explained his own thinking about crossing the cultural divide:

Liaison with the Chinese is based upon friendship, and mutual respect. The Chinese have been exploited by Britishers, Japanese, and other foreigners and so have a natural suspicion of newcomers' motives. It takes time and real sincerity to convince them of our good intentions. It is necessary to speak to them in their own language; one can hardly know the emotional reactions of the Chinese who are always smiling, polite and agreeable. . . . China is a land of human relations, [an] elaborate system of courtesy—family relations and friendships.[11]

Cooperation was not limited to the small joint liaison teams led by Birch and others on the ground. An experimental binational group of pilots and crews was activated in July 1943, known as the Chinese American Composite Wing (CACW). There were two fighter groups of P-40s and one bomber group of B-25s. The Chinese were trained in combat tactics and aircraft maintenance at Malir, India, and on airbases in Arizona, Texas, and New Mexico. One Chinese co-pilot remembered the "cooperation, the harmony, [and] the comradeship between Chinese and Americans."[12] The biggest problem was communicating in a foreign language, especially while experiencing the stress of flying in combat. The Americans spoke little or no Chinese, and the Chinese were expected to learn English.

But Americans assigned to the CACW were sometimes disparaged by their compatriots in other units as members of the "Chinese Foreign Legion" and derided as "slopey lovers." In the early days of the CACW, wrote Ken Daniels, a B-25 mechanic and gunner, "we frequently were lost, often missed our targets, and sometimes could not drop our bombs due to armament system malfunctions." Mountains of unknown height were placed in the wrong locations on maps. Food was poor and monotonous—mainly cabbage soup, rice, and boiled water buffalo—and dysentery, sometimes called the "Yellow River rapids," was common. The CACW was at the bottom of the totem pole for bombs, gas, tires, and parts. Daniels was bitter: "I never felt so abandoned by my country."[13] He counted the days until he had enough missions to return to the United States.

"They think you can buy every man."

After taking over from Stilwell, Wedemeyer set about reorganizing, rationalizing, and consolidating an inefficient and dysfunctional U.S. military system in China. This included intelligence operations, which historian Maochen Yu explains was "plagued by disorganization, jealously, confusion, and opacity of command."[14] The general's decisions would launch a series of events that contributed to the fate of John Birch.

When Wedemeyer arrived, it was the U.S. Navy—oddly enough—that had primary responsibility for intelligence in China. This was explained partly by the need for U.S. ships in the Pacific to have weather information and also by plans for a naval landing on China's coast to prepare for an invasion of Japan—something that never materialized. The Navy's role was complicated by the fact that Captain Milton "Mary" Miles, commander of the so-called rice-paddy navy, worked closely with the notorious Dai Li, head of the Nationalists' secret police, through the Sino-American Cooperative Organization (SACO).[15] Oliver Caldwell, an American intelligence officer, described Dai as "brilliant, imaginative, ruthless, and unscrupulous. He was the Himmler of Nationalist China.... He tried to unify China under Chiang by enforcing iron control. He was cold, crafty, and brutal."[16]

Chennault wrote in his memoirs that he avoided an alliance with Miles and Dai Li. It might have been useful to cooperate with them, he said,

> but since Tai's [Dai's] men were engaged in a ruthless man hunt for Communists, it would have meant the end of our intelligence and rescue relations with Communist armies in the field. Our only effective policy was to stay well out of inter-Chinese and international politics and convince everybody concerned that the only real interest of the Fourteenth [Air Force] was in successful prosecution of the war.[17]

Miles, however, was opposed to working with the Communists, who he said were bargaining, not fighting, with the Japanese.[18]

There was nothing but jealously and mistrust between Miles's Naval Group and the Office of Strategic Services (OSS), the World War II espionage service and forerunner of the Central Intelligence Agency (CIA). Its director was the dynamic William "Wild Bill" Donovan, a World War I hero and influential Wall Street lawyer who had a close relationship with President Roosevelt. Looking for a foothold in China, Donovan turned to Chennault to establish a joint operation between the OSS and the 14th Air Force in March 1944. The new organization was given an intentionally obscure, not to mention laughable name: the 5329th Air-Ground Forces Resources Technical Staff (AGFRTS). Colonel Wilfred J. Smith, its commander, promptly ordered fourteen of Chennault's field intelligence officers, including Birch, to join AGFRTS, which several months later had grown to twenty-nine officers and sixty-two enlisted men.[19]

As fighting in Europe began to wind down in early 1945, the OSS expanded its operations in Asia, where the war was still raging and an invasion of Japan seemed to be unavoidable. It was a difficult adjustment, as one officer recounted:

> In Europe we could move around on the paved roads in automobiles but in China there were only two-lane gravel mountainous roads, primitive by comparison, and no vehicles except the few that the OSS could control. So the teams and their guerrillas had to walk or run and hide most of the time in the rugged terrain, terribly rough by comparison, to avoid capture, torture, and certain death.[20]

As the number of OSS men and women in China increased, Wedemeyer decided to reorganize and consolidate all U.S. intelligence operations under the command of the OSS. Unhappy with the SACO agreement between Miles and Dai because it subjected Americans to Chinese authority, he sidelined the Navy.[21] He also disbanded AGFRTS and ordered Chennault to transfer his intelligence personnel to the OSS chief in China, Colonel Richard P. Heppner.

Chennault agreed with the decision, so long as there would be no delays in receiving essential information. "I don't want you to think that I am getting touchy," he wrote Wedemeyer, "but I would greatly appreciate it if OSS were instructed to establish and maintain close liaison with my headquarters. I need the service that they now control; it is vital to the efficiency of my operations." But he went on to raise one unresolved problem. He had assured the officers who had been transferred to AGFRTS, including John Birch, that they would be returned to the 14th Air Force in the event of a change of policy. "I bring this up, because I am honor bound to do so," he told Wedemeyer. "I gave these officers this assurance when they were transferred from the Fourteenth. There are some personnel now in the organization who will not want to lose their connections with my command."[22] There is no record of a response from Wedemeyer.

Birch especially resented and resisted the change, and had been with the OSS for only a short time when he told Colonel Smith he did not feel right about it. Smith argued for hours, telling him, " 'John, we are Americans whether OSS or 14th Air Force . . . and it is our job to prosecute the war effectively regardless of technicalities.' But John felt keenly . . . and asked me on several occasions to be relieved of his assignment."[23] In fact, Birch was carried on the roster for many months as a member of the 14th Air Force after the other men had been assigned to OSS.

Chennault personally radioed Birch to reassure him that OSS control of intelligence operations "makes no difference in actual working arrangements" and "relations between OSS and Fourteenth Air Force are very close and satisfactory." Chennault deeply appreciated Birch's loyalty and wanted him "to continue your valuable work as in [the] past." He asked Birch to meet with him at the first opportunity.[24]

Dorothy Yuen recalled how unhappy John was because the new OSS commanders wanted to control his activities but they didn't understand the situation.[25] As he himself stated, "I had been transferred into an organization [the OSS] with whose nature, methods, and purposes I felt entirely out of sympathy.... I found out later the other fellows in the field felt the same way as I did, but I was more outspoken than they." It make him "sick" to see liaison work turned over to the OSS. "They will mess up the whole situation as sure as shooting because these men are working on an entirely different basis. Their attitude is: 'Here we want this, and we want that—we have got the money.' They think you can buy every man and every Chinese has his price, and all they are going to buy is the contempt of the Chinese."[26]

He made it clear that he wanted only to work for Chennault. It was a matter of principle for Birch, recalled Wilfred Smith. "John was 100% sincere and was never dishonest in thought or word or deed, to my knowledge, and I knew him intimately." And he was never a person to compromise: "I have never known a young man to be so loyal to his God, and to his friends as he."[27] Yet Birch was not acting just out of disdain for the OSS or blind loyalty to Chennault. He was also being pragmatic. "General Chennault and the 14th Air Force are known all over China," said Birch. "There is no name in China that stands as high as that of Claire Chennault. The Chinese believe him to be the one man who fights the Japanese with singleness of heart. They know the story of his AVG [American Volunteer Group or Flying Tigers]. They believe, and I think they are right, that Chennault is just about the best friend they have and there is no name which opens doors so quickly."[28] Each of the American liaison officers carried letters from Chennault, in Chinese and English, stating they were his personal representatives who were helping the Chinese people in their war efforts and should be given every assistance in performing their duties.

Where regular Army, Navy, and OSS were unsuccessful, said Birch, Americans with the 14th Air Force have "just walked in." Chinese field commanders were willing to do anything for Chennault—cut their own red tape, even risk a reprimand from Chungking. In short, "the name of Chennault is a magic key in China when it comes to opening doors for Sino-American liaison. The 14th Air Force exclusively in China enjoys the confidence, respect and trust of the Chinese. A second lieutenant from the 14th Air Force can get a lot further up north than a Colonel who says he is from Stilwell's or Wedemeyer's headquarters."[29]

Birch felt so strongly that he radioed OSS headquarters in Kunming that Chennault's name was "worth twice all Donovan's equipment and slush funds for effective liaison with Chinese." If he was no longer in the 14th, he wanted to resign his commission as an officer and return to the 14th Air Force as a private. Birch later joked that the message "made me rather unpopular with the OSS."[30] When he was ordered to return all 14th Air Force identifications and to report the serial numbers of his vehicles to the OSS, he sarcastically replied that he had four black mules and they did not have serial numbers. Ignoring orders to send intelligence only to OSS, he continued to forward urgent tactical and weather reports directly to other units.[31]

He was no longer only identifying targets, reporting on weather, and helping to rescue downed airmen. While he continued these functions, he was also an OSS spy. A mission scheduled to start on August 1, 1945, offers an example of the kind of espionage he was asked to do. The top-secret operation code-named Crow was to be under his direction from his base in Anhui Province. A Mr. Xue Yuhua, a former guerrilla leader from Shandong Province, would set up radio and intelligence teams behind Japanese lines near Jinan in Shandong Province and Tianjin, the port city east of Beijing. His men were to collect information on enemy troops; shipping, railway, and highway communications; and industrial production—coal, bauxite, iron mines, steel mills, and factories producing military supplies. They were also instructed to gather intelligence on Chinese puppet military organizations and activities. (Puppet troops were those who collaborated with the Japanese. Some were captured, some conscripted, and some were mercenaries; most such forces were badly equipped and poorly trained.) Birch would provide radio frequencies, schedules, and codes. Xue was to report to Birch, who would relay the information to Chungking and Kunming. In addition to salaries, the OSS would provide expenses for "traveling, entertainment, bribes and recruiting agents in the field."[32] It appears that the war ended before the plan could be put in place.

"I'd rather be a poor preacher."

While Birch felt sorry for the Japanese people, his duty as he saw it was to do everything possible to defeat Japan's godless forces, an essential prerequisite if China was to become a Christian nation. "I want peace," he told his brother George Stanley, "but not that purchased by tolerance of such evils as I saw Japan spreading across this part of the world!"[33] He had become a soldier to fight for a just cause, but "the greater struggle is spiritual warfare against principalities and powers—the evil rooted in men who do not understand and accept Christ's message of love and salvation, in a contest that will continue long after war has ended."[34]

"The thing I liked about John," Wilfred Smith told his mother after the war, "was that although he was a very fervent Christian, he was also a very fine soldier." Smith, himself the son of a missionary, thought Birch actually influenced more Chinese lives in the army than he would have otherwise. "As an officer he moved much more widely than he could have as a private citizen or ordinary missionary." Whenever possible, Birch continued preaching and handing out tracts and copies of the New Testament. Smith allowed him to proselytize, believing it would "help his morale and it didn't hurt the work." Birch believed the boys from Christian homes stood up better and lasted longer under dangerous and uncomfortable conditions. As he and his men hiked through rice fields or traveled on a river, they would sing the old spiritual "We Are Climbing Jacob's Ladder, Soldiers of the Cross."[35]

Toward the end of the war Birch held a Sunday morning service "especially thanking God for bringing us to the eve of victory."[36] A few weeks earlier, he spoke to over six hundred Chinese Christians in the city of Fuyang, the first time he had preached in Chinese since leaving Changsha. Birch, however, was no longer the pious zealot he had been as a college student. He was more tolerant of others, including Catholics. He told Smith that Christianity comes "from the heart" and is not based on the church one joins, something he did not think possible when he was ordained. Smith observed that Birch was no longer a boy but had become a man: "I saw him develop and change from a rather naïve approach to one of maturity."[37]

During the last few months of his life, Birch was stationed in northwest Anhui Province on a small base in a long narrow valley running from south to north. It was called the "Anhui pocket"—and was nicknamed "the island"—because it was isolated from the Japanese by mountains. It was the headquarters for an OSS intelligence network with the radio call sign R2S (Roger Two Sugar). Getting there could be an arduous journey, as Captain James Hart, Lieutenant Laird Ogle, Sergeant Vern Crosby, and Corporal Donald Willmott discovered when they made the trip in early August 1945. The first leg was a harrowing landing at Valley Field airstrip about 150 miles from the R2S base. Willmott recalled that their C-46 transport plane "seemed to be endlessly circling and twisting through mountain valleys and clouds," trying to locate the small runway as daylight was waning and fuel was running very low. "Sometimes we came suddenly out of the mist to find a mountain directly ahead." They spotted the field just in time. Chinese guards and sixteen porters then carried their equipment and baggage to Lihuang, headquarters of the Tenth War Area. The two American officers rode in sedan chairs. Their movements were reported to the local military authorities.[38]

In Lihuang they were introduced to Kim Gu ("short, soft spoken, genial," according to Willmott), who was the leader of the Korean Provisional Government. An estimated two million Koreans lived in Manchuria in the northeast, most of them farmers, and another two hundred thousand in north China, mainly in cities. The Japanese conscripted many of them as workers and soldiers, while others, as members of the anti-Japanese Korean Liberation Army, cooperated with the Communist Eighth Route Army and also worked with the OSS.[39]

The OSS group was extremely well treated, remembered Willmott. They were feasted and toasted by officials. "Along the streets we were greeted by children *and* adults with the familiar '*ding hao*' (very good) . . . In some places we saw posters expressing gratitude for our participation in China's war." It was a complete contrast to Chungking, where "foreigners were so common that they were barely noticed, and American soldiers were widely disliked or even hated for the arrogance or sexual exploitation common among them." The next leg of the journey was a four-day raft trip "floating down a shallow, rocky river through the mountains and out onto the plain."[40] Their diet was mainly eggs—scrambled eggs at every meal, supplemented with cheese, canned milk, and sugar, as well as luscious watermelons. Birch and KMT Major General Wang Zhongmin, the joint commanders of R2S, met them when they reached Fuyang.

From there it was still another fifty miles and a two-day trek to the R2S outpost near the town of Linquan. The station was a "cluster of one-story buildings, barracks, and farm houses scattered among veg-etable gardens, trees, threshing yards, a duck pond, a drill field, and a basketball court." General Wang had some fifty soldiers to guard and assist the OSS men, who numbered about fifteen, including radio operators and weathermen.

Willmott, who was the son of Canadian missionaries in Chengdu, served as a translator and interpreter. He described Wang, a big Manchurian, as "an explosive basketball player, a wicked bridge player, and a tough commander of a company of well-trained soldiers whose job it was to protect us from Japanese-paid assassins." He was "a vora-cious eater, but also a loquacious talker, requiring me to sit beside him and interpret just about anything anyone said as well as his own contri-butions, which ranged from Chinese opera to the necessity for a future war against the Soviet Union." It was probably at one of these meals that Birch and Wang, who "seemed to be great buddies, though very different," both expressed the thought that "with the war with Japan ended, a war with the Soviet Union and the Chinese Communists was imminent."[41]

On one occasion, Birch arranged for one of his men, Lieutenant Toohill, to be treated for a serious case of amoebic dysentery at a Catholic mission located about twelve miles up the Quanhe River. Several days later, Birch and a few others went to pick him up in a captured Japanese outboard motor boat. Traveling up the river, recalled Staff Sergeant Richard Rudeloff, they saw the bodies of several new-born baby girls wrapped in straw and floating in the water. As they reached the mission, Birch maneuvered the boat close to the shore, the propeller hit a submerged rock, and the shear pin broke. He had left a replacement behind when changing shirts, so he asked a Chinese

Chinese and Americans at the OSS base in Anhui Province on August 17, 1945, one week before Birch was shot dead. General Wang Zhongmin stands in the back row center, and John Birch is to the right. Also in the back row are Donald Willmott (second from the left) and Laird Ogle (second from the right). Courtesy of Donald E. Willmott.

soldier to run back to their outpost to retrieve the missing part. The rest of the group decided to return to Linquan rather than staying at the mission but grew concerned about their safety as night was coming on—a night with no moon. Two of the men took turns towing the boat with a rope, trudging along an embankment on the edge of the river. They stopped around 3:00 a.m. and fell asleep. Birch awakened them just before sunrise. "He had gone to a nearby village and brought back a dozen hard-boiled eggs for our breakfast," said Rudeloff. The shear pin soon arrived, and they were back in the village two hours later.[42]

When mail finally caught up with the R2S outpost, Birch was thrilled to find two letters from Marjorie Tooker, although the first one had been soaked and was illegible. "Holding it up to a strong light and figuring out the words make[s] a fascinating but disappointing job," he wrote in reply. He confided that he felt an "unstable mixture of loneliness, affectionate feelings, need for a wife, and genuine friendship." He was wrestling with the "uncertainty of and dissatisfaction with my own nature." He still trusted in God, but confessed "there are still too many things about which I am not sure." He envied the simplicity of a Chinese farmer whose life was complete with the fulfilling of simple basic needs. "Why are we so complex in our emotional and mental make-up?" he lamented.[43]

He also told Marjorie that some people "want me to enter the post-war intelligence service, but they are barking up an empty tree. Apart from a far different vocation I have long felt and only begun to follow"—referring to his intention to return to evangelizing—"I could never stick the game of spying on those for whom I profess friendship. This sounds pompous and self-righteous, but this secret police business, necessary as it may be, has always seemed to me a slimy sort of job. No, ma'am, I'd rather be a poor preacher."[44] Intelligence work and espionage had been necessary to defeat the Japanese, but being a spy after the war would divert him from his true calling. He might have remained in the military if he had been as prescient about communism as Robert Welch later claimed. But a Communist takeover that would prevent him from preaching the Gospel seemed highly unlikely in 1945.

Birch was thinking seriously about the future. He had written to Frank Norris that he wanted to push westward, "possibly in an effort to storm the mountainous Buddhist citadel of Tibet," or else the "little-reached Chinese Turkestan" (today's Xinjiang Province) in the northwest, this "strange part of the empire of Islam," where itinerant native preachers would carry the Word of God via camel caravans or, eventually, airplanes.[45] (The "Chinese Back-to-Jerusalem Evangelistic Band" shared this vision of extending the Christian faith across inner Asia to the Holy Land.[46]) He wrote to his sister, "If I survive the war, I shall never escape the call to serve Christ. I am unsure of the place; it may be in West China, or Georgia, or a television station on some mountain peak ... I shall probably run at least one stock ranch—perhaps in Chinese Turkestan—and may start some Chinese farming Co-ops."[47]

He hoped that Japan's defeat would make China more open to foreign missionaries but was concerned that neither the Nationalists nor the Communists had the best interests of the people at heart. His answer to the dilemma was to escape the machinations of politics and find refuge in a remote part of China. Imagining himself as a "war weary farmer," he wrote to his father, "I do not want a life of monotonous paper-shuffling or of trafficking with money-mad traders." Instead, he longed for a bucolic life using his strength "in making the fields green, and the cattle fat. . . . I want to love a wife who prefers rural peace to urban excitement, one would rather climb a hilltop to watch a sunset with me than to take a taxi to any Broadway play."[48]

Dorothy Yuen remembered that Birch "used to talk about how discouraged he was in the mission he belonged to. He said they weren't out to help bring God to the people but that they were worrying about their own comfort."[49] He expressed these doubts to his sister Betty: "I know I want no part of begging mission boards, bickering denominationalism, or dictatorial hierarchies." He declared, without specific mention of Norris or the Fundamental Baptists, "I'll depend on no board and no church; in these dark days I see all human institutions as unreliable; even churches which are now being led by the Holy Spirit! . . . Some how, I want to stand alone, between a strife-torn earth and wrath-darkened heavens, and thunder out, late in time, a call to repentance and belated trust in Christ, during the lust-ridden years which will follow this war!"[50] This soldier of the cross would chart his own path, as guided by the Lord, without the burden or baggage of institutions: "I want of Government only protection against the violence and injustices of evil or selfish men. . . . I want to reach the sunset of life sound in body and mind, flanked by strong sons and grandsons, enjoying the friendship and respect of my neighbors."[51]

His was a utopian vision of a place far from the madness of war and free of the fetters of politics. A self-envisioned independent Christian community somewhere in the far reaches of China was not the dream of a fanatic cult leader; rather, it was Birch's plea for purity and purpose. Christ-like, he would go into the wilderness to cleanse himself of the world's sins. "Often in these days I feel that these barren years are my apprenticeship, God-given. . . . I know that God is preparing me . . . to stand privation, pain, isolation, fatigue, physical danger, etc., to what end? That I trust in Him to show me in His own time."[52]

War and romance had changed Birch, making him more questioning and self-aware, less absolute. He told Marjorie, "I think both of us have been given too much to introspection; it may be because of the exalted standards taught us as children."[53] Yet even though he had matured, he still sought his parents' approval for his personal life. He wrote home in the aftermath of the failed marriage engagement to Audrey, "Even tho' I picked the wrong girl and messed things up a while, still it's wonderful to know how my folks back home love me, and share my joys and sorrows!"[54]

More than anything, Birch was concerned about living up to his mother's expectations. She was, he had told Audrey, "by far the most noble person I have known on this earth." "God help me to be the man Mother thinks I am!" he wrote to his father. He cautioned his brother George Stanley that their mother "has always seen so much more in me than really exists." He warned his sister to stop idolizing him: "I have changed much, and not all for the good, since we said goodbye in Macon's Terminal Station nearly five years ago."[55] None of these self-doubts would prevent others from remaking his life as a myth.

Although Marjorie and John were far apart and never saw each other after April 1944, their relationship blossomed in their letters. She wrote to him, "God has been awfully good to give me even this much of you." Birch's spirits were lifted after receiving an especially warm and tender message from her. "All my unpleasant feelings melted when I lost myself in your letter. . . . I'm sorry if I gave the impression that I considered our religious convictions incompatible, or that our separate ways of expressing them are antagonistic; I believe the opposite." Since commenting earlier that he needed a wife who would be willing, if need be, to undergo "poverty, privation and prolonged thankless effort in un-evangelized places," Birch had had misgivings. An astounding admission, evidence of his loneliness and depression, followed: "I've had some bad moments in my own thinking, and now doubt that I'll ever find such a woman, and sometimes I doubt that God is calling me to evangelistic work after the war."[56]

Marjorie returned to the United States by way of India after being driven out of Changsha by the Japanese. She joined the U.S. Army Nurse Corps, determined to do her share for the war effort. At the time of Japan's surrender in August 1945, Lieutenant Tooker was in the Philippines, where she was in charge of a dermatology and venereal disease ward. In October, unaware that John was dead but concerned about the absence of any word from him, she wrote from the Lingayen Gulf where she was stationed: "What on earth has happened to you? Mail has caught up with us and still nothing to indicate where you are.... If you are susceptible to moonlight and music with the ocean added, as I am, you would enjoy the evenings, glorious sunsets and white beaches." By now, she hopefully imagined, "you will be adjusting to the business of life in the States and the attention of doting relatives." Most of all, she wanted to know, "What are your plans?"[57]

Part Three

—————

Encountering Communists

MOST AMERICANS, EVEN THOSE in China, knew little or nothing about the Chinese Communists, who were relatively small in number and geographically remote during the Second World War. A handful of outsiders may have read Edgar Snow's *Red Star Over China*, a favorable account of the Long March and the lives of CCP (Chinese Communist Party) leaders published in 1938. In addition to Snow, the few foreigners who made it to the Communists' Yenan headquarters in the northwest wrote uniformly positive accounts. They were impressed by Mao's charisma, Zhou Enlai's charm, and Zhu De's candor. These energetic young revolutionaries were informal, idealistic, and direct—a refreshing change from the stultifying ceremony and formality of many Nationalist government officials. Confusing what they saw with American liberal values, these observers confidently concluded that the Communists were democratic at heart.[1]

The Communists were equally ignorant of the United States. As Marxist-Leninists, they were suspicious of American capitalism and imperialism but positive about President Roosevelt's New Deal and his opposition to colonialism. These policies made it appear that progressive forces were on the rise in America. Ideology aside, it was prudent for the Communists to make common cause with the United States against Japan; they needed whatever help they could get. Moreover, cultivating American good will could enhance the CCP's legitimacy. People in the areas under their control were told that the foreign "big noses" were friends who should be helped, and Mao and Zhou boldly wrote to Roosevelt to suggest they meet with him in Washington.[2] They hoped to have good relations with both the United States and the Soviet Union.

American and Chinese Communist cooperation against Japan was real, although the relationship was episodic and ad hoc. Yet even the most basic questions that could inform crucial longer-term policy decisions went unanswered. From the American perspective, were the Communists patriotic progressives or ruthless revolutionaries? Were they independent actors or did they do Moscow's bidding? The Communists questioned whether the United States was a hegemonic power or essentially benevolent. Were the Americans driven by the demands of monopoly capitalism or could they be enlisted to help China achieve modernization?

There was no resolution of these issues by the time Emperor Hirohito made a radio broadcast announcing the end of the war on August 15, 1945. The surrender came sooner than anticipated, precipitated by America's unforeseen atomic bomb attacks on Hiroshima and Nagasaki as well as the Soviet Union's invasion of Manchuria, where 1.2 million Japanese soldiers were based. Until then, military planners expected an invasion of Japan's home islands would be required and thought it might take as long as two more years to win the war. But in China, the elation of sudden victory was mixed with tremendous uncertainty as the KMT and CCP embarked on a mad scramble for territory.[3]

Recognizing the ebbing authority of the Nationalists and the growing strength of the Communists, U.S. ambassador Patrick Hurley had tried and failed to broker a compromise between Chiang and Mao in 1944. Hurley's misguided efforts infuriated Mao, who believed he had been misled. Immediately after the war, the antagonists once again tried to reach a power-sharing accord. In December 1945, in a final attempt to avoid civil war, President Truman dispatched General

George C. Marshall on a mission to mediate between the two parties. Washington suspended and then resumed military and economic assistance to the Nationalist government to gain leverage in the negotiations, but the Americans lacked both the resources and the political will to intervene decisively in China. An exhausted American public was demanding that the troops be brought home as quickly as possible. In retrospect, all of the attempts to avert internecine warfare seemed doomed from the start. A history of distrust and sheer hatred between the Nationalists and Communists, dating from 1927 and suppressed for the most of the war, was certain to erupt.

Men on the ground, like John Birch, could see the impasse facing China as the war drew to a close. In a letter to Marjorie Tooker, he faulted both the Nationalists and Communists for China's problems. He blamed the "relatively small, non-representative" Nationalist government, with its "abuses, intolerance, and impotence." It never had the enthusiastic popular support necessary for a strong nation. On the other hand, Chiang Kai-shek's government "should be praised for its steadfastness of purpose" in attempting to unify the country and in fighting the Japanese invaders. The picture was no better on the other side: "The equally small, non-representative group of Chinese Communists (whose leaders I consider hypocritical thugs) should be blamed for their lack of patriotism, but praised for their endurance and ingenuity in fighting the Japs."

Birch's sympathies lay not with political and military officials but with the "industrious, fair-minded, friendly, self-respecting people, who have suffered much at the hands both of invaders and their own hard-pressed leaders." The Chinese had endured famines, floods, plagues, bandits, taxes, drafts, and invasions, yet they persisted. "I respect and admire them, and for their sakes alone would gladly do anything in my power to drive out the Japs or help protect a government which sincerely tried to give these farmers enlightenment, peace, and personal freedom." But this, he thought, would not happen soon. China was a patchwork of constantly shifting local and regional alliances without true coherence at the national level. In his opinion, there was still "no such real political entity as China."[4]

The weakness of the central government under the Nationalists was readily apparent. Rampant corruption, galloping inflation, a military weakened by years of fighting, and a regime that shared power with provincial governors and warlords combined to erode the morale and legitimacy of Chiang Kai-shek's regime. Nonetheless, most observers expected that a degree of unity and stability would return under the Nationalists after the war. Even Joseph Stalin, who thought the Communists too insignificant to be serious contenders for power, lent his support to the Nationalists until Mao Zedong began to prove him wrong.

9

The Death of John Birch

FROM HIS FIELD STATION at Linquan on the Quanhe River, Birch was elated that at long last, after so much suffering and bloodshed, "the word has just come over the radio that Japan has unconditionally surrendered! Praise God from Whom all blessings flow," he told his parents.[1] To Marjorie Tooker he wrote, "When the first wild thrill swept thru the little river town where I was last night, as the Chungking radio said Japan was trying to surrender, I realized for the first time how utterly weary, even heartsick this war has made me." The same mixture of excitement, exhaustion, and relief marked the U.S. effort in general. Almost no one could imagine that a horrendous civil war would result in a Communist victory within the next four years.

"I am still convinced, as ever," continued Birch, "of the right that has been ours in fighting Germany and Japan, but I feel that a tremendous load of guilt lies on the heads of our own and other major governments for permitting the development of those circumstances which made such a world-staggering sacrifice necessary." He closed on a longing, wistful note. "Thoughts of you and wishes for your happiness run back and forth thru my mind almost incessantly, and yet these thoughts seem never to tire. God guard you, Marjorie, and grant an early meeting with you."[2]

Celebrations broke out everywhere. As Hart, Ogle, Crosby, and Willmott made their way to the R2S base, the local officials in every town and village came out to greet them and invite them to stop for rest and tea. The streets were lined with people setting off firecrackers as they passed by. "We were treated like General Wedemeyer and the Generalissimo combined!" recalled Donald Willmott. "You would think that we were the inventors of the atomic bomb, or the flyers who dropped it and ended the war for China. It made me feel like a sheep in king's clothing."[3]

Birch finally was ready to go home. Eight months earlier, he was offered but had refused a thirty-day leave to the States with priority air transportation there and back. "My work is becoming more interesting and hopeful, my health is excellent, and when I see home again, I want more than 30 days!" he wrote to Tooker. "Now that the real game is starting, it's not the time to go home!" In a letter to his sister he added, "I did NOT join the Army to fight that stateside war, no, not for one day!" John's mother believed he needed a furlough, but "knowing John's determination, anything we might say or urge would not change him. He will do what he feels is his duty no matter what the cost."[4]

Instead of sending Birch home after Tokyo's surrender, the OSS gave him one last assignment before making his way back to headquarters. Yet something had changed by the time of this final mission. After five arduous years, he was physically and mentally exhausted. He had survived with little food or money as a missionary. As a soldier, he lived in the field for months at a time close to or behind enemy lines. He experienced the uncertainty of dealing with militia groups and secret agents, not always knowing who was friend and who was foe. He had suffered repeated attacks of malaria.

Earnie Johnson, who saw Birch not long before his death, asked if he was afraid of going into an area where the Communists were active. "He replied that he had worked with the Communists many times in the past and had little trouble with them," recalled Johnson. "There was always plenty of danger in being a spy, he said, but he did not feel this mission was any more dangerous than usual. Still, he seemed tired of war and felt apprehensive about going. He told me he was looking forward to going home to Georgia for a rest and to visit with his family."[5]

Captain Oliver Caldwell, the son of Methodist missionaries in Fuzhou and a graduate of Oberlin College, greeted Birch when he arrived at the airstrip in Xi'an where he had come to prepare for his last trip for the OSS. They had met earlier in the war in Kunming, where they became friends and "seemed to share a love of China," remembered Caldwell. They drove to the OSS base outside the city, a compound rented from American Seventh-day Adventists. But when they sat together at meals, Birch "made me very uncomfortable. He answered in monosyllables and his eyes were opaque. There was no communication at all between us. He seemed to be a changed man." James Hart, who joined Birch at R2S, also believed his personality was different toward the end of the war. "He had been there too long. He became arrogant with the Nationalist Chinese and increasingly irritated with the Chinese Communists." Hart thought Birch was showing signs of paranoia.

Birch's own comment that he was "utterly weary, even heartsick," as well as others' observations that he seemed tired and apprehensive, that he "answered in monosyllables and his eyes were opaque," and that his personality had changed and he was showing signs of paranoia suggest that he was suffering from post-traumatic stress disorder (PTSD), or "combat fatigue," as it was called during the Second World War. After a few days in Xi'an, he boarded a plane and "flew east into the evening darkness" to Drill Field airstrip in the Anhui pocket 3,300 feet up in the mountains. "None of us ever saw John again," wrote Caldwell.[6]

Birch was ordered to lead an OSS team north and east to the city of Xuzhou in Jiangsu Province, where one of their tasks was to collect enemy documents before they could be destroyed. They were to make a full report on the conditions of roads and railroads "so that American and [Nationalist] Chinese forces could be dispatched to these areas without delay." They were also directed to check on all airfields.[7] Xuzhou was strategically situated at the junction of railways running north to south and east to west. In 1938, the Japanese fought prolonged battles for control of the area, with horrendous loss of life on both sides. As the enemy closed in on the city, Nationalist soldiers blew up dikes along the Yellow River to slow their advance before escaping southwest into the Dabie Mountains.[8] Ten years later, Xuzhou would be the site of the massive Huai-Hai campaign, one of the decisive Communist victories of the Chinese civil war.

Birch originally planned to go on from Xuzhou to Qingdao, a former German territory and major port on the southern coast of the Shandong peninsula. On August 16, he requested a plane to fly from his Anhui base to Xuzhou, where he would drop off Lieutenant Laird Ogle with other men, and then continue flying east to Qingdao. (He had received reports that the Xuzhou airdrome, still held by the Japanese, was in good condition and would soon be controlled by pro-Nationalist puppet troops.) The plane would then return to the Drill Field airstrip to evacuate his colleague General Wang to Chungking. OSS headquarters approved the request, and Birch asked the crew to bring along seven extra drums of gas, hand fueling pumps, an interpreter, and four radio sets with codes.[9]

There was a large Allied POW camp in the Qingdao area, and liberating these internment camps was a top U.S. priority at war's end. An estimated nine thousand prisoners were held in six camps in China and Manchuria, and another one thousand in a camp in Korea. As historian Ronald Spector explains, the OSS was the only U.S. organization capable of mounting a rescue mission on short notice. When small teams of American paratroopers suddenly appeared in the skies over these prison camps, the Japanese guards were so shocked that they did nothing to resist.[10] There is no indication that Birch expected to be involved in the rescue mission near Qingdao. For one thing, he was not trained to use a parachute; most likely, he wanted to check on his Chinese agents in the area.

In any event, OSS headquarters sent a radiogram on August 18 informing Birch, without any explanation, that the plane scheduled to pick him up "will not have to go to Tsingtao [Qingdao]." In a subsequent message, he was told that the flight to Xuzhou was canceled because there was fighting there and the airport was too dangerous. He was advised to travel instead by land.[11] The last-minute changes, vague nature of the orders, and general confusion about the situation must have been exasperating for Birch and his men.

"Americans have liberated the whole world"

Birch set out from the town of Linquan on the morning of August 20 with a party of three Americans and several Chinese (map 3). Their interpreter was First Lieutenant Dong Qinsheng [Tung Chin-sheng], a twenty-eight-year-old Nationalist Army intelligence officer from Qingdao who had been Birch's adjutant since March. The men knew from various reports that they might encounter Communist troops but saw little cause for concern, especially now that the war was over. They were venturing into the unknown, armed only with .38 caliber revolvers and .45 caliber pistols.

Over the next three days, they made their way north by foot and boat to the city of Shangqiu where they were joined by General Beng Dingyi [Peng Ting-i], a former puppet commander who had collaborated with the Japanese in the Xuzhou area but was now siding with the Nationalists. Beng was reluctant to proceed because of reports about fighting ahead, but felt it was his duty to escort the Americans to Xuzhou if they insisted on going.[12] Two Koreans, who spoke Japanese, also joined the team.

On the morning of August 24, the party—which now included the two Koreans, eight Chinese, and four Americans—boarded a train heading east from Shangqiu toward Xuzhou on the Lunghai railway. The train stopped at Dangshan and could go no further because rail traffic ahead had been disrupted by clashes between Communist, Japanese, and Chinese puppet troops. (The Nationalists had no soldiers in the area.) With the help of the Koreans, Birch requisitioned a locomotive and a baggage car from the Japanese stationmaster. After traveling about ten miles, there was a break in the tracks and they could go no further.

The men unloaded their twenty-seven pieces of baggage, which included three radio sets, and Birch and Ogle went off to a nearby village to find some porters. They met a Portuguese Catholic priest who said the Communists had raided and looted the village the previous night, killing some people and carrying away others. The church had been desecrated and the mission dispensary wrecked. Only a few children could be located to help carry the equipment. In the meantime, a Japanese patrol with about forty men arrived to repair the rails. They were not hostile and allowed the Birch party to use a railway handcar to transport their baggage to the next station at Lizhuang, where they arrived in the dark around 8:00 p.m. Here they spent the night in the barracks of local Japanese troops who were guarding a large supply train. A Japanese officer warned them that Communist troops were operating further to the east.

The next morning, they requisitioned another handcar, but the men had to take turns pushing the car along the rails because it had a broken pump. After another ten miles, they noticed the surrounding area was extremely quiet. They passed through fields ripe with grain, yet no farmers or villagers were to be seen. The three Americans with Birch later recalled, "At one cross-road we met a group of about six workmen and tried to obtain their services for pushing the hand-car to the next station. . . . They refused, stating that they had just escaped from the hands of Communist troops who had confiscated all their possessions. They informed us that there were Communists ahead of us."[13]

As they traveled from Lizhuang, the team saw Communist soldiers tearing up railway tracks and cutting down telephone and telegraph poles. The sight infuriated Birch. General Beng and Lieutenant Dong cautioned him that the situation was dangerous, but according to Dong, Birch scornfully answered, "Never mind, I want to see how the Communists treat Americans. I don't mind if they kill me for America will then stop the Communist movement with atomic bombs."[14]

Birch understood better than most outsiders the Chinese way of doing things. He could have written the OSS instruction manual for Americans in China, which counseled, "Patience and tact will be your most important assets. The Chinese like long negotiations; you can't hurry or bully them into decisions. Above all, don't lose your temper, for you will also 'lose face.' "[15] But mounting frustration and exhaustion were winning out over diplomacy, clouding his judgment.

About three hundred soldiers, presumably from the CCP's Eighth Route Army, surrounded the OSS party further along the tracks. They were armed but most were not in uniforms. Birch and Dong went ahead to speak with their commanding officer. Dong wore an army cap, shirt, and shorts but had no insignia indicating his unit or rank. Birch, who was wearing his U.S. Army uniform, identified himself and explained his mission. He refused to be disarmed and would not allow the Communists to examine or take the team's equipment. The property, he said, belonged to the U.S. government. He threatened serious reprisals if anything untoward occurred.[16]

Significantly, in light of what happened next, the Red Army commander did not insist on holding or delaying them. He informed Birch that Huangkou, the next railway station to the east, was now in the hands of Communist troops, and said Dong should go ahead of the others to explain why the OSS team was in the area. "They further told Birch that he need expect no trouble there," remembered Dong, who left his weapon behind and went first to request a pass. After a short time, the rest of the party was allowed to proceed.

The Communists in Huangkou, who recently had been fighting Japanese and Chinese puppet troops in the area, were not in a good mood. They threatened to hold Dong, who protested that "the war is over and we have no more enemies. The Americans have helped us all a lot. Captain Birch's party is going to Suchow [Xuzhou], under orders, to inspect the airfield. If you want to disarm the Americans, then you may cause a serious misunderstanding between Communist China and America."

A Red Army major decided that Dong could return to his team, accompanied by a soldier. "If anything happens," the soldier was instructed, "kill this man first and then kill the Americans." When Birch and his companions arrived on the outskirts of Huangkou, they found themselves confronted by troops with rifles. Birch stood with his arms akimbo as Dong quietly briefed him. Birch angrily said to the soldier in Chinese, "At present the Americans have liberated the whole world, and you want to stop us and disarm us! Are you bandits?" It was a serious insult since the Nationalists regularly called the Communists "bandits" to suggest they were politically illegitimate.

Birch refused to turn over his sidearm, and several soldiers escorted him and Dong into the town to meet the Communist commander. He and Dong were led to a house, forced to wait, and then walked to Huangkou's north gate. At this point, Birch grabbed a soldier by the back of his collar and shouted in Chinese, "Peace has come to all the world and still you make trouble here. Why? After all, what are you people? If I say bandits, you don't have the appearance of bandits. You are worse than bandits."

An officer wearing a Sam Browne belt cursed and ordered his men to load their guns and disarm Birch. "Wait a minute please," cried Dong. "If you want to disarm him, I will get the gun for you; otherwise a serious misunderstanding may develop." Dong later testified he did this because Captain Birch "would have become violent if any Communists tried to disarm him." But as Dong reached for Birch's weapon, the officer pointed at him and yelled, "Shoot him first!" An enlisted man standing about ten feet away raised his weapon and hesitated. The officer swore and again told the soldier to fire. The bullet struck Dong's right thigh a few inches above the knee and he fell down. A second shot was fired, and Dong heard Birch say in Chinese, "I'm hit in the leg. I can't walk." He then heard another shot. At no time, Dong later said, did Birch move to draw his weapon.

Dong lay on the ground, still and quiet. He heard a voice saying, "This man is not dead yet" and someone then struck him across the bridge of his nose with a rifle butt. Two men picked him up by his legs and arms, carried him to a shallow pit, and stripped him of his clothing. As Dong began to lose consciousness, he felt Birch beside him. He awoke sometime later and heard local farmers say, "We cannot leave the bodies here in the open air. We had better bury them." Dong opened his eyes a little and said, "I am not dead yet; please rescue me. If you cannot, kill me. Don't leave me like this." The farmers told him the Communists were still nearby. "Wait until they go, and we will remove you. The other man is already dead."[17] It was around two or three o'clock in the afternoon on Saturday, August 25th, ten days after the end of hostilities with Japan.

The details concerning Birch were gruesome. His hands were bound behind his back and his feet were tied together with thick rope. His clothing was stripped from his body and there were gunshot wounds to the left thigh and right shoulder. His face had been mutilated beyond recognition with a bayonet or knife. The local school principal, a Mr. Sao, arranged for the body to be cleaned and wrapped in a straw mat. That night, some local Chinese hastily buried Birch and took Dong to a shelter where they placed him on a wooden board. It was starting to rain. A boy brought him hot tea. Japanese soldiers arrived, questioned Dong through an interpreter, and went away. More Japanese came the next morning from Lizhuang, where Birch and his men had spent the previous night. They recognized Dong and took him to a clinic at the Huangkou railway station. There he received treatment from a Japanese army doctor.

Realizing that the death of an American military officer could mean serious trouble, the Communist commander had released one of the Chinese from the OSS party, instructing him to tell the authorities in Xuzhou that the other intruders were being held while he awaited orders from Yenan. The message said the detainees were being treated well. The commander was very sorry for the incident, which he said did not represent the policy of the Communists.[18]

After receiving this news, General Hao Pengju—a former commander under Wang Jingwei's puppet regime who was now allied with the Nationalists—dispatched Colonel Ma Zhengjiao with a detachment of soldiers to Huangkou. (Chiang Kai-shek had recently designated Hao's troops as the New Sixth Army.) They left by train in the middle of the night and arrived at Huangkou station, about thirty miles to the west, on the morning of August 27. The Japanese troops who now controlled the area gave Colonel Ma their version of the story.

Ma and his men returned by train to Xuzhou's East Station with the seriously wounded Dong and the body of Birch, carrying them on stretchers to a military hospital. The bullet wound in Dong's right thigh had developed gangrene, so there was no choice but to amputate the leg about six inches below the hip. His face was badly injured when he was struck with the rifle butt, and doctors thought they might have to remove his right eye. Birch's corpse was examined during an autopsy—a bridge for his missing front teeth confirmed his identity—and photographs were taken. The body was wrapped in white gauze bandages, covered with white silk, and placed in a temporary coffin.[19]

"The most impressive funeral possible"

There was a chill in the evening air when Lieutenant William T. Miller arrived in Xuzhou on a Japanese armored train on August 29. Accompanied by several men, he had come from the same general area as Birch, but on a different route via the Yellow River. He encountered no problems from Communists, Japanese, bandits, or anyone else. Over a cup of hot green tea, the Japanese station master told him the local newspaper had a story about an American officer who was killed a few days earlier by Communist forces to the west of the city.[20] Miller learned it was John Birch and promptly sent a message to General Wedemeyer in Chungking that the murder "should not go unnoticed or unavenged." He assured Wedemeyer that Captain Birch would receive "the most impressive funeral possible."[21]

Miller was a field intelligence officer with the Air Ground Aid Service (AGAS), an organization responsible for rescuing downed pilots. The son of a career Army officer, he was born in the Philippines and attended West Point, graduating in 1944 in three rather than four years because of the war. He was a reluctant cadet and did not achieve a distinguished record at the U.S. Military Academy, ranking 414 out of his class of 474.[22] By the time he reached China, he had missed most of the action, but his association with John Birch would bring him attention and become something of a cause for him in the years to come.

Miller had met Birch a few months earlier on an airbase at Angang in Sichuan Province. While "flat on his back and burning up with a malarial fever," recalled Miller, Birch complained about the OSS. He expressed his fears that their tactics "might seriously disrupt his own quiet but highly effective methods of obtaining information . . . from Chinese irregular forces and Korean Independence Army agents." According to Miller, Birch believed that certain OSS officers "were not aware of the forthcoming danger to China and Christianity posed by the Communist forces." Far into the stillness of the night, "we would lie on our cots and talk about the options open to the United States to stabilize China politically once the Japs had surrendered." The Communist movement was menacing China's only hope of becoming a truly democratic nation, but what worried Birch most, Miller said many years later, was the possibility that the Communists would oppose Christian missionaries.[23] This, of course, is exactly what happened after the CCP took power in 1949. To this day it is illegal for foreigners to proselytize in China.

William Miller was the first American to interview Lieutenant Dong about the events at Huangkou with the help of interpreters. "I hurried to Tung's [Dong's] side and from his feeble but impassioned account I learned the full details of John's death."[24] He promised Dong that the U.S. military would care for him and provide him with an artificial leg, and asked General Wedemeyer to authorize his medical treatment.[25] In mid-September, Dong was evacuated to a U.S. military hospital in Chungking, where doctors decided it was not necessary to remove his eye. When the Americans pulled out of Chungking and transferred their operations to Shanghai a few weeks later, Dong was moved to a Chinese army hospital. There is no record in the OSS files of what became of him; he may have returned to his home in Shandong.

Ironically, the Baptist John Birch would be accorded a Catholic Requiem Mass at the Sacred Heart of Jesus Church (*Yesu Jixin Tang*) in Xuzhou. Miller was a Catholic, and the Romanesque-style church, founded by French Jesuits in 1910, was prominent and centrally located; its two spires were the city's highest structures. The funeral took place on Sunday morning, September 2, 1945, which coincidentally was the same day the Japanese officially surrendered to the Allied forces on the deck of the battleship USS *Missouri* in Tokyo harbor.

The church was packed to the doors with Chinese dignitaries and local residents, despite the fact that American bombers had attacked the city a few weeks earlier. They were targeting rail yards and ammunition and fuel dumps, but one bomb missed its mark and detonated above an open-air cloth market. Spanish priests who surveyed the devastation told Miller that the explosion killed about three hundred and wounded between five and eight hundred Chinese civilians.

Spanish, Italian, and Hungarian Jesuit priests and Hungarian nuns chanted the Latin Mass. "Also present were the only two [Chinese] Protestant lay preachers I could find," remembered Miller. "Never will I forget that bizarre scene as I sat there in the transept of that great church flanked by two as yet un-surrendered Japanese Generals as we gazed at the huge dragon catafalque, resting in the aisle." It was draped with an oversized American flag, which nuns had sewn the night before. Father Saccatini, one of the priests, told Miller that the ceremony was the first occasion the Japanese military had set foot in his church during the entire seven years of occupation.[26]

After the funeral service, a military band led a long procession, and two dozen men carried the massive casket through the winding streets of Xuzhou. It was a twenty-minute walk to Birch's final resting place overlooking the city on Yunlongshan (Cloud Dragon Hill). Both Catholic and Protestant prayers were said, and an honor guard of twenty Japanese and twenty Chinese puppet troops—men who just days before were the sworn enemies of the United States—fired three rifle salutes over the grave. Hao Pengju, the former puppet general, arranged for a tombstone to be inscribed with the Chinese characters and English words: "He died for righteousness." Two other Americans would be buried at the same site: an American P-51 pilot who was shot down and died at the Xuzhou airfield on March 10, 1945; and the remains of Flight Officer Samuel E. Evans, who lost his life in a crash on September 4. They were placed in simple brick vaults on either side of Birch's larger memorial.[27]

It was, of course, a strange twist of fate for Birch to have a Catholic funeral service and to be buried by the Japanese and their Chinese collaborators. Postwar politics made for strange bedfellows. The Allies had instructed some 1.5 million Japanese troops in China and Taiwan to surrender to Chiang Kai-shek's armies and no one else. The Nationalists ordered the Japanese not only to hold their positions but also to recover territory recently taken by any "irregular forces"—meaning the Communists and any local military forces not under the Generalissimo's command. Lieutenant General Mori, commander of Japanese troops in the Xuzhou district, told Miller that China would be lost to Communism "unless the United States allowed the Japanese Army to remain in defensive positions throughout North China until the Nationalist Armies had sufficient time to re-occupy the region militarily."[28]

The odd mélange of former enemies paying their respects to Birch highlighted concerns about America's role in Asia. Birch was not a high-ranking officer and no U.S. official more senior that Lieutenant

William Miller with Japanese soldiers and Chinese puppet troops at Birch's gravesite in Xuzhou on September 2, 1945. Credit: U.S. Army Air Forces.

Ethel and George Birch with Frank Norris at John Birch's memorial service in Fort Worth, Texas, October 1945. Credit: Arlington Baptist College Heritage Collection.

Miller attended his funeral service. But everyone was aware that the United States had emerged as the most powerful nation in the world, a fact underscored by the two atomic bombs dropped over Japan. How would this unparalleled power be used? The unexpected murder of an American officer therefore demanded attention, not because of who John Birch was but because of what he symbolized.

At this uncertain juncture, Birch represented something more than a local conflict gone wrong. His frustrations with the Communists, which had boiled over into self-righteous anger, mirrored America's larger anxieties. What exactly his life stood for would be the subject of debate in the years ahead. Robert Welch believed his death was a "deliberate and unjustified killing," a single event that marked the beginning of a momentous struggle between communism and "Christian-style civilization."[29] For others, it was a senseless tragedy that revealed the limits of U.S. power to determine events in China.

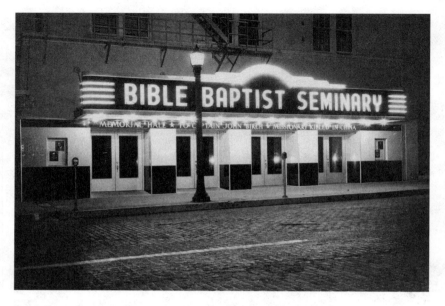

Bible Baptist Seminary's Memorial Hall in downtown Fort Worth, dedicated "to Captain John Birch, missionary killed in China." Credit: Arlington Baptist College Heritage Collection.

When the news about Birch reached Frank Norris in Fort Worth, he wrote George and Ethel Birch to express his deep sorrow and comforted them with the thought that "humanly speaking, his life would seem unfinished, yet how wonderful that he lived so gloriously in so short a time." Norris organized a memorial service at the First Baptist Church in October to honor Birch and to dedicate John Birch Memorial Hall near the corner of Throckmorton and Fourth Streets. John's parents and their fifteen-year-old son Douglas traveled from Georgia. Major General Claire Chennault also attended the ceremony and paid tribute to Birch as a man "who never swerved in his duty to his God, to his country or to his fellow man."[30]

10

Confrontation and Cooperation

THE THREE AMERICANS WITH Birch at the time of his death were Curtis Grimes, Laird M. Ogle, and Albert C. Meyers. Grimes, an OSS civilian, wore the uniform of a U.S. Army captain to reduce the risk of being tortured and shot as a spy if he was captured. Like many others drafted for espionage work, he spoke Chinese, having grown up as the son of missionaries in the city of Tianjin. After graduating from college in the States, he returned to China in 1934 to teach music at Yenjing University, a well-known Christian institution in Peking. Interned by the Japanese after the United States entered the war, he was repatriated in a prisoner exchange, recruited by the OSS, and came back to China as an intelligence officer.[1]

Sergeant Meyers was from Walnut Creek, California, and Lieutenant Laird Ogle came from a wealthy Indianapolis family, studied at Harvard, and was a radio broadcaster with NBC. Before his assignment in China, Ogle served with the OSS in France and Italy where he was involved in the production and distribution of a clandestine German newspaper as part of a black propaganda operation. Corporal Donald Willmott remembers him as an eccentric who walked around with his shirt completely unbuttoned during hot weather, but "he had a tolerant, inquiring mind and interested attitude toward all countries and peoples." Unlike many officers, he did not pull rank.[2]

Birch and other Americans north of the Yangtze River had regular contact with Communist guerrillas while operating behind Japanese lines. After the war, Colonel Wilfred Smith told Ethel Birch that John's attitude toward the Communists was pragmatic. He thought they were "one instrument to get rid of the common enemy. John had no bitterness toward the Communists; his attitude was that anybody who would help defeat Japan was to be worked with."[3] Despite unconfirmed reports of clashes between Communist, Japanese, and Chinese puppet troops, Ogle later testified that he did not foresee danger as the OSS party set off on its mission. "We as Americans expected no trouble. We were feeling pretty good about the war being over."[4] Grimes agreed: "Being American I had expected to meet with friendliness." They were eager to complete the trip to Xuzhou, return to headquarters, and board a plane or ship for home. Instead they found themselves taken prisoner by soldiers clad in the tan uniforms of the *Balujun*—the Communist Eighth Route Army.[5]

On the hot afternoon of August 25 in Huangkou, two Chinese members of the OSS party had gone into a nearby courtyard for fruit and boiled water while the rest of the team was waiting for Birch and Lieutenant Dong to return. There were no signs of danger, but after forty minutes or so they heard a gunshot about one hundred yards away.[6] Fifty or sixty Communist soldiers then emerged from the town walls and surrounded the OSS team near the railway station. The Americans recalled that they "set up a machine gun and trained it on us. Other soldiers crossed the track and covered us." An officer approached Grimes and indicated that all of the party should follow him. Grimes refused, stating that they had been ordered to watch their equipment. The team had located a railway handcar in working order and were transferring their baggage for the rest of the journey to Xuzhou. The officer's mood turned ugly and he ordered the four or five children who had been helping the intruders to leave the group. Beng Dingyi, the ranking Nationalist Chinese officer, walked toward the Communist officer with open palms, saying, "Don't shoot, don't shoot, we'll talk." At this moment, says Grimes, the Communist gave an order to his men who "advanced in a very disorderly fashion and forcibly disarmed us."

The party of twelve men was marched into Huangkou at bayonet point and lined up against a mud wall. Grimes's arms were bound behind his back and he was shoved. "Sweat streamed down my face and body as I looked squarely into the open muzzle of the machine-gun being set up a few yards in front of us." They were ordered not to talk and were stripped of their possessions. Protesting that they were allies fighting for the same cause against the Japanese made no difference. Grimes recalled "the nervously excited and leering grimaces of the undisciplined and rowdy mob surrounding us. . . . Our captors were gleefully buckling on our belts, brandishing our weapons about, and pocketing our money and other personal objects." It was very likely the first time in their lives that most of the young Red Army soldiers had seen foreigners. One of the guards was a smiling sixteen year old.[7]

In the distance, they heard two more shots. Grimes remembered "the wild, far-away expression in the eyes of one of my companions, and his pale, sweat-laden cheeks as he glanced at me and huskily remarked, 'This looks like it, alright. They're going to do us in like rats. Meet you in Heaven or somewhere.'" Grimes could only repeat in Chinese, "But we are Americans. We are friends!" Everyone took cover when two P-51 fighter planes suddenly buzzed the area at low altitude.[8] Unsure about what to do next, the commander of the Eighth Route Army detachment decided the safest course of action was to detain the OSS team, move them deeper into Communist-held territory, report the incident, and await orders from CCP headquarters in Yenan. As the prisoners were marched northwest of Huangkou, they overheard soldiers using the word *sha*—to kill. It was unclear whether they were talking about Birch and Dong, or plans to eliminate them.

Upon reaching a village, Beng and Grimes, the two senior personnel, were questioned. Grimes explained that their orders were to examine the airfield in Xuzhou and observe the activities of the Japanese following the cessation of hostilities. The interrogator told Grimes that the Communists would brook no interference in the pursuit of their goals. He condemned the Nationalists and accused the Americans of being their agents and enemies of the Communists. Grimes replied that the Americans were solely concerned with defeating the Japanese and "were not allowed to participate in any way in Chinese political issues."[9] The CCP commander defended his actions against Birch and Dong, claiming that Birch "had displayed a very bad temper" and had sorely provoked his soldiers by his statements and attitude. Grimes concluded from these statements that Birch and Dong had been either killed or seriously wounded.

They traveled about one hundred miles during the next three days and four nights, "swallowed up in one of the vast plains of the remote interior of China." They had very little food, water, or sleep. Grimes, who had come down with acute amoebic dysentery, wrote, "I know that I stumbled along in my attempt to keep up with our captors, and that when I had become exhausted they still appeared to be fresh and ready to move on as soon as they had taken a short rest." Some U.S. currency and gold coins were returned to the Americans when they reached the village of Gonglou in Shandong Province.

On September 15, three weeks after the incident at Huangkou, three Chinese detainees escaped as the group moved westward toward Puyang in Henan Province. When a General Chen interviewed them there, they pressed for their release, or at least an explanation of why they were being held as prisoners, but the general would only tell them he was awaiting instructions from Yenan. They were allowed to examine their radio equipment, codebooks, and weapons, but were not permitted to send any radio messages. It now seemed clear that Birch and possibly Dong had been killed back in Huangkou. General Chen said that Birch had "physically attacked a Communist officer, had drawn his pistol from the holster, and was shot down by the Communist soldiers present."[10]

Historians have debated how much actual fighting the Red Army did against the Japanese. Based on what Grimes saw while moving through the countryside, he believed the Eighth Route Army had conducted some impressive guerrilla warfare against the Japanese. He also concluded that the Communist army was "guilty of bloodshed, violence, and ruthlessness in the subjugation of its own people" within the confines of territory that it controlled. "Its ability to organize an area is effective and decisive; and its absolute power is achieved through intimidation and terrorism." Grimes thought the Communists were "brutally efficient," even if their troops were ill led and poorly disciplined. The Red soldiers had very little formal military training, traveled almost entirely by foot, and had no equipment except the clothes they were wearing and their weapons. Their rifles, machine guns, and pistols were either captured from the Japanese or bought through underground networks.

Village men were conscripted into military and labor service. Grimes met a man who had been induced to give up much of his personal property and his land. In one tiny village "encircled by an ancient crumbling mud wall," children were being taught Communist slogans. In a town along the Hankou railway line, captured by the Reds four days earlier, there was a feeling of "suspense, fear, and unrest." Another town was "in a state of decay and disrepair. Most of the shops were boarded up and appeared vacant, although families lived behind the closed doors, submissively eking out an existence and attempting to meet their taxes, attending indoctrination meetings when called upon, and generally doing as they were told." A Catholic church run by four or five Hungarian priests was still operating, but other churches were used for offices, classrooms, meetings, eating and sleeping, or even as stables for horses. On one occasion an old farmer bitterly told Grimes, "If only we might be left alone by soldiers. All soldiers! We have learned to hate to see them come. It always means trouble of one kind or another."[11]

As the days dragged on, Grimes grew angry and resentful. Ogle, by contrast, was more positive about the experience, pointing out that Grimes had been quite sick during the ordeal. "Excepting for the humiliation, I felt that they treated us decently," he recalled. "We were at no time brutalized but at all times under strict guard and separated from our radios. After the initial looting [of our equipment], orders came from Yenan to treat us well and to return everything that had been taken from us. John's things were returned to us after about ten days."[12]

The captives and their guards traveled westward for two more weeks, arriving at an airfield near Shexian in Hebei Province on October 18. Here they were met by Lieutenant Haulk, who had been sent from the U.S. Army Observation Group at Yenan, and Lieutenant Sherhoman, a downed flier. On October 20, a 14th Air Force plane arrived at the airfield to evacuate the Americans, Nationalist Army General Beng and his orderly, two Communist officials, and six soldiers. The two Koreans stayed behind, joining about two hundred of their compatriots somewhere in the vicinity. Because the American rescue plane had consumed too much fuel while trying to locate the airfield, the pilot was unable to fly the four hundred miles to OSS headquarters in Xi'an. Instead, they flew one hundred miles to Yenan, where Major J. C. Eaton greeted them. More of their equipment and money was returned to them a few hours later. Still missing were miscellaneous radio parts and accessories, one M-209 cipher machine, two .38 caliber pistols, thirty-four gold coins, seven gold rings, and a significant amount of Chinese and U.S. currency.[13]

The following morning, General Ye Jianying, chief of staff of the Communist army, personally met with the three Americans. "He stated that he regretted Birch's death, and asked us to convey his condolences to his family." General Ye seemed anxious to hear their version of the incident, but the Americans were reluctant to discuss it with him.[14] He ordered a search to recover and return the various missing items. Mao's public criticism of the United States had grown more blunt and outspoken, but Ye Jianying's apology for Birch's death showed how important good relations with the Americans still were to the Communists at this juncture.

Grimes, Ogle, and Meyers flew to Chungking later that day, nearly two months after Wedemeyer had demanded their release from Mao. Wedemeyer ordered "a very thorough interrogation." "This entire matter is still under investigation and there are many loose ends which require tying up due to the scraps of the story coming in from several different sources," wrote an OSS officer.[15] After their debriefing in Chungking, the three men started the long trip home. No doubt they were cautioned to keep their stories to themselves.

"We want to cooperate with the United States."

To fight the Japanese, the Americans had to work with the Nationalists as well as with guerrillas, regional warlords, Communists, and Chinese collaborators (puppets) in vast areas not controlled by Chiang Kai-shek's central government. Politics and ideology were secondary to winning the war. The Kuomintang, however, did its best to keep the United States away from the Chinese Communists. The one exception was the small U.S. Army Observation Group—known as the Dixie Mission, possibly because it was operating in "rebel" territory—which arrived at Mao's Yenan headquarters in July 1944. The Mission's purpose was to gather intelligence on the Japanese, provide weather reports for American fliers, and assist with the recovery of air corps personnel who were shot down. The Dixie Mission was also asked to assess the strength of the Communists. Supplies were flown in from Chungking to set up operations for radio and cryptography, a weather station, kitchen and mess hall, bathhouse, and housing for electrical generators. Five of the original eighteen members were OSS.

The Americans dispatched to Yenan got along quite well with the Chinese revolutionaries. They attended weekly dances and everyone enjoyed watching Hollywood movies flown in on U.S. planes. Laurel and Hardy's slapstick comedies, which required no translation, were big hits with the Chinese.[16] Mao told Colonel David Barrett, the first Dixie Mission leader, "We want to cooperate with the United States in fighting the Japanese, we want to help in the present desperate situation. . . . If you land on the shores of China, we will be there to meet you, and to place ourselves under your command."[17] Another extraordinary offer was made in January 1945, when Zhu De, the CCP's top military commander, wrote to William Donovan, director of the OSS, suggesting that the Communists borrow twenty million U.S. dollars "to be used in strengthening subversive activities among puppet troops."[18] The Americans provided very little in terms of arms or supplies, but in subsequent years the small contingent sent to Yenan would be accused of sympathizing with the Chinese Reds and undermining Chiang Kai-shek's government. Most prominent among them was John S. Service, a diplomat in the U.S. Foreign Service whose career would be destroyed by recriminations over the failure of America's China policy.[19]

One member of the Dixie Mission, Captain Henry C. Whittlesey, lost his life. On February 2, 1945, Whittlesey and a Chinese photographer, Li Xiaotang, learned that enemy documents had been discovered on a derailed train at some distance from Yenan. They happened to be nearby and decided to investigate. Arriving at a village around dusk, they ran into Japanese soldiers and were captured. The Communists mounted a rescue operation but were too late. When they entered the town they found the bodies of Whittlesey and Li where they had been shot.

Colonel Barrett called Whittlesey "one of the finest young officers I ever knew" and wrote that the Communists "appeared deeply distressed over the death. I believe they held him in high esteem, and it was also a great loss of face for them to have allowed him to enter the village on their assurance there were no Japanese there." He doubted the Chinese would have deliberately allowed Whittlesey to fall into a trap. General Zhu De personally expressed his sympathy to the Americans, noting that his own men had suffered some twenty casualties in the effort to rescue the American captain.[20]

The Communists did not allow foreigners to show up in their territory without notification and identification, but they nevertheless went out of their way to help downed U.S. airmen. At the end of the war, General Zhu De informed General Wedemeyer that CCP forces had come to the aid of eighty-four Americans. During these rescues, 110 Chinese officers and men—not to mention numerous Chinese civilians—lost their lives. This, wrote Zhu after the death of John Birch, proved that the Communists were fighting together with America against Japan: "I assure you that this spirit of cooperation has been so in the past and will be continued in the future."[21]

It was thanks to the Communists that First Lieutenant Joseph Paul Baglio escaped and survived after bailing out over Japanese-held territory near the city of Taiyuan in Shanxi Province.[22] Baglio, a pilot with the 26th Fighter Squadron of the 14th Air Force, was on a strafing mission on June 9, 1944, when his plane was hit by ground fire and began to smoke. He bailed out at an altitude of six hundred feet and landed safely. He carried halazone tablets for water purification, an extra pair of shoes, a .45 caliber handgun, and some Chinese money. Every flier wore a "blood chit," which was a piece of cloth with U.S. and Republic of China flags and Chinese characters identifying him as an American assisting China's War of Resistance. A reward was promised for returning downed airmen to Allied lines.

Baglio also had a "Pointie Talkie," a booklet with a list of English questions, phrases, and words on one side of each page and Chinese translations on the other side. Even without a common language, Americans and Chinese could communicate by pointing. One might ask, for example, "Is this area occupied by the Japanese?" and receive a "yes" or "no" response. The PT, as the booklet was called, was a good idea, but neither of the first two peasants Baglio met, both of whom gave him water, could read Chinese characters. He finally met a boy who was literate and who told him the Japanese were about three miles away. Eventually he was taken to a district magistrate who read the PT from cover to cover while Baglio ate some hard-boiled eggs.

Baglio was guided from village to village and was introduced to a Communist guerrilla leader, who asked for his gun, looked it over, and said he would keep it. The guerrilla gave Baglio a Chinese jacket to wear over his uniform to make him less conspicuous. According to a detailed account taken down by the same Captain Henry Whittlesey who was killed by the Japanese several months later, it was obvious that "a large, protective scouting net" had been set up around the American pilot. Telephones and radios were almost non-existent, but word-of-mouth communication was remarkably efficient. "Every few minutes peasants would come in with reports on the Japs." Ordinary people provided food and shelter and served as scouts, guides, bearers, and fighters. Baglio concluded that they would give up anything to help the Eighth Route Army.

On June 18, a Captain Qing agreed to escort Baglio across the Yellow River in the direction of Yenan. His pistol was returned to him, and he was given a Chinese-style pair of pants and a wide-brimmed hat for the trip. About a week later, Richard T. Frey, a young Jewish doctor who had fled Austria after the Nazis took over, came from Yenan to see if Baglio needed any medical attention. Frey arranged a much-appreciated bath, good food, and a decent bed.[23]

Baglio became a living propaganda exhibit, useful in showing that the United States was fighting alongside the Communists. Baglio was "paraded through streets lined with cheering people" who had likely never seen an American. Signs of welcome were pasted up everywhere and he had to make speeches. As they moved north, he saw areas devastated by the Japanese campaigns of the previous year. On July 4, he arrived at the Jinqiaji military region, where he would spend the next twenty-one days as a local celebrity. The newspapers ran stories about him and he was photographed more than 150 times. He finally left for Yenan in late July, accompanied by an interpreter and three men. One night along the way, Baglio's horse fell into a canyon and was killed. On another occasion, he found himself "hidden in a coal mine with a number of others, mostly women and children who were avoiding a Jap raiding party." In one area he saw large poppy fields and was told they were raised to sell opium to the Chinese puppet soldiers. The Communists used the cash to buy arms and supplies.

Baglio said the Eighth Route Army troops, who clearly had been fighting the Japanese, were "well-fed and neatly uniformed" and had excellent morale. He thought the civilian populations under the Communists were much better off than Chinese in the south under the Nationalists. The Americans in Yenan were impressed that none of the Communist guerrillas who helped Baglio walk out expected any reward. On the contrary, they had spent money on him for shoes, clothing, food, cigarettes, and a bedding roll. Whittlesey added in his report, "Nor is there the slightest intimation on the part of the government here [in Yenan] that we owe them anything. They feel it is part of their contribution to the war. This is a pleasant contrast," he said, "to some of the ridiculous and high demands made by certain [Nationalist] Chinese generals for expenses in connection with the saving of our fliers." After reaching Yenan on September 2, eighty-five days after bailing out of his plane, Baglio sent his pistol to the guerrilla leader who had disarmed him—a man with no gun of his own—to thank him for saving his life.

William Taylor told an equally dramatic rescue story. The twenty-four-year-old civilian from Ogden, Utah, was building a military base for the Morrison and Knudsen Construction Company on Wake Island—a U.S. territory about halfway between Hawaii and Japan—when he and 1,600 other Americans (civilians and military) were captured by the Japanese in late December 1942. They were transported by ship to Shanghai, and for the next three and a half years, Taylor managed to survive the ordeal of the Woosung and Kiangwan prison camps.

In early May 1945, Taylor and Jack Hernandez, another American, jumped through the window of a moving train in the middle of the night while being transported north from Shanghai with other POWs. Hernandez broke his leg, was unable to walk, and was recaptured by the Japanese. Taylor fled and several days later stumbled into a village where he was surrounded by troops from the Communist Eight Route Army, one of whom told him in perfect English: "Your country and mine are friends." They bathed, clothed, and fed him. Officers gave banquets in his honor and treated him "like a visiting potentate."

Over the course of the next several weeks, Taylor was escorted westward through Japanese-occupied territory into western Shandong, where he was given a horse and a bodyguard of twenty soldiers. His escorts skirted around the enemy through the Taihang Mountains in Hebei Province—a kind of no man's land in between the cities and towns—and "protected me at the risk of their own lives." Along the way they saw puppet troops who were friendly to the Communists. Taylor also met a Nationalist general who had gone over to the Red Army a few months earlier. Allegiances were rapidly shifting as the end of the war was in sight.

In late June, the Communists helped Taylor make radio contact with members of the Dixie Mission, who arranged for a B-25 to pick him up at an airstrip. He was thrilled to see the U.S. flag flying from a tall flagpole when he reached the Communist headquarters in Yenan. Zhu De and other leaders gave a dinner in his honor, and Mao Zedong came to the airstrip on July 5 to see Taylor off as he boarded a C-47 transport plane for Chungking. Mao shook his hand, congratulated him on his escape, posed for a photo with him, and gave him two small hand-woven rugs. Taylor returned to the United States a few weeks later and met with a group of military officials in Washington. "I told them as soon as the war ended, Mao would conquer all of China within a short time. They listened politely, but didn't believe me."[24]

Mao wanted U.S. support to fight the Japanese; to gain legitimacy in his struggle against the Nationalists; and to counterbalance the influence of the Soviet Union. Nevertheless, it seems clear that the treatment of Baglio, Taylor, and others was not simply an orchestrated propaganda campaign but rather a genuine outpouring of appreciation for Americans who were risking their lives to defend China. Within a short span of time, these sentiments of friendship and cooperation would be overwhelmed by the forces of ideology and nationalism. Americans would find themselves at first bewildered and then deeply angry over this tectonic shift.

The Fuping Incident

There were many different types of men in the clandestine OSS. Frank Miller, who was in charge of special operations north of the Yangtze River, writes that some were soldiers of fortune, explorers, and Wall Street bankers. Some were "dashing, flamboyant, hard drinking, devil-may-care soldiers" and others were "serious-minded, cool, analytical thinkers." There also were "ranchers and farmers, and Ivy-Leaguers, doctors, missionaries, and a few Catholic priests."[25]

Independent and courageous, the OSS could also be reckless and inept. The Spaniel mission—which led to the Fuping incident—was an especially ill-advised endeavor. On May 28, 1945, five OSS men took off from Xi'an and parachuted into Communist-held territory close to Japanese lines, about 230 miles southwest of Beijing in Hebei Province. Coming down near the city of Fuping at dusk, the team included Major Francis L. Coolidge, Captain R. G. Mundinger, Sergeant Elmer B. Esch, Private First Class Mort S. Bobrow, and Mr. Deng, a Chinese working for the OSS who assured them the Communists would be helpful. They carried money and gold, but no identification papers. Containers with weapons, radio equipment, and food supplies were dropped one-half to one mile away. The Red Chinese had not been informed about their arrival.

Their objective was to make contact with Chinese collaborators in order to test their willingness to break with the Japanese and work with U.S. forces. As these puppet troops began realizing that Japan would lose the war, the OSS saw an opportunity to co-opt them into setting up intelligence networks and sabotaging Japanese communication lines. The collection of materials for counterintelligence ("black operations") was also of interest, according to an OSS memorandum, especially "the securing of [enemy] proclamations with chops and seals, so that fake Japanese military orders may be promulgated."[26]

Major Coolidge, the team's leader, kept a daily journal which became the basis for a detailed report on the Fuping incident. After they landed, he wrote, some Communist soldiers politely greeted, questioned, and fed them. A local commander, who initially suspected the Americans might be Germans or Italians, asked why they did not have the CCP's approval for travel in the region. They were treated well, and in the coming days, local college students practiced their English, sang songs, and played basketball with the Americans. Their hosts asked them to prepare the students "to help when the Americans land on the China coast" in preparation for an invasion of Japan.

Repeated attempts to make radio contact with OSS headquarters in Xi'an or Kunming—which the Communists allowed—were unsuccessful. The distance was too great, the frequency too high, and their radio set too small. After a few days of hiking through the countryside, the team reached an area close to Fuping where they met Geng Biao, a high-ranking CCP commander who would go on to have a distinguished political, military, and diplomatic career in China's new government after 1949. Despite his misgivings about the Americans' highly irregular arrival, Geng at first seemed willing to help them set up intelligence operations—but only after receiving approval from Yenan. Meanwhile, the Communists took the OSS team's weapons, "since it is their policy to disarm anyone until officially informed otherwise by higher authorities," wrote Coolidge. (John Birch was confronted with the same demand but had refused to turn over his gun.) They were also asked to turn over their radio equipment, "less one receiver that we might enjoy swing music."

The biggest question and apparent sticking point concerned Mr. Deng, who the Communists suspected of being an agent of Dai Li, the infamous head of the KMT's intelligence service. The CCP interpreter, Mr. Ma, told the Americans they could have carried out their intelligence work if they had come without Deng, a representative of Chiang Kai-shek whose purpose was to unite the puppet soldiers "to fight not merely the Japs but the [Communist] 8th Route Army." Deng was interrogated separately from the Americans.

By late June, Coolidge and his men were convinced they were being held incommunicado, not as guests but as prisoners, at the same time that William Taylor and other Americans were being rescued by the Communists. They had periodic bouts of malaria and dysentery, and Sergeant Esch suffered the pain of an impacted wisdom tooth. In despair Coolidge noted, "We have come on a military mission and have run into a political mess." It was an observation that aptly characterized U.S. policy as a whole.

In July, a few Frenchmen and a Vietnamese showed up, having fled from the French consulate in Japanese-occupied Tianjin. This group was detained until early August when the Chinese gave the French permission to leave. The Vietnamese, a man named Phinh, was told he would have to stay behind "to work for his country's independence from France." The French major protested, and the Vietnamese, who was a member of the French army, expressed no desire to remain behind since "his thoughts and culture were entirely French," according to Coolidge. A guard led Phinh away, while the French put on their packs and walked off; the OSS men heard nothing more of them or Phinh.

Growing uncertainty led the four Americans to consider an escape either to join the Russians in the north or to meet up with Nationalist troops to the east. In preparation, Coolidge and his men used some of their gold to buy local clothing and food. Then, without warning, they were sent to an airstrip at Linqiu, where they were to be released and evacuated by air to the south. But this plan changed as the war came to an abrupt end in mid-August, and they were told they would be sent north to help release American prisoners of war held by the Japanese. In the meantime, two downed American airman, Lieutenant Fred Joy and a Captain Smith, were brought to their location. All of them set up a five-dollar-per-person pool, betting on the day and hour that the U.S. rescue plane would arrive.[27]

On September 8, more than three months after the Spaniel mission was dispatched, a C-47 airplane landed on "a beautiful windy day" to fly the Americans to Yenan and from there to Xi'an. They were picked up at Varoff Field, an airstrip built by the Communists and named for George Varoff, the captain of a B-29 crew that was rescued by People's Militia and the Eighth Route Army in late 1944.[28]

"In general," Coolidge summarized after returning to Chungking, "our physical treatment was good. We were given reasonable quarters and ample food was available." But the lack of information, inability to communicate with OSS headquarters, and constantly changing signals from the Communists was nerve-wracking. He also faulted OSS planning. The Japanese would have captured the team, he believed, if not for the CCP, whose organization was "so extensive it would have been impossible to have lived in the hills without their knowledge." He was impressed with efforts to reduce rents, lower taxes, set up schools, and educate soldiers. However, unlike Curtis Grimes, he was convinced that the amount of actual fighting being carried on by the Eighth Route Army against the Japanese or puppet troops "has been grossly exaggerated."[29]

In response to the detention of the OSS team near Fuping, U.S. China Theater headquarters issued an order on August 1, 1945, effective immediately, that no special operations would be carried out or staged in areas controlled by the Chinese Communists north of the Yellow River. In addition, each field commander "will be made responsible to insure that his equipment and supplies are not used in Chinese civil strife." On August 17, two days after Japan announced its surrender, Wedemeyer issued a further order stating that "American personnel will take such action as is necessary to protect American lives and property against anybody whether Communist, Nationalist, or provincial. Act accordingly."[30]

Birch nevertheless was ordered into an area being contested by the Communists. After he was killed one week later, the OSS immediately requested a complete list of all personnel "who are close enough to Communist forces to be possible victims of another Birch incident." Wedemeyer wanted to know why Birch and others had received instructions for "tracking the activities of non-Nationalist armies and bandits." Colonel Paul Helliwell responded that all OSS field teams had received directives "to report in detail on movements and activities of all Chinese troops, including Communist and irregular troops, as well as to perform their primary function of securing intelligence on the Japanese." At the same time, all OSS teams had been told, "political partiality or sympathy for one side or the other is under no circumstances to be displayed. . . [and] an attitude of absolute impartiality will be maintained." Helliwell pointedly added that the OSS had been "precluded from working directly with Communist forces."[31] As the Birch party would learn, the policy of "absolute impartiality" was not realistic.

The Fuping incident, as well as the death of Birch and the capture of his men at Huangkou, underscored the risks of miscommunication and the potential for misunderstanding between the Chinese Communists and Americans. It was not an auspicious beginning. The two sides worried that these events might be harbingers of further discord. Slowly but surely, they were being swept into the swirling vortex of a fearsome postwar world.

II

The Aftermath

THE ONE-THOUSAND-MILE FLIGHT FROM Yenan to Chungking was Mao Zedong's first time in an airplane. Patrick Hurley, the flamboyant U.S. ambassador from Oklahoma, accompanied him on the two-engine American transport. The chairman of the Chinese Communist Party had come to negotiate with Generalissimo Chiang Kai-shek, head of the Nationalist Party. Both leaders professed a desire to avoid civil war; both needed to buy time to gather strength and to reinforce their positions. Zhou Enlai, who spent much of the war as the CCP's representative to the Nationalists, joined Mao for the talks. They would remain in Chungking for forty-three days discussing a formula for sharing military and political control, but no concrete results would emerge. Neither side had any intention of ceding power to the other.

Two days after Mao's arrival on August 28, General Wedemeyer received a top-secret radio communication informing him that an American officer, Captain John Birch, had been shot and killed by Communist troops in north China. Three other Americans with him at the time had been taken prisoner. The news was alarming. Wedemeyer was already concerned about another OSS team—designated as the Spaniel mission—captured three months earlier and being held by the Communists near the city of Fuping. The reasons for the two incidents were unclear to Wedemeyer. He needed to know whether the murder of Birch was deliberate or simply an accident. Was the detention of the men with Birch and those on the Spaniel mission intended as a warning to the United States not to interfere in China's affairs, now that Japan had surrendered? Were these actions against Americans meant to sabotage the U.S. role in brokering a peace between the Communists and Nationalists? Or were these events simply the result of uncoordinated decisions by local commanders?

Foreseeing the possibility of civil war, Washington was specific about its policy to avoid entanglement in China's internal politics. Chennault issued an order on June 3 forbidding all 14th Air Force officers from discussing political questions or future military plans with "any Chinese in a position of authority in any area of China." Wedemeyer wrote to Mao on July 30 declaring that the United States would not get involved in clashes between the Communists and Nationalists: "I have very carefully refrained from participation . . . in the political affairs of this great country. My one purpose has been to help the Chinese help themselves in their struggle against the common enemy, the Japanese."[1]

CCP chairman Mao Zedong and U.S. ambassador Patrick Hurley as they arrived in Chungking on August 28, 1945. Credit: Bettmann/CORBIS.

But maintaining a neutral position would prove extremely difficult if Americans were being killed and captured.

After receiving the report on Birch, Wedemeyer telephoned Hurley to say he urgently needed to see Mao and Zhou, who were scheduled to meet with the ambassador at his residence that evening. The general arrived at Number 2, Jialing Village, at 7:45 p.m. on August 30. Pointing to a map of Jiangsu and Shandong provinces, he informed the Communist leaders about the death of the American officer, shot by Red Army soldiers in the vicinity of Xuzhou at a nearby railway station. It was, said the American commander, "a very serious and very grave incident."[2]

"Why was he there?" asked Zhou. "He was sent there by me several weeks ago to obtain information about the Japanese," answered Wedemeyer. "I feel that I can and must send Americans anywhere in China to carry out my mission." "You mean any place?" "Yes," replied said Wedemeyer.

Mao seemed to be caught by surprise. "We cannot say the Communist troops killed him or not. If this is true that the Communist troops shot this American officer, I extend my deepest apology." "I would like assurance that this will not occur again," demanded Wedemeyer. "I cannot have Americans killed in this Theater by Chinese Communists or anyone else. I am directed by the President of the United States to use whatever force I require to protect American lives in China."

Wedemeyer then asked why the three Americans with Birch had been taken prisoner. "It must be due to a misunderstanding," replied Mao. "It might be—I hope it is," said Wedemeyer. "I want Mr. Mao to investigate and report to me the circumstances. I must make a prompt and thorough report to the President of the U.S." Mao: "I will investigate this incident and also hope that from now on if anyone goes into those areas where Communist troops are operating that they notify the Communist troops beforehand so as to avoid unnecessary incidents." (Nothing was mentioned about the Chinese Nationalists and Koreans in Birch's OSS party.)

Wedemeyer stated that prior notification of U.S. military movements was not always feasible; "I have Americans operating all over the China Theater." He very much hoped that China would not become involved in a civil war and that the "various political factions" could settle their differences without resorting to warfare. "We have Republican and Democratic Parties in the United States—they have violent differences—but do not use force of arms."

Mao agreed on the need to avoid bloodshed now that the war was over. "That is the reason why I am here to confer with the Generalissimo." As for the United States, Mao reassured Wedemeyer and Hurley that the Communists welcomed the Americans, starting with the U.S. Military Observer Group sent to Yenan one year earlier. "It is true that Americans are our friends, not our enemy. We have only one enemy and that is Japan," said Mao. He asked the Americans to "have faith in the Communist troops since they have helped your fliers in the past." Zhou added, "We have assisted American fliers as recently as June and July."

Wedemeyer acknowledged that the Communists had been very kind and very helpful to American airmen who were forced down during combat with the Japanese. But cooperation had not been good since the members of a U.S. team (the Spaniel mission) were taken prisoner near Fuping in late May. Hoping to resolve that problem quietly, Wedemeyer said he had not reported the incident to the U.S. War Department. But he had received no response to the letters and radio messages sent to Yenan. Growing more agitated, he demanded, "I want those four men returned at once.... Now I have had a Captain killed and three other Americans taken prisoners. This has got to stop." Mao replied, "This is very unfortunate. I will investigate at once."

The American general asked Mao, "Why did they capture these men [at Fuping]—why did they take them as prisoners? You should have had the courtesy to at least wire me and say, 'Wedemeyer, who are these people that just came into this area?' Do I have your assurance that these four men will be sent to me immediately?" "I consider the Fuping incident very unfortunate," offered Mao. "As soon as I heard about the four Americans, I . . . [issued] instructions not to treat the Americans badly." He claimed the messages Wedemeyer had transmitted to Yenan had not been received. "So far as I know they are not being retained as prisoners but are free and are being treated very well. When they parachuted down our people thought they were the enemy. They will be sent back immediately."

As for the death of Captain Birch, Mao said he knew nothing about it until this meeting. If Communist soldiers were responsible, he repeated, "I extend my deep apology, and will instruct my troops to investigate at once. I hope that General Wedemeyer will look at it from my angle—that the shooting must have been done by the local guerrillas who were fighting the Japanese and during the fighting some misunderstanding very probably could have happened."

In an effort to be more diplomatic, Wedemeyer then told Mao and Zhou that he also would report the Birch incident to Chiang Kai-shek. "It may have been caused by forces of the Generalissimo," he allowed. "I am going to talk to him just as earnestly as I have talked to Mr. Mao." He apologized to Mao and Zhou for taking so much of their time, but "this is a terribly important matter." Ambassador Hurley summarized the extraordinary meeting in a telegram to Secretary of State James Byrnes in Washington.[3]

General Wedemeyer followed up with a memorandum asking Mao to make an immediate investigation of the Birch and Fuping incidents and to "inform this Headquarters as to what steps are being taken by you to preclude similar unfortunate occurrences involving U.S. personnel, and the measures adopted to insure that U.S. personnel and property are given full and adequate protection without molestation." He acknowledged that Chinese Communist forces had assisted the United States with collecting intelligence and assisting downed airmen in the past. "It is difficult therefore to understand how the two incidents could have happened."[4]

The August 30 confrontation between Mao and Wedemeyer effectively marked the end of cooperation between the CCP and the United States. Whatever hope there may have been for deeper understanding was pushed even further into the distance. It was an ominous foreshadowing of things to come.

Wedemeyer wrote to Chiang Kai-shek—since technically the Communists were under the Nationalists' command—asking him to demand of Mao that "the officer responsible for this outrage be severely punished and the prisoners be released." He wanted the Generalissimo to secure a pledge that incidents of this type "will not happen in the future, for they weaken the friendship between China and America. . . . I am certain that you are aware that the U.S. Government and the

American public will view such occurrences as being of the gravest importance and possibly of direct consequences."[5]

In response, the Nationalist authorities ordered General Zhu De, commander-in-chief of the Red Army, to "investigate the incident and punish the responsible persons for the crime."[6] Zhu soon replied directly to Wedemeyer, promising an investigation and expressing his "deep condolences over the unfortunate death of Capt. Birch which is entirely unexpected on our part." He confirmed that the three Americans who had been with Birch as well as the four Americans being held near Fuping were being escorted to airfields for evacuation to Chungking.[7]

Mao—who was apologetic during the discussion with Wedemeyer—was incensed and humiliated by what he perceived as the American commander's blatant lack of respect.[8] His resentment was understandable. While he knew about the Americans being held near Fuping, it seems entirely plausible that he had no information about the Birch incident five days earlier; Red Army radio communications in the field were rudimentary, one reason why the Eighth Route Army troops at Huangkou were so interested in U.S. equipment. Yet he had been lectured like an errant schoolboy. Knowing that U.S. policy favored the Nationalists, Mao also would have viewed the U.S. general's professions of political neutrality with considerable skepticism, if not cynicism. Sensitive to the history of foreign interference in China's affairs, he must have bridled at Wedemeyer's statement that he would "use whatever force is necessary to protect American lives." Despite being insulted by Wedemeyer, the CCP could not risk further alienating the Americans. The Nationalists had the stronger military, and Chiang's government recently had signed a treaty with Stalin, who feared the Chinese Communists might trigger a major U.S. military response if they were too aggressive.[9] Diplomatic recognition of the Republic of China did not, however, prevent the Soviets from aiding the Communists in Manchuria.

The KMT and CCP had been placed on a collision course earlier in August when Zhu De issued an order to Communist troops to seize strategic towns, cities, and rail lines controlled by the Japanese. If the enemy refused to surrender, they would be annihilated. "Those who oppose or obstruct such actions will be treated as traitors."[10] U.S. authorities ordered the Japanese in China and Formosa (Taiwan) to surrender only to the Nationalists. (The Japanese troops in Manchuria were instructed to surrender to the Soviets.) More than one hundred clashes broke out between Communists and Japanese and puppet troops between late August and the end of September.

The strategic problem facing Chiang Kai-shek was that the Communists, who claimed control over ninety million people, were strong in the north where the most of Japan's troops were based. The Nationalists had almost no presence there, and it would take weeks for their armies to arrive from the south. The result, as historian Suzanne Pepper writes, was "an extended period of time during which the Japanese or their collaborators continued to function in authoritative positions with the explicit sanction of the Kuomintang Government." The KMT's overriding concern, which turned out to be only too real, was the threat posed by the Chinese Communists. But Chiang's expediency in using the enemy as proxies against the Communists alienated many Chinese citizens who had suffered so terribly under Japanese occupation. The incompetence and corruption of officials who were sent north further weakened the Nationalists' authority and legitimacy.[11]

"Explosive and portentous possibilities"

It was with a deep sense of foreboding that Wedemeyer looked to the future. "I view Asia as an enormous pot, seething and boiling," he wrote to the Joint Chiefs of Staff in Washington in mid-August 1945. He was alarmed about the "explosive and portentous possibilities in China when Japan surrenders." Chinese Communist forces might precipitate civil war and the Japanese Army might continue to fight "either in force or in isolated areas," he told George Marshall. The corruption and incompetence of the Nationalists was a cause for concern, but Wedemeyer argued that the sole viable U.S. option was continued support of the Generalissimo, who heads "the only officially and universally recognized constituted government in China."[12]

U.S. postwar policy toward China would not, however, be determined by the international legal status of Chiang Kai-shek's regime. The overwhelming concern was not China per se but America's increasingly uneasy relationship with the Soviet Union. Would some form of Roosevelt's wartime cooperation with Stalin be possible, or would Soviet expansionism preclude a peaceful relationship? What would Soviet domination of a China under Mao mean for U.S. policy in Asia? Choosing the least bad option, Washington sought a middle way, encouraging the Chinese to settle their differences, while at the same time dispatching American planes and ships to transport Nationalist armies and equipment to the disputed north. Fifty thousand U.S. Marines were sent there to disarm and repatriate Japanese forces while helping to keep the peace.[13]

In light of such important events, the arrest of two groups of American soldiers and the murder of a low-ranking American officer in a backwater Chinese town did not loom especially large. General Zhu De nevertheless responded to Wedemeyer's demand for an explanation of the Fuping and Huangkou incidents. He reported that the Communists had been informed in early 1945 that Captain John Birch was working in Anhui Province. The CCP's New Fourth Army was notified of his presence and was ordered to "give protection if and when necessary." But Yenan received no further information after this communication.

The Communists were fighting Japanese and Chinese puppet forces when Birch appeared without notice at the Huangkou railway station on August 25, wrote Zhu. As the battle continued, the Japanese brought in reinforcements on three trains from the east. "Small groups of plain-clothes men had infiltrated our flank and rear," and sentries discovered two armed persons, a foreigner and a Chinese, coming toward them from the direction of the enemy. They were ordered to halt and be recognized, but instead "they pulled out their arms, and dashed forward" to the place where Deputy Commander Zhang Chuansheng was located.

According to the CCP's investigation, the two intruders—Birch and Dong—were taken to regimental headquarters in Huangkou where they "argued and struggled, cursing: 'You people are traitors, bandits.'" They were very aggressive and "pointed their pistols at

Commander Chang [Zhang]." At this critical moment, two of the Communist soldiers, acting in self-defense, opened fire killing both men. The nationality of the foreigner was not known at the time, and "due to the urgent withdrawal of our troops there was no opportunity to bury either our own dead or Captain Birch." The other foreigners and Chinese were disarmed and taken to the rear while the commander awaited instructions from Yenan. (Zhu's report omitted any mention of the Chinese or Koreans who were also detained.) After receiving confirmation that the three surviving foreigners were U.S. Army personnel, they were being released and evacuated. Zhu again expressed his "deepest regret over the unfortunate death of Captain Birch."[14]

As we have seen, Lieutenant Dong portrayed himself as a mediator who was trying to keep Birch calm in order to avoid conflict. Even if we accept the possibility that Dong was belligerent—since it appears that he was shot first—the claim that both Birch and Dong "pointed their pistols" at the Communist officer does not seem credible. Dong testified that he was not armed when he reached Huangkou and said that "at no time . . . did Birch or I draw our weapons."[15] Being heavily outnumbered by Red Army soldiers, it would have been suicidal to do so. It is conceivable, however, that in the heat of the moment the Communists thought Dong was being hostile when he reached for Birch's sidearm in order to disarm him.

Turning to the Fuping incident, Zhu stated that the CCP's investigation confirmed that four Americans had parachuted into a Communist-controlled area in north China in late May without notification. "They were surrounded and disarmed by the local militia and people. They claimed that they were U.S. Army personnel but they presented no credentials to testify as to their mission." They were given preferential treatment, allowed to keep their sidearms, and permitted to set up their radio. In June, General Ye Jianying sent a message through the U.S. military mission in Yenan asking Wedemeyer about their purpose, but there was no reply from Chungking. Zhu said that Wedemeyer's letter dated July 14 requesting the release of the Americans was never received. Only after hearing from Wedemeyer in early August were arrangements made for the

OSS team's evacuation, which did not take place until September 8, one week after the August 30 meeting between Mao and Wedemeyer in Chungking.

Why the Americans were detained for so long near Fuping is uncertain. Colonel Wilber J. Peterkin, acting head of the Dixie Mission, blamed it on miscommunication inside Wedemeyer's Chungking headquarters.[16] Maochen Yu, professor of history at the U.S. Naval Academy and author of a detailed history on the OSS in China, speculates that Peterkin decided against delivering Wedemeyer's initial messages to Mao because the OSS "badly needed the Communists' goodwill" for an ambitious radio communications intelligence network and "did not want to let a direct confrontation between Wedemeyer and Mao Zedong ruin their already fragile cooperation with the Communists." It is hard to imagine that Peterkin would have interfered with a message from his commanding general in this way. Yu also thinks the CCP wanted to prevent the Americans held at Fuping from finding out about their collaboration with puppet armies.[17] Yet if this were true, why would the OSS team have been allowed to stay for more than three months in areas where they could observe the Communists?

Ren Donglai, late professor of history at Nanjing University, believes that the lack of an immediate American response to the detention of the OSS men "created an illusion on the side of the CCP leaders that the Americans knew they were wrong and had no choice but to suffer the humiliation."[18] Most likely, writes Ren, the Communists were waiting for an explanation and an appropriate apology from the U.S. command. Whatever the explanation, it seems clear that the CCP's response to Fuping contributed directly to the Birch incident. Mao was already unhappy with Ambassador Hurley and U.S. policy, which he saw as duplicitous. It appears that the Fuping episode was further evidence of U.S. conceit as far as the Communists were concerned, and the Americans needed to be taught a lesson about acting with impunity in CCP territory. Yenan therefore instructed all Red Army units "to arrest and disarm and hold all unauthorized Americans encountered anywhere." Peterkin reported this new order to the U.S. headquarters in Chungking on June 9.[19]

Partly in response to the Fuping incident, the CCP's Central Military Commission imposed additional restrictions on Americans. A July 7 directive stated that the U.S. mission in Yenan was no longer allowed to send its staff to the frontlines; the Americans were not permitted to set up radio communication networks in local military branches; and all Communist troops were warned about the "Special Commando Force" (i.e., the OSS) being trained in Xi'an. As soon as any U.S. personnel entered Communist-controlled areas, Communist troops were to "disarm them first, stop them from making communications, monitor their activities, but still provide accommodation and report to Yenan for instructions."[20] It seems that Birch and his companions were unaware of these new regulations.

After the Birch incident—which alarmed both the Americans and the Communists—the CCP reversed the order to disarm and detain U.S. soldiers. Zhu De told Wedemeyer that he had instructed all Communist units to give "all possible cooperation, protection and assistance to American personnel in their legitimate operations against Japan." He urged the Americans to "adopt a similar attitude and possess proper identifying credentials in contacting our personnel." This would help to prevent any further misunderstanding. Zhu reassured the U.S. commander that the past spirit of cooperation between Chinese and Americans would be continued in the future. The postwar situation remained dangerous, he wrote, since most of the Japanese and puppet armies "have not yet laid down their arms and continue to fight our troops."[21]

An internal CCP document spelled out the rationale for the sudden policy reversal:

Currently we must be extremely careful dealing with our diplomatic relations with the Americans. The principle remains avoiding conflict with the U.S. military. American military personnel or civilians are not to be detained upon encountering at the frontline. No harm should be done to them. They also need to be protected. Do not take away the weapons or radio equipment they carry. If they move along with Kuomintang agents towards our areas, detain the Kuomintang agents only, but do not involve the Americans.[22]

While the possibility of another clash had been reduced, the United States and CCP remained far apart on the fundamental issue of sovereignty. Wedemeyer was adamant about being able to send American troops anywhere in China without necessarily informing the Communists or other Chinese beforehand. Mao was equally firm about the principle of noninterference in China's internal affairs. He bitterly resented the long history of privileges extracted from weak Chinese governments—as did Chiang Kai-shek—and was determined that the special status of foreigners must end. And yet the unexpected death of a U.S. Army officer forced Mao to modify his position, at least for a time, and allow Americans freedom of movement in areas controlled by the Communists.[23]

"A close examination of the evidence"

Robert Welch would make the claim that U.S. officials intentionally suppressed any news about John Birch because of their communist sympathies. While it is true that the official investigation was not disclosed, there is nothing in the now declassified records to suggest there was a plot to cover up the incident. It does not require a conspiracy theory to explain why the U.S. government kept information about the Fuping and Huangkou incidents secret. First, in the OSS—as with the CIA which succeeded it—secrecy was its stock in trade and the details of missions were not to be openly discussed. Sweeping wartime censorship policies reinforced the ability to keep information from the public. Second, neither incident put the OSS in a good light. Miscommunication and confusion surrounded the botched mission near Fuping, and the details about Birch were potentially embarrassing. Third, as some critics would later charge, it would have been unwise to antagonize the CCP given the delicate political situation in China at the time. The United States was trying to encourage a peaceful resolution between the KMT and CCP. It was better to keep quiet, take actions to avoid future incidents, and move forward.

To determine exactly what had happened to Birch, General Wedemeyer ordered a thorough investigation of his death. Lieutenant Colonel Jeremiah J. O'Connor, U.S. China Theater Deputy

Judge Advocate, delivered a carefully considered legal opinion in mid-November 1945. The ten-page document was based on Lieutenant Dong's testimony; William Miller's account; the joint report by Grimes, Ogle, and Meyers; and an investigation prepared for the OSS by Navy Lieutenant John Thomson. O'Connor also had seen Zhu De's version of the events. After weighing all of the available information, he reached these findings:

> A close examination of the evidence contained in the file on this case leads to the conclusion that although Captain Birch's conduct immediately prior to his death indicated a lack of good judgment and failure to take proper precautions in a dangerous situation, nevertheless the actions taken by the Chinese Communist Army personnel fell short of according the rights and privileges due even to enemy prisoners of war and constituted murder. . . . If the story related by Lieutenant Tung [Dong] is true, and he tells it with clarity and conviction and under rather rigid questioning, it is abundantly evident that the shooting was done maliciously and that the killing was completely without justification.

It was "entirely proper" for the Communists, who were in the midst of battle, to hold Birch and Dong to determine if they were friendly troops, O'Connor's report continued. Their arrival had not been announced. It was understandable, furthermore, that the Communists "were to a degree properly resentful at being termed 'bandits' and were not inclined to be immediately helpful." It was clear from Dong's testimony that Birch had not exercised caution and that his actions toward the Communists were "belligerent and contemptuous."

In no event, however, was the use of violence justified. "Clear evidence of malicious and inhuman conduct is seen in the smashing of Lieutenant Tung's face as he lay helpless on the ground; in firing a second shot at Captain Birch after he was already disabled; in the manner in which Birch's body was trussed up; in the way in which the bodies were abandoned; and in general in the contemptuous and accusatory manner in which the Communists dealt with Birch and Tung."[24] Wedemeyer agreed with the finding that Birch's behavior offered an explanation but not a justification for his being shot and killed. There was, in his view, no excuse for the Communists' actions, even if it was clear that Birch had provoked them when he lost his temper and refused to be disarmed. This still left unanswered the question of whether the death was intentional or not.

Dong's testimony suggests the murder was not premeditated: "It is my opinion that if Captain Birch had been calm, nothing would have happened. I was afraid that there would be shooting if Captain Birch continued his manner. He would have become violent if the Communists tried to disarm him." Historian Maochen Yu disagrees, asserting that the death was no accident. He writes that Birch was killed "because the Communists tenaciously tried to keep all American influence out of the geographically important Shandong Peninsula and Northern Jiangsu." Yu believes that "CCP troops were actively searching for the Birch party" in order to stop it from meeting the former puppet collaborator who had gone over to the KMT, General Hao Pengju. He writes that Communist agents had infiltrated Hao's headquarters and were in the midst of secret negotiations with him. A message from Chungking instructing him "to cooperate with the incoming Birch party" was intercepted by CCP intelligence. "Fearing any undue influence upon the ongoing secret parley, the CCP promptly dispatched a team belonging to the Eighth Route Army to intercept Birch."[25]

Ren Donglai disputes Yu's claim that the CCP sent people to stop the Birch team. He points out that Yu's evidence is based solely on two articles about General Hao. Both mention that the Communists secretly managed to convert two of his division commanders, but neither account makes any mention of the OSS party led by Birch. Ren concludes that Yu's interpretation is based on conjecture.[26] Yu's view seems problematic for other reasons. First, Wedemeyer and Chennault were adamant that American military personnel were to keep out of Chinese politics and avoid "fratricidal warfare," which makes it very unlikely that Birch would have been authorized to negotiate with Hao Pengju. Second, Birch's OSS orders for the mission to Xuzhou (now declassified) made no mention of collaboration or coordination with the former puppet commander. Third, if indeed the CCP was determined to intercept Birch, why did the first group of Red Army soldiers allow the team to proceed, telling them there was fighting and more Communists ahead?

———

A few reports about the incident appeared in the U.S. press soon after Birch was killed, although these stories were later ignored. Constantine Brown, a columnist for the *Washington Evening Star*, wrote in mid-November 1945 that "long dispatches" were being sent from China about incidents between Americans and Chinese. "They are all marked top secret . . . [and] no one has yet been officially informed about the murder of Capt. Birch by the Chinese Communists when that officer, after the Japanese surrender, was trying to make his way back to the American lines."

Two days later, Brown wrote a longer piece about Wedemeyer's confrontation with Mao Zedong in Chungking but did not identify his source. The gist of Brown's column was accurate. He reported that Mao "disclaimed responsibility, but when it was proved to him conclusively that the Americans had been attacked in an area under Communist control, he apologized and explained that his men were under the impression that the five Americans [there were four] were Japanese in disguise." General Wedemeyer "warned the Yenan leader that any further attacks on American lives and property would be dealt with drastically by the Americans." Mao promised that "the most stringent orders would be issued to the forces in the field to treat the Americans as friends."[27]

An Associated Press story, dated November 21 from Peiping [Beijing] and citing a Nationalist general as the source, correctly reported that "an American Army officer was killed and three other Americans and a group of Chinese taken prisoner by Chinese Communist guards while on a special mission in North China shortly after the end of the war," but included no further detail.[28] On November 23, the New York edition of the *Shanghai Evening Post and Mercury* carried a brief front-page article reporting that Birch had been slain while attempting to return from a formerly Japanese-occupied area through a Communist-controlled area to Free China.[29]

In Georgia, the *Macon Telegraph* printed a longer front-page story on November 22 with the headline "Captain Birch, Macon, Killed by China Reds, Reports Say: Local Officer Dies a Hero."[30] It was based on Constantine Brown's columns and an exclusive account by Adeline Gray, an American who had lived in China for nine years writing for the *China Weekly Review* in Shanghai and teaching English at Nankai University in Tianjin. Gray, who married and later divorced a Chinese professor, left China a couple of years before the war's end. It is doubtful that she ever met John Birch.

Gray told the editor of the *Telegraph* that Birch lived "a glowing, near fantastic life in China, a life of adventure and heroism all crowded into a few years." He helped rescue General Doolittle in 1942 after the Tokyo raid and "was the hero of a hundred daring exploits in war years in China, during which he made countless secret trips into Japanese areas, often in disguise as a Chinese coolie." Gray asserted that the Chinese Communists deliberately murdered Birch. "The murder was kept a 'hush affair,' and no China correspondent was able to send out the story." The U.S. government had not protested or demanded that the murderers be punished because of "delicate" relations between the Americans and Communists. "It is believed he was murdered due to the Communist dislike of Americans, and because he was an officer and knew China too well."[31]

Gray wrote personally to Ethel and George Birch voicing the suspicion that American authorities were afraid to "annoy" the Communists in China with an official request about their son's fate. She acknowledged that the U.S. Army in China had expressed "displeasure" over the murder, but claimed they received only a "feeble excuse" from the Reds in response. She told the Birches that if this information had not been suppressed, John's death would have been the headline in newspapers all over America.[32]

Adeline Gray's story was full of exaggeration and several statements made to the *Macon Telegraph* were plain wrong. She asserted that Birch stayed with Doolittle for some weeks; that he made "a painstaking trip into nearly inaccessible Tibet"; and that he was engaged to an educated Chinese girl.[33] We know that Birch spent less than twenty-four hours with Doolittle, never visited Tibet, and was engaged to a Scottish nurse. But in the absence of more reliable information, Gray's inflated prose would feed the idea of conspiracy and help foster the image of Birch as anti-communist martyr.

The story received no further coverage in the U.S. press at the time. None of the news reports mentioned Lieutenant Dong's eyewitness account or the fact that he was shot and lost his leg. The fates of Grimes, Ogle, and Meyers, and the Chinese and Koreans, who were captured by the Communists, were not revealed. And nothing was said about the OSS team led by Francis Coolidge and detained by the Communists through the summer of 1945 near Fuping.

The absence of more reliable information left room to conjecture that Birch's death was something more than a random act of violence. Robert Welch would write that the Chinese Communists had murdered "in cold blood, without the slightest excuse, one of our most heroic officers; one of the best known and most widely loved by the Chinese people; and one of those most highly esteemed by Chiang Kai-shek's Nationalist Government." He was convinced the Communists had shown their true, contemptuous colors. Adding insult to injury, they had taken Birch's companions as prisoners. And yet the United States "went to extreme lengths to hush the whole thing up," for fear that it might upset negotiations between the Communists and Nationalists.[34]

Echoing Adeline Gray, Welch would make the claim that Birch was killed because "he knew too much." But how could a junior American officer with a small group of men have the ability to influence General Hao's negotiations with the CCP? Even if the Communists were worried about Birch's "undue influence" as Maochen Yu contends, the cost of murdering him was far outweighed by the benefits of maintaining good relations with the Americans, at least for the time being. Even though Mao was speaking out against the United States, he was still hedging his bets at this juncture.

The sad reality seems to be that Birch was exhausted—as were the Chinese who confronted him—lost his temper, and provoked a lethal response. It was a tragedy that would never have happened if any one of the links in the chain of events leading up to it had been broken. The Communists were grabbing territory and had orders to disarm all intruders, but there is no compelling reason to believe there was a policy to intercept and kill Americans. If this were *not* the case, why were the other members of the Birch party spared? Why bother to release a prisoner to tell General Hao in Xuzhou that the Communist commander was very sorry for the incident and to say that it did not represent CCP policy? Why would soldiers take the trouble to butcher Birch's face in order to prevent identification? If the incident was an orchestrated, intentional act, what were the reasons for Mao and Zhu De to apologize to Wedemeyer, and why would Ye Jianying go out of his way to express his condolences to Grimes, Ogle, and Meyers when they reached Yenan?

The men who killed Birch and wounded Dong were never publicly identified or punished. General Xu Yongzhang [Hsu Yung-chang], director of the KMT's Board of Military Operations, sent telegrams to Zhu De on January 8, January 27, and February 11, 1946 ordering him to "send in custody all personnel concerning the death of Captain Birch to Chungking so that they can be court-martialed."[35] The Nationalist general received no reply, which is hardly surprising given the CCP's position that its soldiers had acted in self-defense.

Relations between the Americans and Chinese Communists would continue in a slow but steady downward spiral. In November 1945, Communist infantry stopped a train carrying U.S. Marines led by General DeWitt Peck on the Peking-Mukden line. Fighting broke out, but no one was killed. Early in July 1946, seven Marines were kidnapped by Communists in eastern Hebei, but were released several days later. A more serious incident occurred on July 29 when a Marine truck convoy on the way from Tianjin to Peiping [Beijing] was ambushed by Communist troops near Anping. Three Americans were killed and twelve wounded. Two other incidents inflamed anti-Americanism among the Chinese public. In September 1946, a U.S. Navy sailor shot and killed a Chinese rickshaw puller in Shanghai in a dispute over the fare. And in December 1946, the rape of a Peking University student by two American soldiers ignited major protests across China.

The Truman Administration faced a colossal dilemma. A Communist takeover was unacceptable to the United States, but Chiang Kai-shek increasingly lacked legitimacy and seemed incapable of reform. Without the resources or political will to ensure a Nationalist victory, the best the United States could hope for would be a power-sharing coalition between the Nationalists and Communists. Indeed, President Truman became so concerned about China's instability that in December 1945 he sent General George C. Marshall, one of America's most respected military figures, to mediate between the contending forces.

China was in turmoil as independence movements were breaking out across Asia. Now that the Japanese had demonstrated the vulnerability of white colonialism, attempts to restore French rule in Vietnam, Cambodia, and Laos; Dutch rule in Indonesia; and British control in Burma, Malaya, and India were destined to fail. Simultaneously, the world was divided into pro- and anti-communist ideological blocs as the Cold War took shape. The story of John Birch was overshadowed by these transformative events, but his life and death would re-emerge in unexpected ways in years to come, taking on a different meaning and purpose.

Part Four

⸺◦◊◦⸺

Making a Martyr

AMERICA'S HOPES FOR CHINA and China's optimism about the United States disintegrated within a year of the October 1949 Communist victory. New boundaries were drawn and the U.S. government—which had been so intent on avoiding entanglement in China's internal affairs—found itself engulfed in the politics of a divided nation. One was communist and one anti-communist, one on China's mainland and one on Taiwan (then known as Formosa).

Despite this troubling outcome, President Harry Truman and Secretary of State Dean Acheson expected that the United States would, in due course, establish diplomatic relations with the new People's Republic of China (PRC). The primary reason for Washington to consider this option was to prevent Mao from rushing into Stalin's embrace. Acheson signaled this policy publicly, making it clear that the United States would not send troops to defend Taiwan, where Chiang Kai-shek had fled with the remnants of his army, because the island was not critical to the U.S. line of defense.

Mao had announced in June 1949 that China would be willing to set up diplomatic relations with any country on the basis of independence and equality. The Communists wanted American trade and investment for the sake of China's economic recovery and realized that U.S. recognition would give Beijing further international legitimacy. Even after the PRC announced a policy of "leaning to one side"—that is, aligning with the USSR—Zhou Enlai told U.S. ambassador John Leighton Stuart through an intermediary that the policy should not "be misinterpreted as implying dependence on others."[1] The United States and China were using one another to hedge against the Soviet Union. This was precisely the rationale Nixon and Mao would employ to renew Sino-American relations during the 1970s.

Diplomacy, however, would be overwhelmed by nationalism and ideology, tools that were essential for Mao's mobilization and unification of the new state. As historian Chen Jian explains, Mao was "unwilling to compromise the CCP's revolutionary principles" to gain Western support for economic reconstruction. Without any common language or common codes of behavior, "it was easy for each side to misperceive the intentions of the other." Warren Cohen adds, "If there was to be a generous gesture, an attempt to appease, it would have to come from the Americans. China had been on her knees too long. New China would not beg the imperialists for recognition."[2]

The relationship unraveled step by step as Angus Ward, the U.S. consul general in Shenyang [Mukden], and four of his men were placed under house arrest, tried as spies, and expelled from China in December 1949 after nearly one year in detention. The State Department recalled all official personnel from China after the U.S. consulate in Beijing was seized in January 1950. When China and the Soviet Union signed a Treaty of Friendship, Alliance, and Mutual Assistance in January 1950, it seemed to confirm Washington's worst nightmare: that Beijing was taking orders from Moscow. Any possibility for reconciliation between the United States and China ended definitively after the outbreak of the Korean War in June 1950, when Kim Il-sung's forces invaded South Korea.[3] Determined that the advance of communism must be stopped, the United States and its allies entered the conflict in response. Convinced that China's national security was in jeopardy, Mao sent 250,000 members of the People's Volunteer Army across the Korean border on October 19, 1950. China and the United States were now military as well as ideological enemies. In December 1950, two months after China entered the Korean War, Washington imposed a trade embargo and froze all PRC assets held in the United States. Beijing retaliated by seizing all American-owned property in China. The U.S. declared its support for the Republic of China in Taiwan, and the contours of the Cold War in Asia were fixed.

The PRC's new leaders organized widespread anti-American campaigns to rally support for the defense of North Korea. The Chinese made an example of foreigners, arresting and trying them as spies. Christianity was branded as a subversive force that threatened the nation's sovereignty, and some four thousand Protestant and Catholic missionaries were ejected from China in an effort to cleanse the society of Western cultural influence. Even if John Birch had survived, he would not have been allowed to stay and evangelize in China. Like a number of Southern Baptist missionaries, he might have gone to Taiwan.

As the Iron Curtain fell in Europe and the Bamboo Curtain came down in Asia, global communism took the place of fascism as an existential threat to the United States. For the new regime in Beijing, U.S. imperialism replaced Japanese aggression as a fundamental danger to China's survival. *How to View the United States*, a document issued by the CCP, stated that the United States was a "deadly enemy of the Chinese people," a "corrupt imperialist state headquarters of worldwide decadent reactionary forces," and "nothing but a paper tiger"—meaning it easily could be defeated.[4] Chinese who had been educated in America were denounced for their liberal "bourgeois individualism." Americans who had fought in common cause with the Chinese against Japan were now treated as adversaries. All the good will and good works bestowed by missionaries over decades represented "cultural imperialism." Schools, orphanages, relief programs, and hospitals—labeled as expressions of colonial occupation—were nationalized. There was a parallel anti-communist movement in the United States, but on a much less violent and extensive scale.

The United States adopted a three-pronged policy toward Red China—no diplomatic recognition, no trade, and no admission to the United Nations. The corollary was continued relations, economic and military aid, and moral support for the Republic of China, which continued to represent all of China in the United Nations until 1971.

Chiang Kai-shek perennially announced that his forces would one day return to recover the mainland from Communist imposters. Washington maintained the fiction that the ROC was the legitimate government of China until 1979. Even after breaking with Taipei—a requirement for recognizing Beijing—the United States to this day maintains a commitment to Taiwan's security.

Assistant Secretary of State for Far Eastern Affairs Dean Rusk summed up the U.S. attitude in a speech to the China Institute in New York. The Communists were subjecting the Chinese people to "trial by mob, forced labor . . . , the arbitrary seizure of property, the destruction of loyalties within the family, [and] the suppression of free speech." The "real Chinese" were being coerced and controlled by Marxist radicals who were manipulated by the Russians. "The peace and security of China are being sacrificed to the ambitions of the Communist conspiracy," said Rusk. "We do not recognize the authorities in Peiping for what they pretend to be. The Peiping regime may be a colonial Russian government—a Slavic Manchukuo on a larger scale. It is not the Government of China. It does not pass the first test. It is not Chinese."[5]

Robert Welch realized it was this geopolitical context that gave the John Birch story greater significance. He noted that Birch "commanded no armies, headed no government, converted no nations to his creed." But his murder at the hands of the Communists illuminated "a crossroads for civilization" leading in one direction toward "slavery, stagnation and increasing darkness," and in the other direction toward "greater freedom, further growth and more enlightenment." As Welch put it, "With his death and in his death the battle lines are drawn."[6] Only one system could emerge victorious in a historic confrontation between the opposing forces.

If Birch had sacrificed his life in some other country, say Greece or India, it would have mattered far less. The fact that he was murdered by *Chinese* Communists imbued the event with much more meaning because the unforeseen "loss" of China was so dismaying and disorienting to Americans. China's rejection of capitalism and democracy in favor of Marxism-Leninism represented a profound failure of U.S. leadership. Accusations blaming the Truman Administration—ranging from poor judgment to appeasement—transformed a complex foreign policy problem into a potent domestic political issue.

12

Grief and Anger

HIS MOTHER'S LETTERS CAME back to her stamped: "Addressee Enroute To U.S.A. Return To Sender." But the U.S. military had informed her that John was gone, killed while traveling in north China as "a result of stray bullets." How was it possible that her beloved eldest son, so full of promise, would not be coming home? "We are still hoping against hope that there may have been some mistake, but no word has ever come from John," Ethel Birch lamented to Marjorie Tooker. "It is so very hard for me to be reconciled to the fact that John's work is finished, just as he had had all these years of pioneering and perfecting the use of the language, for a life of missionary effort in places where no missionary had ever gone, to be taken on what would have seemed an apparently safe trip, especially after all the danger and hardship of all those years."[1] She later told Dorothy Yuen that she trusted God "will make plain why John had to be taken when his whole life purpose was to make the Lord known to those in China who had never had a chance to know Him."[2]

While the family was trying to come to terms with their loss, questions were raised about the circumstances of John's death when an officer from Robins Air Force Base, to the south of Macon, came to Ethel's home. It was about one week after receiving official notification from the War Department. She noticed a message on the officer's clipboard that stated: "Birch, Captain John M., 0-889028, killed by Chinese Communists on the Lunghai Railroad, enroute to Hsuchow [Xuzhou], China on August 25, 1945." This was different from what she had been told, she said to the officer. "He snatched the clip-board away and said I wasn't supposed to see it," adding that he would be in trouble with his superiors if they knew that she had this information. "This was the first inkling we had of suppressed truth, though later it became very evident," recalled Ethel.[3] Years before meeting Robert Welch, seeds of doubt would grow in her mind and blossom into a full-fledged conspiracy theory.

Determined to learn more, Ethel asked Marjorie for the names of anyone who had known John and might be able to explain what he was doing in China. She planned to write a book using excerpts from his letters "as the basis for what I hope will be a consecration and the sending of many consecrated young people to China to bear the fruit that John's short service prevented." Anything Marjorie could do to help would be greatly appreciated. "I believe if he had not been taken that perhaps as no other man of this generation, he would have been a mighty power for the Lord in China." The book, which was never written, was to be called *Captain John Birch of China*. "In this way John, like Borden of Yale, may in death prove a blessing to many."[4] At this point, she envisioned her son as an inspiration for Christian missionaries, not as a rallying point for anti-communism.

Tooker, who was still in the Philippines with the U.S. Army Nurse Corps, not only replied with the names and addresses of people who could offer information but also forwarded copies of the private letters John had sent her. Ethel expressed her deep appreciation: "I think it is just wonderful of you to write just as you did. . . . I am not surprised at what you write of yourself and John,—from his letters I guessed it. You are indeed a wonderful girl and Christian,—you would have been the real help-meet he needed. Why these things have to be, we don't understand, but someday we will."[5]

Marjorie did not learn about John's death until October when one of her letters to him was returned marked "Deceased." She then heard that he had been shot by mistake soon after the war ended and shared the terrible news with her parents:

That is the saddest waste of all, somehow, that those who had to die by accident, and those who still had to die after the victory was won. It was an awful shock; John and I had been waiting for a year and a half to get together again and he had refused his furlough last spring, not wishing to quit till the war was over. It's hard to understand why God would want to take anyone so utterly devoted to Him and so perfectly prepared for a life of service in China. . . . Well—it all leaves my future temporarily blank, but I know time will heal, and change my perspective. Forgive me for burdening you with my sorrows.[6]

Marjorie's mother, Mary, sent a heartfelt reply to her daughter: "I had not the slightest idea that you and he loved one another—you seemed simply to be giving a passing opinion when you wrote,—'he is the finest I know',—though I have often remembered it. I wish you could really find a mate that is the finest you know. . . . God grant you may only grow stronger and more beautiful in this great loss and suffering. You must never apologize to us for telling us of your sorrows. It only brings us all closer together." John's life, wrote Marjorie's mother, "will always be a standard for you, not to be lowered when you are tempted to love other men."[7]

Ethel and Marjorie finally met each other in Georgia in February 1946, not long after Marjorie returned to the United States and was separated from the Army. When he was alive, John had repeatedly urged her to meet his mother:

She is (or was, when younger) like you in many ways, and is a person far more worthy of your friendship than I. Please don't aggravate her misconceptions by singing my praises—I'll have enough disillusioning to do when I reach home, as it is! I hope you do accept Mother's invitation and spend some time at Macon this summer. She will be slightly dismayed by your cigarettes and your excellent dancing, but these trivial differences will not blind her to your true nobility. So please do her the kindness of letting her know and love you.[8]

He joked to his mother that Marjorie would be "disillusioned of course, when she sees our middle Georgia surroundings, as she has always heard of the 'Old South,'—all white pillared mansions, oak-shaded lawns, softly singing slaves, etc., but she would be awfully happy to know you, and you will like her. She is a very noble and brave person who kept a great hospital running thru battles, fires, floods, famines, and plagues."⁹

Heartbroken over John's death, Tooker felt that meeting his parents and seeing the place where he had grown up might offer some consolation. Unfortunately, the Birchwood farm that John had so fondly described to her had been destroyed in a fire on September 12, 1943, the date of Ethel and George's wedding anniversary. A breeze had blown embers from a passing locomotive up the hill toward the house while the family was attending church that Sunday morning. Robert and Douglas Birch remember fighting the flames with pine boughs. The attic of the house was full of books, but "nothing was saved except the clothes we wore and our Bibles," Douglas told me. (The Birches didn't believe in insurance but eventually received some compensation from the Southern Railway.) After the disaster, Ethel lived in a room in the dairy while the two boys lived in a nearby shack and milked the cows every day. Their father preferred the comfort of staying with one of his relatives in town. Sometime in 1945, the family moved to a house on Ridge Avenue in a Macon suburb, although the Birchwood property was not sold until the 1990s.¹⁰

Tooker spent a weekend with the Birches in Macon; Douglas gave up his room and slept in the attic during her visit. She wrote to a friend at the British consulate in Shanghai that Ethel and George were "warm, informal and very eager to get acquainted with this girl that John had written so much about." She went to a little Baptist church with them and was pleased to play the organ for a hymn but a panorama on the wall, depicting the tortures of hell, made her uneasy. She concluded the family was "awfully fine, tho' conservative, the kind of Christians who don't believe one can be a Christian and play cards, smoke, or dance. I don't know quite how they class me, as they know I smoke, tho' I don't do it before the family. It makes me realize what I would have gotten into if I had married John." Ethel was going to drive back north with her, and "she will just have to get used to my vices."¹¹

Marjorie carried on with her life, quietly mourning John's death, which she believed was the result of a senseless misunderstanding. In 1947, she signed up again with Yale-in-China and went back to Changsha, where she met and fell in love with Stephen Whittlesey, a Yale graduate who had flown missions in bombers over Germany during the war and was now teaching at the Yali Middle School. (He was not related to Henry Whittlesey, the American officer killed by the Japanese while based in Yenan with the Communists.) They married in China; settled in Burlington, Vermont; and had four children. She became a writer. As she lay dying in 1991, she was handing out copies of her memoirs, which included a final chapter about her relationship with Birch, quoting extensively from his letters to her. "With John's death," she wrote, "a shining light had gone out of my life and out of the world and all I felt was emptiness." Her daughter Jean told me that her mother's years in China were when she seemed the happiest and most alive. "The relationship with John Birch was not resolved. She always loved him." Not being allowed to return to China, the land of her birth, only added to her unhappiness.[12]

"Not an accident"

Ethel Birch had become obsessed with learning the truth about her son's fate. She needed some form of closure, some measure of justice. Surely God must have planned for John's legacy to be vested with greater importance. Shouldn't someone recognize the magnitude of his sacrifice?

During the December 1945 school holidays, she and her sons Ellis and Douglas drove their A-model Ford to Washington, DC, to seek information from the Pentagon and the Casualty Department in the Munitions Building. She was asked about the disposition of John's body, which she decided should remain in China because he wanted to stay there after the war. Ethel and the boys also went to the OSS headquarters, which she described as an imposing building with very tall colonial pillars and steps leading to many doors at 2430 E Street, NW. With considerable persistence she was able to locate addresses for the three Americans who had been with Birch at the time of his death as well as others who served with him in China. She also secured the name and address of John S. Thomson, a U.S. Navy officer who conducted an official investigation of the incident.[13]

Ethel contacted Major General Clayton Bissell in Washington, asking for his help in obtaining the facts about John's intelligence work in the military: "Because of the nature of his work, his activities during the more than three years that he was in the service are unknown to us," she wrote to him.[14] She requested, but did not receive, access to John's reports on his military missions, which were classified. In the coming months she interviewed Captain William Drummond in Washington; General Charles Stone—who later became a member of the John Birch Society's council—in Dayton, Ohio; Wilfred Smith, who was now a professor at Ohio University in Athens; Laird Ogle and John Thomson in New York City; Colonel Paul Helliwell in Coral Gables, Florida; and others, including Paul Frillmann and Bryan Glass.

Claire Chennault met with Ethel, George, and Ellis at the Henry Grady Hotel in Atlanta on December 10, 1945. The general praised John as a man who was respected and well liked. John had contacts with Chinese leaders in Henan, Anhui, Fujian, Shandong, and Zhejiang provinces, said Chennault, and as a result of his work "many an American airman was rescued and taken out safely by Communist and Nationalist parties." On several occasions he continued his duties in spite of being sick with malaria.

Chennault left China in early August 1945, after being pressured to resign from the Army, and had only second- and third-hand information about Birch's murder, but in his opinion, the death was "uncalled for and unnecessary." He blamed the OSS for sending Birch on his final assignment, saying he "never would have sent a skillful, highly trained intelligence liaison officer on a commando mission." "What actually happened near Hsuchow [Xuzhou] remains obscure," Chennault wrote in his memoirs published in 1949. "But if I had still been in China, there would have been a squadron of B-25s blasting that Communist position with no further questions asked." Suffering from lung cancer toward the end of his life in the late 1950s, Chennault told Paul Frillmann in a New York taxi that just before leaving China he had sent Birch to examine a new kind of Japanese fighter plane that was shot down in the Xuzhou area. The fanciful tale made little sense to Frillmann, and there is nothing to support it in the official records.[15]

Ethel and her husband arranged to meet with General Albert Wedemeyer in Washington, DC, in November 1947. They found him cordial but guarded, and he told them nothing that changed their minds about their son's death. "Capt. Birch's parents, a fine old couple, came to visit me," he recounted, "and I could not tell them the entire story."[16] Ethel subsequently criticized Wedemeyer, who had said he would demand reprisals from the Communists but achieved no results. Wedemeyer "is not living up to his responsibility when the war dept. writes us that John was accidentally killed, and then suppresses the truth, not allowing any news agency from China to tell of John's death."[17]

Based on her own investigations, she reached the awful conclusion that her son's death "was not an accident as the War Department led us to believe, from the official telegram and confirming letter,—but a deliberate murder on the part of the Chinese communists." Repeating Adeline Gray's hearsay, she surmised that John "had information regarding the Civil War that the Communists did not want to get back to U.S. headquarters or the Generalissimo, and that John was the target for cruel bullets, and that the four GIs [there were only three] accompanying him were held prisoners . . . so that nothing would interfere with their plans."[18]

Ethel's frustration with officials in Washington started with skepticism and gradually swelled into full-fledged disbelief. If John had given up his life in service to his country, why was the truth being withheld? Why had he not received the awards and recognition he deserved? Did the suppression of information mean there were traitors inside the military and State Department? Robert Welch eventually would answer these questions and give credence to her suspicions. But it would take the eulogy of a powerful U.S. senator for this narrative of alleged betrayal to come to light.

13

The First Casualty

THE RAPID COLLAPSE OF the Nationalist forces and victory of the Chinese Communists set off a political earthquake in U.S. domestic politics. The Truman Administration tried to explain and justify the outcome by releasing a massive report and collection of documents titled *United States Relations with China with Specific Reference to the Period 1944–1949*, otherwise known as *The China White Paper*. But instead of dousing the fire, the volume only fanned the flames. Opponents said Secretary of State Acheson was blaming Chiang Kai-shek without taking any responsibility himself. Four Republican senators issued a blistering response, calling the *White Paper* "a 1,054-page white-wash of a wishful, do-nothing policy which has succeeded only in placing Asia in danger of Soviet conquest."[1]

"We have broken our word time and time again," charged Senator William Knowland. "We have abandoned a friend and ally in need and we have contributed to the disaster of allowing China, with her 470,000,000 people, to be almost overwhelmed by militant communism."[2] Even across party lines, a consensus emerged that the so-called loss of China represented a colossal failure of American diplomacy and leadership. Some politicians and pundits went even further, saying the Truman Administration was not just incompetent but guilty of betrayal.

The indictment was not new. When Patrick Hurley resigned as U.S. ambassador to China in November 1945, he made the sweeping charge that "a considerable section of our State Department is endeavoring to support Communism generally as well as specifically in China." He complained to Truman that "the professional foreign service men sided with the Chinese Communist armed party and the imperialist bloc of nations whose policy it was to keep China divided against herself." After the *White Paper* was published, Hurley said it was "a smooth alibi for the pro-Communists in the State Department who had engineered the overthrow of our ally, the Nationalist Government of the Republic of China and aided in the Communist conquest of China."[3]

Recriminations over the failures of American foreign policy multiplied, fueled by disclosures about Roosevelt's concessions at the Yalta Conference and the Soviet Union's successful test of an atomic bomb. Fears of espionage and subversion combined with the specter of communism marching across Europe and Asia to produce anger, bewilderment, and scapegoating. Headlines were dominated by the trials of Julius and Ethel Rosenberg—who were tried, found guilty, and executed for espionage—and of Alger Hiss—a high-ranking former State Department official accused of being a communist spy and found guilty of perjury—proving that communism was not just a distant threat. A potent brew of concern, opportunism, and paranoia gave birth to a second Red Scare, which would in turn spawn a number of anti-communists groups, including the John Birch Society. At this time, however, Robert Welch was still a businessman selling candy. He had not yet heard of the missionary-soldier and had no thought of founding an organization in his name.

"The Senator from Formosa"

In September 1950, a few months after the outbreak of the Korean War, an unlikely source breathed new life into the Birch saga. Senator William F. Knowland, an influential Republican from California, rose on the floor of the Senate to pay tribute to a young American whom he proclaimed as "the first casualty of World War III." He told the "simple story of a lone American officer, who was willing to sacrifice his life so that this Nation might find out whether these Communists were friends or enemies." The incident, claimed Knowland, was "one of the least known and most significant" indications of communist intentions in China. It was none other than William Miller, the Army lieutenant who arranged Birch's funeral, who quietly alerted the senator to the existence of a secret report on the death of Captain John Birch, which Knowland was able to obtain from Army files.[4]

A big man with a booming voice, Bill Knowland was known for his honesty and integrity. The *Saturday Evening Post* profiled him in 1953 as "a clean-looking, moon-faced man with thinning brown hair, a determined chin and a resolute expression." He never attacked opponents on personal grounds, boasted a *Time* magazine cover story. Best recognized for his interest in the Far East, he was characterized as "the loudest, the most relentless and probably the most articulate critic of the State Department's hapless China policy during the last several years." Knowland was convinced that China—except for Manchuria, which was occupied by the Russians at the end of the war—could have been saved if only the United States had given the Nationalists enough moral and material support. He spoke so frequently in favor of Chiang Kai-shek that he became known in some quarters as the "Senator from Formosa." *Time* said that he had only three set speeches during his 1952 re-election campaign: "One took five minutes, one took 15 and one half an hour, but each said the same thing: the Truman-Acheson Far Eastern policy was catastrophic."[5] He was relentless and effective in his opposition to Red China, working to prevent trade and diplomatic recognition and to keep the PRC out of the United Nations.

Knowland was not a figure on the political fringe. He was a respectable, mainstream politician who had grown up around power. His father, J. R. Knowland, served in the U.S. House of Representatives for five terms, and the family owned and operated the *Oakland Tribune*. The young Knowland was elected to the California state assembly when he was only twenty-five and entered the state senate two years later. At the age of thirty-seven, while serving with the U.S. Army in Europe in the summer of 1945, he read in the *Stars and Stripes* newspaper in Paris that California governor Earl Warren had appointed him to fill the seat left vacant by the death of Senator Hiram Johnson. Knowland rapidly rose through the Senate ranks. He gave the speech placing Richard Nixon's name in nomination for vice president at the July 1952 Republican National Convention in Chicago, became Senate majority leader after the death of Robert Taft in 1953, and served as minority leader from 1955 to 1959.[6]

William Knowland, who was called the "Senator from Formosa," and Chiang Kai-shek in Taipei, Taiwan, November 1949. Credit: Bancroft Library, University of California, Berkeley.

Knowland and Representative Walter Judd, a Minnesota Republican who had been a medical missionary in China, were the two most outspoken members of Congress on Asia policy. Both were internationalists who supported the United Nations and the Truman Administration's Marshall Plan in Europe—which others in their party opposed—but they believed it was inconsistent to fight communism in one part of the world and ignore it in another. Because the scourge of communism was global in character, it "did not make sense to close the door in Europe if the door in Asia was to be left wide open," said Knowland. He also suggested that American policy was racist: "Are we now to take the position that human freedom is less worth supporting in Asia than it is in Europe?" And on another occasion: "Is it the color of a man's skin or his geographic location that determines his right to be in a free world of free men?"[7]

Judd said it was "most disturbing" to have the Truman Administration ask Congress "to put $20 billion into helping the people on the European front withstand the attacks of Communist-led groups and nothing as yet to help those on the Asiatic front." He wrote in the *Saturday Evening Post* that the Administration was willing to confront the dangers of communist aggression in Greece but "closed its eyes" to the threat of Russian imperialism in China. U.S. policy for years "was based on inexcusable ignorance regarding communist objectives and wishful thinking about 'agrarian reform.' These [blunders] were skillfully exploited by the Communist agents, sympathizers and fellow travelers who were permitted to infiltrate the State Department."[8]

After meeting with Chiang Kai-shek in Taiwan and Douglas MacArthur in Japan in December 1946, Knowland became convinced that the entire region was threatened by communist domination. Anticipating the so-called domino theory which would be used to justify the Vietnam War, he predicted the possibility of chain reactions: "If the free people of China on Formosa are sacrificed where do you draw the line?" He feared a "far eastern Munich" in the making that would be "a green light for the communist conquest of Korea, Japan, the Philippines, Indochina, Thailand, Burma, and countries beyond." He warned that "all of Asia hangs in the balance."[9]

As relations with the new government in Beijing worsened, Knowland seized on the fate of John Birch to show that U.S. policy was misguided: "If the Secretary of State and the President of the United States have not read the eyewitness account of the death of Captain Birch, I think it is unfortunate that it was not called to their attention as soon as it was available in 1945. If they have read it, I do not see how they could have approved the policies we followed in China subsequent to 1945."

The senator asked rhetorically, "If the Members of Congress had had this information in August or September 1945, is there any person here who feels they would have tolerated the subsequent activity of the State Department in trying to force a coalition between the Government and the Republic of China and the same Communists represented by the man who shot Captain Birch in cold blood?" Birch was willing to sacrifice his life to test the Communists, who pretended to be cooperating with the United States, said Knowland.

Is there any person here who does not know that this simple story of a lone American officer . . . would not have warned us in time that these Chinese Communists were the same ruthless killers that

Communists are the world over? Does any person here think that, if the story of Captain Birch had been known to the American Congress or the American people, that any American would have been taken in by the theory of fellow travelers that Chinese Communists were also agrarian liberals?[10]

Knowland's assertion that history would have been different if only Birch's murder had been known implied that conspiracy was involved. It was a charge that Robert Welch would make far more explicit. But the senator's statements were not especially shocking; numerous critics already had expressed outrage over Truman's failed policy believing it was the product of deceit. The revelations about Birch did not ignite public outrage or produce calls for official investigations, and the exposé received little attention beyond brief summaries by the Associated Press and United Press International. (The *Macon Telegraph* confused the disclosure in a headline reading "Macon Officer Revealed as Victim of Korean Atrocity Five Years Ago."[11]) The lack of a reaction was not surprising. With a steady stream of reports on U.S. casualties in Korea in the autumn of 1950, Knowland's speech merely confirmed an already widespread perception of Red China as a threat.

It was gratifying, however, for Birch's parents to finally have their son's sacrifice publicly recognized. Upon learning about Knowland's emotional tribute, Ethel Birch left a telephone message with the senator's office asking for his help to gain the military awards that John had been denied. Knowland responded with an airmail special delivery letter enclosing a copy of his remarks from the Congressional Record on "the story of your gallant son" and a pledge that "you may rest assured that this matter will continue to have my personal attention until the sacrifice that Captain Birch made is given the proper recognition by his government."

She replied to the senator, "There is much that Mr. Birch and I would like to tell you regarding the apparently deliberate suppression of truth, the misrepresentation, and even actual lies we met at every turn, while those in authority went through the motions of cooperating." She added that it was "just a matter of time until Formosa [Taiwan] falls into Communist hands, unless something very drastic is done at once. To us it is tragic that with one hand our government gives aid to communists and with the other sends out boys to be killed by the very ones our State Department is aiding."[12]

Ethel sent Knowland copies of various materials she had collected for her book: John's letter to the American Military Mission in Chungking volunteering for service in the Army; the letter from the War Department informing her that her son had been killed "as the result of stray bullets"; Lieutenant John S. Thomson's detailed account of John's death; a letter from Major General Ray Maddocks with photographs of John's casket, funeral parade, and burial service in Xuzhou; and a letter from Major General Charles B. Stone III stating that Birch had been recommended for the Distinguished Service Cross for his "unassuming manner, unswerving loyalty, and personal courage" in circumstances of "extreme personal hardship and immediate danger." Knowland had all of these documents inserted into the Congressional Record.[13]

Ethel was by now thoroughly convinced that John had given his life in an effort to warn Americans about the dangers of communism, and she believed the U.S. government had deliberately kept this information from the public. Her frustration in discovering the truth about her son had morphed into a deep cynicism. She expressed her anger and dismay in a letter to James Burke, a former war correspondent who was from Macon, bitterly complaining that John's loyalty and bravery had not been appreciated and that he had "served in vain":

> There are not words in my vocabulary strong enough to express my disgust and resentment. It seems to me that there has been chicanery on the part of those high in military authority. The suppression of truth, the misrepresenting of what they did give, the refusal to give addresses that we might get facts, and many other things, among them the urgency in insisting on our signing the papers relinquishing the government from responsibility for bringing John's body home, etc., all indicate that there is something crooked somewhere.

Echoing Adeline Gray's suspicions and anticipating Robert Welch's conspiratorial claims, Ethel asked if it could be that communists high in U.S. military circles knew that John "knew too much and wished

him dead?" There was, she believed, "something significant in the manner in which John died, more than just Chinese-American relations."[14]

"I am not a Republican."

The outbreak of war between communist and anti-communist forces
in Korea in June 1950 was quickly followed by U.S. intervention under
the umbrella of the United Nations. China shifted troops that were
poised for an invasion of Taiwan up to the Korean border, but did not
yet enter the war; Truman ordered the U.S. Seventh Fleet to patrol
the Taiwan Strait. U.S. Army general Douglas MacArthur, the World
War II hero who was heading the occupation of Japan, was chosen to
lead the U.N. Command in Korea. He successfully turned the tide
against the North Koreans, who had been winning, with a surprise
amphibious landing at Inchon on the peninsula's west coast. But as the
U.N. forces pushed north, MacArthur advocated bombing China as
well as using Nationalist troops from Taiwan, openly disagreeing with
the Administration's policy to avoid the risk of bringing China and the
Soviet Union further into the conflict.

The dispute became public, and on April 11, Truman made the shocking announcement that he was relieving MacArthur. The president's
popularity plummeted to a new low in the wake of the controversial
decision. Not allowing MacArthur to attack the Chinese across the
Yalu River border, said William Knowland, meant that American soldiers were being asked "for the first time in our history . . . to fight and,
if necessary, to die with one hand tied behind them." Removing the
general represented a willingness to compromise that would result in
the admission of Communist China into the United Nations, warned
Knowland. Secretary of State Acheson should "resign or be removed by
the President."[15]

Truman defended his decision to limit the war in Korea in a national
radio broadcast from the White House on the evening of April 11, 1951,
the same day that MacArthur was fired. "In the simplest terms . . . we
are trying to prevent a Third World War," said the president. He did not
by any measure underestimate the intentions of the communists, who
were "engaged in a monstrous conspiracy to stamp out freedom all over
the world." When communists spoke of "liberation," it was double-talk

for conquest. Nonetheless, said the president, becoming "entangled in a vast conflict on the continent of Asia" would be a mistake. "What would suit the ambitions of the Kremlin better than for our military forces to be committed to a full-scale war with Red China?"[16]

Ethel Birch was furious after hearing Truman's speech. She wrote the president a letter—which she copied to various senators, newsmen, and radio commentators—directly linking her son's death to the failure of American foreign policy. If Truman had known as early as 1945 the "overall Communist plans for world domination," then it was his responsibility "NOT TO SUPPRESS THE TRUTH AND IGNORE THE INCIDENT, but to check Communism then, when our forces were still mobilized and China as a whole was still free." Harking back to Patrick Hurley's charges of communists and fellow travelers in the State Department and Foreign Service in 1945, she asserted that the opportunity to stop communism in China "before it reached momentous proportions" had been ignored. When President Truman sent General Marshall to negotiate a peace agreement between the Nationalists and Communists, she continued, his policy of placing an embargo on military supplies to Chiang Kai-shek "further expedited the overthrow of democracy in China and hastened Red aggression." Truman's failure to act was "inexcusable and traitorous" to the "liberty-loving people" who elected him. "America has been led step by step toward Communism and dictatorship. . . . This is not 'hokum' and I am not a Republican. On the contrary I am proud of the past record of my own personal reps [representatives] in Washington, the Democrats from Georgia."[17] It was the first time she publicly expressed her disillusionment with her own government.

She certainly was not alone in taking up the cause of conspiracy-minded anti-communism. Stunned by Truman's unexpected election victory over Thomas Dewey in 1948, Republican senators Patrick McCarran of Nevada, William Jenner of Indiana, and Joseph McCarthy of Wisconsin, as well as William Knowland, Congressman Richard Nixon of California, and others joined the fray, attacking the Administration for what they saw as the single greatest diplomatic defeat in the nation's history. These politicians and men from other professions—including Henry R. Luce, the influential publisher of *Time* and *Life*—were members of the China Lobby, a loose collection of high-profile personalities deeply opposed to Mao's new regime and working to isolate the People's Republic.

MacArthur was treated as a celebrity after his ignominious recall from Korea. There were parades in his honor, and he was invited to address a joint session of Congress. His speech was forcefully unambiguous and unapologetic: "There are some who for varying reasons would appease Red China. They are blind to history's clear lesson, for history teaches with unmistakable emphasis that appeasement but begets new and bloodier war. It points to no single instance where this end has justified that means, where appeasement has led to more than a sham peace."[18]

In May and June 1951, Congress convened closed hearings to investigate MacArthur's dismissal. During seven weeks of testimony, the case of Captain John M. Birch was mentioned on three occasions. Knowland asked George Marshall, who was now retired from government service, if he was aware of the Birch case—Marshall said he had heard about it in China—and urged that the classified file on the incident be made available to the Senate committees responsible for the hearings, which was done. Knowland went on to repeat his claim that Birch's death was a harbinger: "I think as early as 1945 there was a clear indication by an overt act on the part of the Chinese Communists" of their intentions—nearly one year before the attack on U.S. Marines in north China at Anping.

A few weeks later, after reading the Birch file, Senator Richard Russell, a Democrat from Georgia and chairman of the Armed Services Committee, asked General Albert Wedemeyer to comment. "I should like to pay tribute right now to John Birch," replied Wedemeyer, "because that boy was a hero, an unsung hero." Two days later, Russell asked Wedemeyer about the investigation of Birch's murder. The general said he had protested directly to Mao, who "was most cooperative and said he would do his utmost to determine the events that led up to this boy's murder, and take up appropriate action," although Wedemeyer "never did ascertain exactly what they did do." He added that Birch was "a very fine American boy, and very courageous, and had done good work for me behind Japanese lines, and he was murdered in cold blood by Communists."[19]

Wedemeyer did not elaborate on whether Birch had been killed accidently or intentionally. Nor did he or any of the senators refer to the Judge Advocate General's legal opinion faulting Birch for his "lack of good judgment and failure to take proper precautions in a dangerous situation," even though "the shooting of Captain Birch constituted murder" and was "completely without deserved justification."[20] Divulging this information might have embarrassed the Army and given the impression that Wedemeyer was soft on communism. Ten years later, the general would tell the more complete story, after Robert Welch decided to appropriate Birch's name for his new organization.

"The same type of bullets"

John Birch was already a legend in some circles. Frank Norris had burnished his image as a brave and selfless Christian warrior. Birch's encounter with Jimmy Doolittle and the Tokyo Raiders was a claim to fame. Chennault added to his luster, praising his courage and personal loyalty, and a number of others joined in memorializing him after his untimely death. Former missionary and fellow intelligence officer Paul Frillmann wrote that he was very proud to have known and worked with John. He extolled Birch's "zeal and enthusiasm for the Chinese," writing to his mother that his death was "filled with glory and conviction."[21] Arthur Hopkins, who served with Birch in Changsha, assured Ethel Birch that "everyone who met John was tremendously impressed with him, and he was by far the most able intelligence and liaison officer that I saw in China. . . . I am quite sure that John's life was not sacrificed in vain, and he had accomplished more in his brief span of life than most men achieve in half a century."[22]

Glowing testimonials like these reinforced Ethel's resolve to have the U.S. government recognize her son's sacrifice. Chennault had awarded him the Legion of Merit in July 1944; the Republic of China posthumously bestowed on him the Order of the Cloud and Banner in November 1945; and the U.S. Army approved an Oak Leaf Cluster to the Legion of Merit in January 1946. These honors were respectable but not especially noteworthy. General Charles B. Stone, commanding general of the 14th Air Force in China after Chennault's departure, had recommended Birch for the Distinguished Service Cross, the nation's second highest military award, for "invaluable services which greatly aided the achievement of ultimate victory." Chennault told John's father he could not think of any one of his officers who deserved it more. Colonel Wilfred Smith nominated Birch for the Silver Star. Captain James Hart went so far as to say that Birch should receive the Congressional Medal of Honor. But none of these recommendations were approved. In fact, much to Ethel's distress, General Edward Witsell informed her that John was not even eligible for the Purple Heart because in 1945, as she quoted him, "the Chinese Communists were our allies and the Purple Heart was given only when one was wounded by the enemy."[23]

Undaunted by these rejections, she remained resolved that her son should receive the greater military recognition he deserved. She met in Washington with her congressman Carl Vinson to enlist his support and to ask that Birch posthumously be promoted to the rank of major. "We do think that if the facts of John's service and death were known he would be given the nation's highest award, instead of the next highest," Ethel wrote to Marjorie Tooker. This had been denied, she believed, because the government had suppressed the truth. Why had John been so "belittled," she asked? Perhaps the fact that he opposed the OSS was one reason: "John never played politics and the OSS did."[24]

Senator Knowland took up the case with the secretary of the Air Force at the new Pentagon building, twice requesting the Awards and Decoration Board to reconsider the recommendation for Birch to be recognized for his service in the face of death. Secretary Thomas Finletter replied after reviewing the complete file that "the heroic actions of Captain Birch could not be considered as a basis for the award of the Distinguished Service Cross or the Silver Star inasmuch as they did not meet the criteria as established by law. The circumstances surrounding Captain Birch's death do not reveal evidence of a heroic act in conflict with the enemy forces," which was a requirement for being considered for any of the nation's highest awards. Finletter explained the decision on the grounds that the United States was not at war with the Chinese when Birch was killed.

Knowland fired off a two-page letter to the secretary in response, forcefully arguing that "some of the same conditions existed at the time of Captain Birch's death as exist in Korea at present." Then as now, the United States recognized the Nationalist Republic of China and did not have diplomatic relations with the Communist forces of China. There was no declaration of war against the Communists at the time, but neither had there been a formal declaration of war against the Chinese who "are now openly engaged in aggression in Korea. . . . The same type of bullets that killed Captain Birch in 1945 are now killing American troops in Korea. The same communist military direction existed in 1945 as exists today."[25]

A prominent U.S. senator had given national attention to Birch's bravery, promising that he would receive "proper recognition by his government." But his best efforts proved unsuccessful. Little wonder that Ethel Birch was receptive to Robert Welch, who vowed to expose the wrongs done to her son and bring him the honor and respect that he had earned.

14

The John Birch Society

HAD IT NOT BEEN for Ethel Birch, the John Birch Society would have been organized under some other name. Angry that American officials refused to recognize John's bravery, determined that his sacrifice should be known, and convinced that his death had been covered up, she worked tirelessly to piece together the story. If it had been a different era, she might have accepted her son's fate without protest. If the postwar world had been a period of peace and tranquility rather than an age of fear and insecurity—if China somehow had avoided civil war and a communist takeover—she might not have pursued the story so doggedly. Most likely she would have avoided politics, acceding to God's will in the matter. But communism was not a distant menace; it was an immediate threat. Americans were confronted by an ideology that denied the very existence of God. It seemed necessary to speak out and to allow the use of her son's name to oppose such a scourge.

It was not from Ethel Birch, however, that Robert Welch first learned about John Birch. In the summer of 1953, while sifting through documents in a committee room of the Senate Office Building in Washington, DC, Welch happened upon William Knowland's speech claiming that history would have been different if only Americans had been aware of the cold-blooded murder of Birch by the Chinese Communists. The story struck an immediate chord. Here in the life of one individual were precisely the ingredients needed to dramatize a larger narrative of American virtue in the face of a communist conspiracy.[1]

Welch soon wrote a rambling three-page letter to Birch's parents telling them why he wanted to write a book about their son and asking permission to visit them in Georgia. The more he reflected on what seemed at first glance to be an insignificant event, the more he became convinced that the story must be told. He told them their son was a great American patriot, comparing him to Nathan Hale, the American Revolutionary War hero hanged by the British. According to Welch, Birch represented the epitome of patriotism, honesty, decency, and courage. His devotion to God and country was an inspiring example in a world so deeply threatened by the insidious force of communism.

Welch told George and Ethel Birch he was not a wealthy tycoon but an experienced businessman and a member of the board of directors of the National Association of Manufacturers. Although he had lived in the Boston area for more than thirty years, he was born and raised as a Baptist on a farm in North Carolina. He therefore appreciated and understood John's upbringing, even if he could not claim to be a faithful Baptist, "nor even as good a Christian as was your son John." He went on to present his political opinions, telling the Birches why he had taken it upon himself to sound the alarm against the rising threat of communism. He deplored the collectivist agenda of Franklin Roosevelt and the duplicity of Harry Truman. After traveling to England in 1946 and again in 1948 to learn about the Socialist government there, he had made over two hundred speeches in the United States warning about the dangers of following the same path.[2]

Welch met with the Birches at their home in Macon on the afternoon of Sunday, August 2, 1953. Faced with declining health, Ethel realized she would not be able to author a book of her own. Impressed with what Welch had to say, she approved his plan to write about John and gave him copies of all the letters, interviews, photographs, and documents she had painstakingly collected during the preceding eight years. She recalled that when Welch saw how disappointed she was about the military awards that John had been denied, he told her "not to feel too badly because he had something in mind that would be worth a great deal more than any awards the Government could give." She later observed, "This has proved to be true."[3]

The Man Who Created the Myth

Robert Henry Winborne Welch Jr., the oldest of six children, was born in 1899 in Woodville, North Carolina, where his father was a farmer and his mother a school teacher. A precocious student with a restless mind, he was homeschooled until he started high school when he was only ten years old. He graduated from the University of North Carolina, Chapel Hill, in 1916 at the age of seventeen, by far the youngest and the shortest in his class. "Partly because I had been admitted to the college while entirely too young," Welch later recalled, "I was the most insufferable little squirt that ever tried to associate with his elders."[4] After college, he attended the U.S. Naval Academy in Annapolis, where he had an excellent record, but he decided to change course and resigned after two years. The First World War was over and his enthusiasm for a military career had waned. Next he enrolled at Harvard Law School, but grew bored and dropped out in the final year without completing his law degree. He married Marian Probert from Akron, Ohio, a recent graduate of Wellesley College, and they had two sons, Robert and Hillard.[5]

Welch now put aside his eclectic intellectual interests—he loved mathematics, history, philosophy, poetry, and chess—and set out to find his fortune making and selling candy. He reckoned it was a product that required little equipment, had rapid turnover, and everyone liked. He set up the Oxford Candy Company in Cambridge, Massachusetts, and thanks to hard work and a caramel on a stick (later known as a Sugar Daddy), found success within a few years. After expanding the business to Chicago, he ran into financial problems and had to declare bankruptcy. He started over in New York; moved back to Chicago to work for Brach and Sons, a large candy company; and from there started another business of his own in Attica, Indiana.

In the meantime, in the midst of the Great Depression, his younger brother, James, had built a prosperous confectionary business back in Cambridge. In 1935, still struggling with his own company, Welch swallowed his pride and accepted an offer to work for James as vice president for sales. It turned out that Bob Welch had a real talent for marketing. He was congenial, gregarious, loved to travel, and even wrote a short book called *The Road to Salesmanship*.[6] By 1956, the James O. Welch Company—which made Junior Mints, Sugar Babies,

Welch's Fudge, Pom Poms, and other popular brands—had around one thousand employees and twenty million dollars in annual sales. The two brothers had become wealthy men.

With financial success came the opportunity to volunteer for various organizations. Welch was elected to the Belmont School Board, served as director of a local bank, and did volunteer work for the Massachusetts Republican Party, giving speeches opposing price controls and collectivism. In 1950, he decided to try full-time politics and made an unsuccessful run for the Republican nomination for lieutenant governor of Massachusetts. In his stump speech, he warned against the exchange of freedom for security, "the management of ever larger segments of our national life and our individual lives to the control of government." This clearly was the road to poverty, want, and serfdom. Put simply, said Welch, a "welfare state, carried far enough, is a socialist state." The enemy's divide-and-conquer strategy was designed to strangle businessmen with controls and taxation, to bribe farmers with their own money, to infiltrate labor unions, and to discredit the medical profession. "The forces on the socialist side amount to a vast conspiracy to change our political and economic system."[7] Big government was destroying free enterprise, undermining traditional values, and sapping individual initiative. It was a common refrain in American politics, and still very much in evidence today.

Welch ardently supported Senator Robert A. Taft in his bid for the presidency in 1952. The Ohio Republican also was outspoken about the concentration of power in the federal government. Before Woodrow Wilson instituted a federal income tax and the Federal Reserve System, there was self-reliance, said Taft. Harry Truman's policies were paving the road to socialism, increasing the "danger of complete government control. . . . There was a time when men expected to solve their own problems, when they were solved by cooperative effort and local effort. Today the first thought is to turn to Washington for money and action."[8]

Taft, who unlike some Republicans was no isolationist, linked America's domestic woes to its foreign policy debacles. He blamed communist sympathizers in the State Department for surrendering to every demand of the Russians at the Yalta and Potsdam wartime conferences, which in his opinion had led to a string of Communist victories in Asia and Eastern Europe. He charged that the Department's Far Eastern Division "promoted at every opportunity the Communist cause in China until today Communism threatens to take over all of Asia."[9] Welch later asserted that Taft's bid for the presidency had been snatched from him "by purchase, theft, secret deals, and other tactics." Taft would have cleaned out communist agents by the thousands and therefore had to be defeated "at any cost."[10] Disillusioned with the collapse of Taft's campaign, Dwight Eisenhower's nomination, and Taft's death soon thereafter, Welch became convinced that he could not rely on "politicians, political leadership, or even political action except as a part of something much deeper and broader, to save us."[11] Taft had been the last great hope for restoring the free enterprise system and a sane foreign policy.

Welch began speaking, writing, and publishing about a widespread conspiracy within the U.S. government. Borrowing heavily from Victor Lasky, a newspaper columnist who wrote about the Alger Hiss trials, he spelled out his thinking in a tract titled *May God Forgive Us*. Published in 1952, it argued that nation after nation had been betrayed to communism "through either the active or the passive collaboration of agencies of our government." Chiang Kai-shek had been abandoned by the United States, setting the stage for a Communist victory. The power brokers in Washington were self-serving, misguided, and even worse. Welch agreed with other critics that Truman's decision to remove Douglas MacArthur was ignorant and irresponsible, although he reached the convoluted conclusion that Stalin—rather than Truman—actually fired MacArthur to prevent him from winning the Korean War. To Welch, the only plausible explanation was treason, but all Americans needed to share the blame:

> For the pusillanimous part that we have played in all this spreading horror; for our indifference to the grief of others; for our apathy to the crimes we saw and our blindness to those we should have seen; for our gullibility in the acceptance of veneered treason and our easy forgetfulness even when the veneer had been rubbed off; for all our witting and unwitting help to the vicious savages of the Kremlin and to their subordinate savages everywhere, may God—and our fellow men—some day forgive us![12]

To give more weight to his arguments and to bolster his foreign policy credentials, Welch traveled in 1955 to South Korea where he met President Syngman Rhee and to Taiwan where he met President Chiang and Madame Chiang Kai-shek. He also made stops in Japan and Hong Kong. Upon returning home, he wrote and published biographical sketches of Rhee and Chiang, praising their stalwart anti-communism.[13] Communism, like Nazism, was another form of totalitarianism, and the United States could not afford a Far Eastern Munich.

Too young for the First World War and too old for the Second, Robert Welch perhaps saw in John Birch the heroic figure that he always wanted to be—a brave patriot fighting for a righteous cause, opposed to oppression, standing up for America's finest values. Both men were firstborn sons raised by strong-willed mothers in large families. Both were intellectually gifted, personable, ambitious, and determined. Both viewed life as a struggle between the forces of good and evil, light and darkness. But their differences outweighed these similarities. Birch was consumed by theology, while Welch was obsessed with politics. Welch resolutely pursued a life of business and financial gain, while Birch cheerfully accepted a vow of poverty and a military oath of service. Birch believed none of us is without sin, but that everyone can find forgiveness through Christ, who offers the promise of salvation in the life hereafter. Welch thought a conspiratorial force exists among an amoral elite who are beyond any hope of redemption and cannot be absolved. Good and virtuous Americans were threatened by a group he called "the Insiders," who were motivated by greed and the desire to bend others to their will. Collectivism and communism, not warfare, were their weapons of choice

The Life of John Birch: In the Story of One American Boy, the Ordeal of His Age was Welch's effort to ensure that Birch "did not die in vain." Henry Regnery, who had published the young William F. Buckley Jr.'s *God and Man at Yale* and Russell Kirk's *The Conservative Mind*, issued Welch's slim volume in 1954. Welch wanted the book to help rescue Birch from the "temporary oblivion" consigned to him by "our Communist enemies." Echoing the words of William Knowland, Welch hailed Birch as "the first, or very nearly the first, casualty in American uniform in a war still being waged against us." The example of his life and the "spark of his courage" would be a source of inspiration to "awaken his countrymen to their danger and their duty." Birch's "purity of character and nobility of purpose" merited great admiration in the face of "political tyranny" and "moral anarchy." His unyielding Christian faith was an undeniable rebuke to the sinister atheism of communism. Americans would learn "essential truths about our enemy from the lesson of his murder."

Virtually all of the information about Birch came from the materials that John's mother had collected. His daring exploits were highlighted: assisting the Doolittle Raiders, guiding pilots to their targets, training Chinese agents, and operating in the field, often behind enemy lines for weeks and months at a time. The young missionary-soldier was an authentic American hero who fought bravely to defeat the Japanese enemy and was determined to share Christianity with the Chinese people. He was a loyal patriot devoted to flag, family, and God—a man who was modest and unpretentious, yet resolute and dependable. Beyond these admirable traits, wrote Welch, Birch anticipated and understood, as few others did, the communist threat that America's leaders chose to ignore.[14]

The Life of John Birch, with no footnotes or documentation, suffers from exaggerated claims, convoluted reasoning, and various factual errors. Welch wrote, for example, that Birch was instrumental in saving Doolittle and the American airmen who bombed Japan: "Without him it is doubtful that any of these flyers, or their commander himself, would have escaped capture or torture by the Japanese."[15] Yet as the subtitle—*In the Story of One American Boy, the Ordeal of His Age*—makes clear, the book was intended as more than a biography; it was a platform for Welch's own political agenda.

Welch did acknowledge that the "deliberate and unjustified killing" of a U.S. Army captain on an official mission might have been the direct responsibility of the local Communist detachment and its commanding officer. But he went on to state that the murder "was in accord with general policy, established at the top and well understood throughout the Communist forces." Suppressing the story was a "minor chore" in a much larger scheme skillfully designed by the Communists and their dupes and allies to "eliminate or play down every item of unfavorable truth." To such people, the murder of John Birch would have seemed "an inconsequential trifle."[16]

As one of the finest examples of "Americanism," Birch "personified everything that the Communists hate." He was deeply devoted to his family. Despite growing up in poverty, he was not susceptible to the idea that it was the duty of the state to provide for the lives of its citizens. He believed in the ownership of property, regularly sending money to his parents to help them buy land. Birch's intense religious convictions were a "great bulwark" opposing Communist advances, even to the point that he was willing to die for his beliefs. Welch admitted that Birch, "in the ardent certainty and fervor of his own early faith, had been guilty of intolerance" when he conducted a militant campaign against his Mercer University professors, accusing them of heresy. But he had grown more tolerant and had become a more charitable Christian. Welch chose to ignore Birch's relationship with the controversial J. Frank Norris and his studies at the Fort Worth Bible Institute.

Welch disclosed to his readers that Birch "willingly cooperated with the Chinese Communists" during the war, but this was because he was not yet aware of the "nature and extent of the Communist conspiracy." As soon as the Communists began to reveal their true aims, Birch became a foe who "could not be silenced except by death." He realized their "specific purpose of causing misery and despair to the civilian population" when he witnessed them tearing up railroad tracks and tearing down telephone wires on his way to Xuzhou.[17]

Welch quoted Lieutenant Dong, the Nationalist officer who witnessed Birch's death, to reinforce Birch's image as hero and martyr. Dong remembered Birch saying it was of "utmost importance that my country learn now whether these people [the Chinese Communists] are friend or foe. . . . I want to see how the Communists treat Americans. I don't mind if they kill me, for America will then punish them with atomic bombs."[18] Birch almost certainly was using dark humor if he actually said these words. He was not suicidal and there is no reason to believe he hoped to become a martyr; he wanted to leave the military and continue his life as a missionary in China. He had worked with the Chinese Communists in the past, as Welch acknowledged, and his team had no trouble when they encountered a band of Red Army soldiers just one day before his death. Birch was well aware of the fact that U.S. policy did not permit Americans to be involved in Chinese politics. For Welch, however, the U.S. government's alleged suppression of information about his death proved beyond any shadow of a doubt that a communist threat existed not only in foreign lands but also within the halls of U.S. power. Traitors had kept the story of Birch from the American people.

The popular *Saturday Evening Post* favorably reviewed Welch's book, observing that the "little-known case of Capt. John Birch is useful material for a study of the 'climate' prevailing in official Washington in 1945 and after." Despite many rumors, claimed the editors, the American people did not learn about Birch for at least five years afterward. "Amazingly, there were in Washington responsible officials who were willing to suppress news of the murder of an American officer, apparently to prevent the American people from rising in their wrath and vetoing further appeasement of communism. Not a great deal can be said for the 'judgment, discretion and reliability' of those responsible for suppressing the tragic and revealing story of Capt. John Birch."[19]

A jubilant Welch wrote to Alfred Kohlberg—one of the most active voices on the Committee of One Million Against the Admission of Communist China to the United Nations—that his biography of Birch might be just the answer that ordinary Americans needed to clarify and dramatize the issues in the struggle against communism.[20]

For Ethel Birch, Welch's biography vindicated her son's memory and justified his sacrifice. For her fortieth year reunion report to Wooster College in 1955, she announced that she would send a copy of *The Life of John Birch* to any classmates who expressed an interest. She wrote that her son was "the first to die at the hands of the Communists. However, because his death never became public, the warning it might have given the American people was lost."[21]

"Less government"

With permission from Ethel and George Birch to use their son's name, Robert Welch announced the formation of the John Birch Society at a meeting with eleven businessmen, many of them former members of the National Association of Manufacturers, in the brick Tudor home of

Marguerite Dice in Indianapolis on December 8 and 9, 1958. Standing at a podium borrowed from a local church and set in the corner of her living room, he held forth with a marathon two-day monologue.

Welch was hardly a charismatic figure. He was of medium height, somewhat overweight, and had thinning white hair. With his hat, cane, and a bulging brown briefcase, he arrived at meetings wearing a dark blue suit, white handkerchief in the breast pocket, white shirt and blue tie. There was nothing magnetic about his personality or fiery about his speaking style, although his grandiose rhetoric could be compelling. One observer said his delivery of a speech, with traces of a North Carolina accent, is "flat, ponderous, [and] monotonous as he shuffles through and reads card after card of manuscript."[22] More professor than demagogue, he was tedious and polite, garrulous and forceful, long-winded and high-minded, serious and occasionally witty. With an air of confidence and authority, he relentlessly built one argument upon another, exhausting the listener with bits and pieces of historical evidence, finding patterns in seemingly random events, and arriving at what seemed to be irrefutable conclusions.

Welch was clear about his leadership but made no effort to promote a personality cult. The organization's stated purpose was thoroughly mainstream—to promote "less government, more responsibility, and a better world." This primarily meant less federal government, said Welch, because "that is where our greatest danger lies." The objectives were "stopping the Communists, and destroying their conspiracy, or at least breaking its grip on our government and shattering its power within the United States."[23] The fifty-nine-year-old Welch had resigned from the James O. Welch Company and was prepared to devote himself and his own money to his cause. During the next twenty months, he held a series of twenty-eight two-day meetings with small groups across the country. There was no charge and no obligation for these seminars, and Welch wanted no publicity while he was laying the groundwork for the new venture. He explained to William Buckley that the goal was to maintain a low profile while the nascent group was being established.[24]

John Birch, of course, had nothing to say about the right-wing organization named for him thirteen years after his death. His parents, however, not only gave their permission but were made honorary life members of the JBS. Any reservations they may have had about Welch were not voiced. They were pleased that he understood John's bravery in standing up to the Chinese Communists and that he exposed the guilt of American officials who, in their view, deliberately suppressed information about John's murder. They had no way of knowing about the deluge of criticism that would pour down on the Society and spill over onto their son's name within a few years' time.

The transcript of Welch's lengthy remarks at the Birch Society's founding meeting, first published in 1959 as *The Blue Book of the John Birch Society*, includes relatively little about the man for whom the organization was named. Welch did not elaborate on his many reasons for choosing the name, nor did he spell out Birch's heroic role in the war against Japan or his prophetic opposition to the Chinese Communists. Welch simply asked his Indianapolis colleagues "not to give undue thought, at present, to the name" and encouraged them to read *The Life of John Birch*. Curiously, he said nothing about the purported plot to conceal Birch's death. But Welch professed that his own obsession with the growing power of evil in the world was due "in large part to my admiration for John Birch; to my feeling that I simply had to pick up and carry, to the utmost of my ability and energy, the torch of a humane righteousness which he was carrying so well and so faithfully when the Communists struck him down."[25]

Addressing the question of Birch's religious faith, Welch said he envied the certainty of true believers. He understood the power of religious fundamentalism, having been raised as a Baptist himself, and respected the fact that Birch and others like him possessed "an unwavering obedience to ancient and divine commandments. We desperately need their unshakable confidence in absolutes, in eternal principles and truths, in a world of increasing relativity and transitoriness in all things." True fundamentalists—whether Catholics, Protestants, or Jews—are "the moral salt of the earth." Christianity for centuries had supplied the moral fabric for the Western world, opined Welch, but now that fabric was wearing thin, as a vast majority of Christians "do not really and literally believe in either the punishments, the rewards, or even in the physical and biological existence of a Divine Father with any interest in their personal lives and actions." The resulting collapse of social values was an open invitation for atheistic communism, he concluded.

Welch confessed to the Indianapolis audience, as he had to Ethel and George Birch, that he was not himself a fundamentalist. He explained that as a teenager he had parted ways with "the intellectually restricting bonds" of the "unusually narrow" Southern Baptist faith in which he was raised. "I loved everything about it except the specific details of its dogma." He realized, he told his colleagues, that even "a tiny pretense to more fundamentalism in the Christianity which I follow" would help to spur the growth of the John Birch Society in some parts of the country, but he was "not willing to make the slightest concession in that direction." He did not want to "reimpose all or any of the strands of a fundamentalist faith" on those who held other convictions. For that would be "like trying to tie the waves of the ocean together with ropes, or to confine them with fishing nets." What Welch advocated was "a broader and more encompassing faith to which we can all subscribe," a faith that would draw strength from all religions without violating the beliefs or doctrines of any.[26]

The universal belief system he espoused, empty of specific doctrine and dogma, would have been anathema to John Birch and most certainly was contrary to the faith of his parents. No mention was made of the Almighty in the Society's original motto, but in 1965, members of the Society's national council debated whether it should be amended. Ethel Birch wrote to one council member that a dedicated local John Bircher had phoned her, much distressed because his preacher said in his sermon that the Society was "against religion." Adding the words "under God" to the motto would "reduce grounds for criticisms of this kind," said Ethel. Another council member noted it was only appropriate to acknowledge a belief in God since the JBS carried the name of a man who was not only a patriot but also a Christian missionary. Soon thereafter the Society's motto was changed to read, "Less government, more responsibility, and—with God's help—a better world."[27]

While Welch remained cautious about crossing the line between religion and politics, there were preachers on the right who did not hesitate to mix fundamentalism and politics during the 1950s and 1960s. Dr. Frederick Schwarz, an Australian physician, led the Christian Anti-Communism Crusade, based in Long Beach, California. Reverend Billy James Hargis advanced anti-communism on radio and television through his Christian Crusade. Carl McIntire, another voice on the far right, ran the 20th Century Reformation Hour radio broadcast out of Colllingswood, New Jersey. Some people active in these organizations also joined the JBS.[28] The common denominator for these groups was fear that a growing federal budget, higher taxes, increased deficits, expansion of bureaucracy, centralization of government, and other factors would certainly lead to socialism, collectivism, and communism. Unbridled government could only lead to limits on individual liberties, including religious freedom.

"Education is our total strategy."

The John Birch Society rapidly became the most effectively managed and best financed grassroots conservative movement in the United States. Its success was due in no small measure to Welch's considerable business acumen. It seemed that marketing ideas was not so different from selling candy. High-quality products, well-organized distribution networks, carefully orchestrated advertising campaigns, and plenty of hard work would produce results. McCarthy used the platform of a U.S. senator to issue subpoenas and captivate the media but lacked a mass movement to back up his accusations. Welch held no political office but effectively mobilized people who wanted to contribute to the anti-communist cause at the local level. Repeating the mantra that "education is our total strategy and truth is our only weapon," the JBS offered concerned citizens a sense of community and purpose. It was not a debating society, said Welch, and no factions were permitted, although a diversity of individual opinions on any given topic was to be expected.[29]

The Society's headquarters was a red brick building at 385 Concord Avenue in the quiet Boston suburb of Belmont, Massachusetts. Framed photos of Douglas MacArthur and Joseph McCarthy hung on one wall in Welch's office, and behind his desk was an oil painting of John Birch in his Army uniform.[30] Members were organized as clubs or chapters, which met at least monthly to plan and coordinate various activities. Annual dues were $12 for women, $24 for men, and $1,000 for a lifetime membership. Paid regional coordinators assisted local volunteer leaders.

Perhaps as many as one hundred thousand Americans—most of them white, suburban, and middle class, and many of them women—joined the JBS at its height. The Society mounted letter-writing

Robert Welch with a portrait of John Birch in the background at the John Birch Society's headquarters in Belmont, Massachusetts, May 1966. Credit: Bettmann/CORBIS.

campaigns, circulated petitions, placed newspaper ads, organized study groups, managed a speakers' bureau, and issued publications. By 1964, Welch reported an income of about $3.2 million—more than a three-fold increase in three years—a paid staff of about one hundred in the Belmont home office, and another one hundred nationally, including some sixty regional coordinators. Literature was distributed through about 240 American Opinion bookstores and libraries. The JBS was strongest in southern California, but branches existed in thirty-five states with strongholds in Alabama, Arizona, Illinois, New Jersey, Louisiana, Texas, and Washington State.[31]

Welch, a prolific writer and speaker, drove himself harder than ever. Believing that one of the main communist strategies was the "principle of reversal," he sometimes carried his ideas to ridiculous extremes. The Eisenhower Administration, for example, placed the U.S. Seventh Fleet in the Taiwan Strait to protect Taiwan from an invasion by Red Chinese troops from the mainland, but in reality American forces were preventing Chiang Kai-shek from invading China. The U.S. government intentionally had double-crossed the East German uprising in 1953 and the Hungarian uprising in 1956. The American invasion of Cuba—the Bay of Pigs fiasco—was a phony assault to consolidate Castro's alliance with the Soviets. Support for the non-communist opposition in Vietnam disguised a plan to turn that country over to the Communists. Washington justified foreign aid as a means to oppose communism, but foreign aid actually supported the international conspiracy. So far as Welch was concerned, Orwellian doublethink infected virtually every policy issue.

He warned of "the unceasing efforts of our government to carry out all programs and take all steps required to bring about the merger of the United States with Soviet Russia and all of its satellites into a one-world socialist government."[32] He mounted a nationwide protest against the 1959 Eisenhower-Khrushchev summit called the Committee Against Summit Entanglements (CASE). Federal government policies on foreign aid, civil rights, and even fluoridated water were communist-backed plots to stir up strife and lead the way for the Soviet Union to take over America. Federal income tax and Social Security should be repealed. The United States should withdraw from the United Nations. Members of the Council on Foreign Relations and the Trilateral Commission were communist sympathizers, or "comsymps" for short.

How, asked Welch, did the communists ever gain "such tremendous direct and far-reaching indirect influence in our government and throughout our nation?" The origins, he explained, went back to the 1930s when it was fashionable for almost everybody to express admiration for the "Soviet Experiment"; to Franklin Roosevelt's decision for the United States to join the International Labor Organization; and still further to "the fulminations of Karl Marx and the elucidations of Friedrich Engels" and to the writings of John Stuart Mill, Jeremy Bentham, and Robert Owen. These men and others created an idealized "glittering mirage" of state socialism and collectivism.[33] He eventually traced the origins of global conspiracy back to the late eighteenth-century Bavarian secret society called the Illuminati.

Statistics, Welch claimed, proved the conspiracy was growing and real: "From the summer of 1945 to the summer of 1958 the Communists have averaged adding to their empire seven thousand newly enslaved subjects every hour." An annual scoreboard published in Society's

American Opinion magazine listed the extent of communist influence in 105 countries around the world. Measurements were made of communist infiltration of labor unions, sympathizers in government, activities of political parties, and evidence of agitation. The overall picture was frightening. In only three years, from 1958 to 1961, communist influence in the United States had increased from an estimated 20 to 40 percent to as much as 50 to 70 percent. "The Communist Conspiracy is now three-quarters of the way to its final goal: enslavement of the whole world."[34]

Many Americans perceived the JBS as being bigoted and racist, but Welch disputed the label. The Society, he protested, had "no similarity or sympathy with the Klans [the Ku Klux Klan] or with any other group that tries to divide the American people along racial or religious lines." He reported that an estimated forty percent of the JBS membership was Catholic, "many of our finest chapter leaders are Jewish, and we are very proud of our small but growing number of Negro members."[35] As historian Samuel Brenner explains, Welch and other conservatives opposed school desegregation and denounced the civil rights movement on the grounds that enforced desegregation was an abridgment of states' rights and "unrestrained federal interference in local affairs would lead to a communist takeover of the country." It followed that Martin Luther King Jr. was a dedicated communist agent—a view that FBI director J. Edgar Hoover shared. Forced integration would "weaken the country" by fomenting "racial violence and political turmoil," said Welch.[36] Racial equality was an admirable goal, but not if it was imposed and compromised individual liberties.

What worried many observers even more than the specter of racism was the idea that Welch was subversive and the JBS was a threat to the very freedoms that it purported to defend. *Life* magazine editorialized, "Welch scorns not only democracy ('a perennial fraud') and both major political parties ('ubiquitous opportunism') but the U.S. political process itself." The Society set itself apart in its "political desperation and its romantic pessimism about our system's capacity for self-correction."[37]

Regardless, one year after the Indianapolis meeting establishing the JBS, Welch was feeling quite optimistic about the future. He was certain the John Birch Society was the sole organization that could protect the independence and freedoms guaranteed by the U.S. Constitution.[38] In reality, enthralled with his own ideas and unable to rein in his imagination, he had been reckless and would soon face the consequences. In the process, the name of John Birch would become controversial, and the actual man would become increasingly distant and obscure.

15

Right-wing Extremism

AFTER PUBLISHING *May God Forgive Us* and *The Life of John Birch*, Robert Welch embarked on a more ambitious and far more inflammatory account of conspiracy and subversion in the United States. Different versions of a manuscript titled *The Politician* were privately circulated to a number of trusted colleagues between 1954 and 1958, before the Birch Society was founded, with the warning that the contents were strictly confidential. Each copy of the 302-page typewritten text, bound in a black cover, was numbered and was to be returned to Welch.

There was good reason for such precautions since the politician referred to in the title was President Dwight D. Eisenhower. Welch made the astounding charge that Eisenhower was "a dedicated, conscious agent of the Communist conspiracy." He also contended that Milton Eisenhower, the president's brother, probably was his boss within the Communist Party. Secretary of State John Foster Dulles and his brother, Central Intelligence Director Allen Dulles, had been communist supporters. George C. Marshall was a "conscious, deliberate, dedicated agent of the Soviet conspiracy."

Welch's bitterness was rooted in the idea that Ike had usurped the presidential nomination from his hero Taft in 1952. But he claimed his accusations were based on "an accumulation of detailed evidence so extensive and so palpable that it seems to me to put this conviction beyond any reasonable doubt." Only one explanation could account for Eisenhower's incredibly rapid rise to power in the military and politics. He "has been sympathetic to ultimate Communist aims, realistically willing to use Communist means to help them achieve their goals, knowingly accepting and abiding by Communist orders, and consciously serving the Communist conspiracy, for all his adult life." President Eisenhower, moreover, had done everything in his power to insult, hamstring, undermine, and destroy Joseph McCarthy. There was only one possible word to describe Eisenhower's purposes and actions: "That word is treason."[1]

Jack Mabley, a reporter with the *Chicago Daily News*, broke the story about Welch's outlandish charges in August 1960, but the exposé did not gain traction until the *Santa Barbara News-Press* in California published a series on the JBS in January and February 1961. In March, the conservative *Los Angeles Times* ran a string of five articles on the purposes and operations of the Society. Publisher Otis Chandler followed with a forceful editorial: "Every loyal American agrees that Communism is a threat which must be halted; every informed American must agree that the United States is actually now engaged with Soviet Russia in a struggle for the survival of our system." But what will happen, he asked, if the John Birchers use the same methods as the communists to fight communism? Chandler did not believe that the argument for conservatism could be won "by smearing as enemies and traitors those with whom we sometimes disagree. Subversion, whether of the left or the right, is still subversion."[2]

Eisenhower, now out of office, dismissed the idea that he had any sympathy for communists, telling reporters after a round of golf in Palm Springs, "If I thought the people of America believed that I had done anything but oppose communism—fought it bitterly—then I'd be disappointed. I don't believe the American people believe I have any use for it. The American people are going to fight Communists by positive means . . . not by making false accusations against anyone." As for Robert Welch: "I don't believe in giving such a fellow publicity."[3]

Publicity is exactly what Welch got in a flood of newspaper and magazine articles. *Time* equated *The Politician* with Hitler's *Mein Kampf* and labeled the JBS "the most formidable of the extremist groups."[4] The secretiveness of the Society, with "cells" in thirty-five states, caused alarm. Welch was accused of using his members to set up front organizations, infiltrate local political groups, run for school boards, and harass librarians about textbooks. A statement issued by the board of directors of Freedom House read in part: "The John Birch Society is not conservative: it is not even reactionary. . . . Its declaration of war upon 'the greatest enemy of man [which] is government' is a call to anarchy. Disguised in that call is the threat of new tyranny and oppression."[5]

The widely circulated *Life* magazine carried a multi-page photo essay on the JBS, questioning whether it was "patriotic or irresponsible." The Society "has its roots in the frustration that many Americans feel at seeing the nation baffled, thwarted and humiliated in the cold war." But it was an illusion to imagine that "by condemning a few 'devils,' the U.S. can be magically restored to some nostalgic Utopian conditions." The *Life* story profiled Welch and introduced the Society and members of the JBS council. It also featured a full-page account written by William T. Miller on "How the Chinese Killed John Birch," quoting from his interview with Lieutenant Dong at his hospital bedside in Xuzhou. In one photograph, Miller and three European Jesuit priests solemnly stand beside Birch's flag-draped coffin at his gravesite.[6]

An editorial in the same issue of *Life*, titled "The Unhelpful Fringe," commented on the striking growth rate of the JBS. Its leader Robert Welch was "not all that charismatic," nor was the Society a standard "hate group." Its appeal rather was a natural reaction to the growth of the welfare state. "Welch is a fundamentalist Whig who believes that all forms of government don't matter much, since all government is dangerous to liberty; the quantity is what matters, and the more the worse." In and of itself this was not overly worrisome. The Society differed from "healthier organizations" in its "political desperation and its romantic pessimism" about the America. Added to this brew was "a patriotic foam of uncompromising war on Communism, at home and abroad. Here, where they should be most useful, the Birchers go most wrong."[7]

Welch excused his irresponsible remarks about Eisenhower and other leaders by saying they were made in a personal letter to friends before the Birch Society had been established. Nothing from *The Politician* had been sent to the vast majority of JBS members. The use of words written in private to discredit the Society was unfair and misleading, he protested. But such statements and his appearance on NBC's national telecast of *Meet the Press* on May 21, 1961, did nothing to quell the storm.

The founder of the JBS was hardly alone in his opposition to communism, the New Deal, and big government. But his tirade against Eisenhower, a widely-admired, moderate Republican, was a spectacular failure of good judgment and common sense, making Welch an easy target for politicians from both sides of the aisle. Ohio senator Stephen Young, a Democrat, described Welch as a character assassin and a "little Hitler."[8] Republican senator Jacob Javits of New York told students from twenty-one colleges at a symposium at Princeton University that "the principles of a free society can be eroded from the extreme Right as well as the extreme Left.... Can we be complacent when men of position and influence seriously fight for the impeachment of Supreme Court [Chief] Justice Earl Warren?"[9]

Senator Kenneth Keating, also a Republican from New York, said it was "completely contrary to our system for any organization to set itself up as an infallible arbiter of what is correct and to smear all those who disagree with charges of being traitors or Communists." Democratic representative John Shelley of California shared Keating's concerns. The JBS should be subjected to "relentless public exposure" because of the tactics it uses, he said. These include the same methods as "the enemy it claims to be combating: front organizations, pressure campaigns, apparatus of intimidation with the smear its hallmark and a crippling of the democratic process its outcome."[10] The *New York Herald Tribune* reported that George Romney, Republican candidate for the Michigan governorship, issued "a stinging repudiation of the John Birch Society and called for the ouster of a powerful state GOP leader active in the controversial organization." Attorney General Robert Kennedy blasted the JBS and other right-wing organizations as "a tremendous danger" to the United States. He had no sympathy with those "who in the name of fighting communism, sow the seeds of suspicion and distrust by making false or irresponsible charges." FBI director J. Edgar Hoover said, "Anybody who will allege that General Eisenhower was a Communist agent has something wrong with him."[11]

Richard Nixon, a man who made his reputation by fighting communists in the late 1940s, also condemned Welch for demagoguery and totalitarianism. Nixon, who was positioning himself to run for governor of California, sounded what was by now a common refrain: "The irresponsible tactics of Robert Welch and others like him have hurt the fight against communism. His statements have been so unreasonable that a question has been raised as to whether or not there is any danger at all of Communist subversion in the United States." The danger from communism was real, said Nixon, and it was "not enough to tell people they should quit the John Birch Society and that they can do nothing in the fight against communism. What they need is a positive alternative."[12] In fact, Welch's propensity toward conspiracy obscured an important debate about the appropriate extent of government, although by this time the balance had long since shifted in the direction of more federal regulation of society, not less.

Arizona senator Barry Goldwater, a staunch anti-communist who paved the way for the modern conservative movement, also had misgivings about Robert Welch and decided to distance himself after meeting with William Buckley and four other men at the Breakers Hotel in Palm Beach, Florida.[13] Buckley took the lead with a five-thousand-word editorial assailing Welch in *National Review*, a semi-monthly publication he started in 1955. He rhetorically asked how the John Birch Society could be "an effective political instrument" while the views of its leader on so many current issues were "so far removed from common sense?"

Welch was a likable and honest man, wrote Buckley, and the idea that he was "an aspiring tyrant, or a megalomaniac, or an opportunist" was "unthinkable." His intentions were good, and he had inspired a spirit of patriotism in many people. Nonetheless, his opinions on the root causes of America's difficulties were "disastrously mistaken," and he actually was "damaging the cause of anti-Communism." Welch distorted reality and refused to make "the crucial moral and political distinction" between active pro-communists and ineffectual anti-communist liberals. For all his good intentions, Buckley concluded, Mr. Welch "threatens to divert militant conservative action to irrelevance and ineffectuality." The members of the John Birch Society were in a position to make a strong case for conservative causes, but "only as they dissipate the fog of confusion that issues from Mr. Welch's smoking typewriter." Out of a love of truth and country, they should reject "his false counsels."[14] Buckley's diatribe reverberated throughout the world of conservative American politics.

The next issue of the *National Review* carried a letter from Senator Goldwater attacking Welch but defending the membership of the JBS:

> Mr. Welch is only one man, and I do not believe his views, far removed from reality and common sense as they are, represent the feelings of most members of the John Birch Society. . . . I believe the best thing Mr. Welch could do to serve the cause of anti-Communism in the United States would be to resign. . . . We cannot allow the emblem of irresponsibility to attach to the conservative banner.[15]

The *National Review* lost subscriptions and financial support after condemning Welch, but Buckley gained wider credibility.[16] His biographer John Judis writes that the assault on the John Birch Society "transformed Buckley into a public figure. He was no longer the pariah of the McCarthy days." He had become a respectable voice of "the new conservatism that television producers and college deans could invite to appear without provoking an outcry."[17] Goldwater, too, had positioned himself as a "responsible conservative" but would be branded as an outlier after he famously proclaimed in his acceptance speech as presidential candidate at the Republican Convention in 1964 that "extremism in the defense of liberty is no vice . . . and . . . that moderation in the pursuit of justice is no virtue."[18]

The terms "Bircher," "Birchite," "Birchitis," "Birchism," and "Welchism" entered the national vocabulary to signify radicals, extremists, paranoiacs, and super patriots. Yet, as Goldwater maintained, the image of JBS as a lunatic fringe or a ridiculous sideshow did not jibe with the fact that most members were reputable citizens who might very well be your friends, coworkers, or neighbors. Local chapter volunteers typically were solid citizens in their communities. As one letter to Buckley put it, "Many of us in the John Birch Society are sincere, worried citizens trying to preserve our Christian faith, our self-respect, and our liberty."[19]

The Society's national council, comprising about two dozen men, included prominent business executives, a former law school dean, retired military officers and government officials, and a Catholic priest. Two Congressmen, Edgar W. Hiestand and John H. Rousselot, both Republicans from southern California, identified themselves as Birch

Society members. Welch's pro-business, anti-government, anti-communist philosophy expressed the feelings of many. His zeal for traditional "Americanist" values—individualism, constitutionalism, and religion—was comforting and reassuring. Yet despite the thoroughly middle-class character of its growing membership, the JBS had become a lightning rod for liberals and a foil for conservatives. An editorial in the *Macon News* expressed the opinion that the JBS, "made up of self-styled dedicated patriots, is nothing but an organization of 'Main Street McCarthyites.' "[20]

Why was Welch—who so clearly was eccentric and erratic—seen as such a serious threat? Why did anyone care what he said? After all, by the mid-1950s there was virtually no opposition to anti-communism in the United States; it was a battle already won. No American politician could afford to be "soft on communism." Welch, of course, made good copy for the press because his statements about Eisenhower and other leaders were so sensational. He was an easy punching bag. A deeper concern, voiced in a *New York Herald Tribune* editorial, was that the JBS would "revive the dormant divisions and suspicions and fears of the McCarthy era."[21] A California newspaper editorialized, "The prospect of another McCarthy era, in which half-truths, slander and invective replaced reason, fills us with dread."[22] Americans had no stomach for returning to the paranoia of the Second Red Scare. And, as historian D. J. Mulloy suggests, attacking Welch offered a kind of redemption for those who failed to stand up against McCarthyism a few years earlier. Here was a chance to fight a weaker opponent and discredit the far right.[23] Energized by the election of John Kennedy, liberals vowed that such reckless scaremongering would not be allowed to happen again, while conservatives like William Buckley understood the need to protect themselves from guilt by association.

The key link between Joseph McCarthy and Robert Welch was their belief in subversion and conspiracy. Like McCarthy, Welch asked his members to keep lists of suspected communists. Just as McCarthy questioned the allegiance of many Americans—including those who had contact with the Chinese Communists during the Second World War—Welch questioned the loyalty of Protestant clergy, alleging that the National Council of Churches "harbors Communists." He told an audience in Amarillo, Texas that seven thousand Protestant ministers were communists or communist sympathizers.[24] He wrote to members of the JBS council and a few others that the "forces that are out to destroy us are almost incredibly sly, vicious, brazen, extensive, entrenched, and determined. This is because we constitute the first serious threat to the Communist take-over of this country since the destruction of Joe McCarthy."[25] It should be noted that all of the damage done by the likes of McCarthy and Welch paled by comparison with the massive ideological witch hunts in China under Mao.

Welch saw conspiracy everywhere he looked. One especially strange episode involved Newton Armstrong Jr., a nineteen-year-old student at San Diego State College, who was found dead one night in March 1962, hanging from a beam in his parents' house in Coronado, California. His father, who was a dedicated Birch Society member, insisted that his son—a clean-cut young man who was active in conservative politics on campus—had been "murdered by Communists." The district attorney investigated and ruled the death a suicide, although friends said he had not been despondent.

Armstrong's father contacted Robert Welch, who took up the cause before the official investigation was completed and compared Armstrong's death to the murder of John Birch. Both men, said Welch, gave their lives so that others could understand "the nature, methods, and purposes of the Conspiracy that seeks to enslave us." He announced a memorial fund in Armstong's name and urged JBS members to write their local newspapers asking why the "unsolved murder" had not been given the national attention it deserved. Public officials began receiving anonymous postcards with the words: "Dear Comrade: Did your Communist friends murder Newton Armstrong, Jr.?" Some cards were stamped at the bottom: "We never forget."[26]

"I do question your judgment."

"Thunder on the Right" was the headline for a lengthy article on American conservatives, radicals, and the fanatic fringe in *Newsweek* in December 1961. The cover featured a portrait of U.S. Army Major General Edwin Walker, commander of the 24th Infantry Division in West Germany. He was a member of the JBS and agreed with Welch that a communist conspiracy had infected all sectors of American society. Questions were raised about Walker when he was accused of distributing anti-communist materials to his troops; *The Life of John Birch* was on Walker's list of recommended books. For mixing politics with his military duties, he was relieved of his command, subsequently resigned from the Army, and ran unsuccessfully for governor of Texas. *Newsweek* called him "the new hero of the extreme right wing in America."

The same *Newsweek* article included an interview with Albert Wedemeyer, the American commander in China when Birch was killed, in which he seriously questioned Robert Welch's choice of John Birch as a figurehead for his organization. He was quoted as saying that Birch "was one of a number of men who participated in operations in China. He provoked the attack on himself [when he was killed by the Chinese Communists]; he was arrogant." Wedemeyer also told the reporter, "I warned Welch not to make a hero of Birch. That's why I quit as an adviser" to the JBS.[27] This contradicted the testimony he had given in closed session during the MacArthur hearings when he said Birch was "a very fine American boy, and very courageous, and had done good work for me behind Japanese lines, and he was murdered in cold blood by Communists."[28]

Wedemeyer's statement to *Newsweek* was a surprising admission for someone who was a staunch anti-communist and supporter of the Nationalists on Taiwan. Before the war ended, he was well aware of Chiang Kai-shek's weakness but had grave reservations about the Communists as an alternative. In 1947, after civil war erupted, George Marshall, who was by then secretary of state, asked him to investigate the situation in China and Korea. Upon returning from the trip, Wedemeyer recommended large-scale economic and military aid for the Nationalists on the condition that they would agree to major reforms. Because this option was contrary to the Truman Administration's policy to let the Chinese civil war run its course without further American intervention, Marshall decided not to release the report. Wedemeyer was infuriated and Senator William Knowland would charge that withholding the document showed "the grave negligence and incompetence of the administration."[29] Suppression of the report was one more quiver in the bow of Truman's opponents, one more indication of a widespread cover-up as far as they were concerned.

After retiring from the Army in 1951, Wedemeyer made his criticisms public, giving speeches across the country. He defended Senator McCarthy in his memoirs "not as a person but [for] what I believed he was striving to accomplish in the struggle against Communism."[30] He praised *May God Forgive Us*—Welch's condemnation of Truman's decision to fire Douglas MacArthur—calling it "the most comprehensive and objective treatment of the complex situation in the Far East that I have yet read." Although he was not a JBS member, he wrote an article for Welch's magazine *One Man's Opinion* and joined its editorial advisory committee.

But in September 1961, Wedemeyer decided to draw a line between himself and Welch. Welch's irrational statements about Eisenhower, Marshall, and other high-profile Americans must have disturbed him, and he was especially offended by Welch's characterization of the Birch incident as a cover-up, insisting that a full report was made to Washington immediately after the event occurred in China. "Despite my efforts to insure that you maintained a defensible course of action, . . . you proceeded to organize the Society, with the name of John Birch, and with an explanation which is full of distortions of the facts," he complained to Welch. "I have been giving considerable thought to my continued association with you and your activities and have decided irretrievably to sever all connections with you and your organization. . . . I do not question your sincerity of purpose or motives but I do question your judgment."[31]

Welch replied with a five-page rebuttal imploring Wedemeyer to reconsider his decision. Nothing Welch had written was meant to criticize the general's actions. He did not dispute Wedemeyer's statement that a full report had been made. But the story of the murder of John Birch had been hushed up, insisted Welch, due to the leftwing bias of journalists in China and pro-Communist influences in Washington. As Birch's parents had discovered, the Pentagon knew what had happened, but someone in a position of power was determined to keep the American people in the dark. He assured Wedemeyer that "some of America's leading conservatives" saw the JBS as "the one last best hope of saving our country and our civilization from Communist destruction."[32] Wedemeyer was not persuaded. He wrote back to Welch that he resented the suggestion that he was "concerned mostly about myself in connection with the facts pertaining to the Birch case. . . . I would have been just as vociferous in my denunciation of your story if the [China] Theater Commander had been someone else." He repeated his decision to sever all connections with the Birch Society.[33]

Regardless of what Wedemeyer and other critics said, Welch remained as determined and combative as ever. The Society continued its crusade with letter-writing campaigns, newspapers ads, and publications. As far as Welch was concerned, the assault on the JBS only confirmed the existence of powerful, communist-inspired forces determined to conceal the truth. The conspiracy's "concerted attack on the John Birch Society," wrote Welch, "succeeded only in making obvious the [Communist] infestation of press and radio." The communists have "beguiled a lot of very good Americans into attacking us."[34] Slanders and smears simply demonstrated that the Society was effective.

During a television interview with Ladies of the Press, Welch said he had no recollection of General Wedemeyer ever telling him that he should "not make a hero of John Birch," as reported by Newsweek. He dismissed the idea that Birch provoked his own death. Birch's arrogance was appropriate, since "we would expect a man like that to stand up against being disarmed by a bunch of communists who were supposed to be our allies."[35] Thanks to the new round of publicity, Welch claimed that the JBS gained as many new members as it lost.[36]

"Our hero just the same"

Some Americans warmly endorsed the Birch Society, there were those who saw it as a dire threat to democracy, and still others found it more ridiculous than menacing. A report by the California Attorney General's Office famously described members of the Birch Society as "wealthy business men, retired military officers and little old ladies in tennis shoes." They are "bound together by an obsessive fear of 'communism,' a word which they define to include any ideas differing from their own." Employing an Alice in Wonderland "principle of reversal," Robert Welch contends that many American organizations generally supposed to be anti-communist are really communist, said the report.[37]

Welch's hyperbolic language and implausible conspiracy theories were easy to mock. Students on a few campuses lampooned the JBS by creating the Tao Chu Kuang Society, named for a fictitious Chinese soldier supposedly responsible for bayoneting Birch in 1945. Welch lamented that "these American college youngsters have now been so brainwashed of communism that they promote an organization for the specific purpose of honoring the murderer of John Birch."[38]

Humorist Art Buchwald wrote in his newspaper column about organizations like the JBS. The truth was revealed to him by a Russian he met in a Paris café, Mr. Serge Orlov, who once was in charge of all communist subversive activity in the United States. Orlov came to realize that "the only people willing to wreck the U.S. government were the extreme right wing groups. They were being ignored, and yet they were the key to all internal subversion," he confided with Buchwald. So his plan was first to have the right wing accuse Eisenhower of being a communist. "Then I would get them to call their own high government officials traitors." After that he would see that the right wing attacked American United Nations representatives.

"Then," continued Orlov, "I would encourage rumors that everyone in the State Department was either a Communist or a homosexual." He even proposed they impeach Chief Justice Earl Warren. "And the topper was that any one who disagreed with this would be accused of being a card-holding Communist." An incredulous Buchwald asked Orlov, "Then you mean all these extreme right-wing groups are really Communist dupes?" "Exactly, they're doing the Lord's work for the Soviet Union, and most of them don't even know it."[39]

Bob Dylan's *Talkin' John Birch Paranoid Blues* was a parody about joining the JBS and fearfully looking for "them Reds" everywhere he could imagine—underneath his chair, in the sink, up the chimney, even inside the toilet. No communists were to be found, but he couldn't shake the idea, so he sat at home investigating himself. Dylan's satire was touchy enough for CBS television executives to tell the twenty-one-year-old to change the lyrics or sing a different song on *The Ed Sullivan Show*, a hugely popular Sunday evening TV program. Dylan refused and did not appear.[40]

The Chad Mitchell Trio, a popular young folksong group, joined the fray with a rollicking tune called "John Birch Society." The lighthearted lyrics poked fun at the members who were "here to save our country from a communistic plot." The song had Birchers telling themselves,

"You cannot trust your neighbors, or even next-of-kin; if mommy is a Commie then you gotta turn her in!" Like most Americans, the trio was confused about the Society's namesake: "We only hail the hero from whom we got our name; we're not sure what he did, but he's our hero just the same."[41]

The *New Yorker* magazine compared a "Birchist" to a man who, before the invention of fire, "wanders helpless among malignant forces, his only consolation inner knowledge of how terrible things are, his only protection an amulet in the form of a 'Blue Book,' his only weapon a postage stamp."[42]

Yet the JBS was hardly a laughing matter for Claire Conner, who wrote about her experiences in *Wrapped in the Flag: A Personal History of America's Radical Right*. Her devout Catholic parents were devotees of Joe McCarthy and became leaders of the local Birch Society branch in Chicago. At the age of thirteen her father gave her a JBS membership application, telling her, "Your country is calling. You are old enough to join the fight." She had her doubts, but no choice in the matter. After *Life* magazine featured a photo of a group of well-dressed Birchers—including Claire and her younger brother—reciting the Pledge of Allegiance in the Conner's living room, the family was ostracized by friends and shunned even by their own relatives. It was a wrenching experience for the teenager.

Robert Welch came to the Conner's home on one occasion to discuss the damage done by publicity about his far-fetched accusations of President Eisenhower. Claire remembered he was wearing "a charcoal-gray fedora that almost covered his eyebrows and a baggy beige trench coat. . . . In one hand, he carried his overnight grip and a briefcase. In the other, his cane." He did not make much of an impression on her and barely acknowledged her existence. A more sinister and frequent visitor was Revilo P. Oliver, a founding JBS member and professor at the University of Illinois whose name was a palindrome. He denied the Holocaust, calling it a hoax, and became so controversial that Welch expelled him from the Society and its national council, but not before considerable damage had been done. Conner writes, "I wish I could say that Oliver was the last Jew-hating, race-baiting, Nazi-loving extremist my parents brought home for supper."[43]

A prominent historian of Japan, who also grew up in Chicago and whose father was a member of the JBS, has a different story: "My father was a staunch Republican, concerned about communism, growing government, and increasing taxes," she told me. "He didn't agree with everything the Birch Society advocated, but believed the basic message was important." A highly respected China specialist said to me that his mother, a perfectly reasonable and rational person, was a loyal member of the Birch Society in southern California, despite all of the criticism. These supporters and others distinguished between what Welch sometimes said and what the JBS stood for.

Few members, however, had more than a vague understanding of who John Birch was. Welch tried to remedy this by paying homage to Birch and his parents from time to time. Ethel Birch was active in the Society's Macon chapter and attended a meeting of the JBS national council in Belmont, Massachusetts. She was a guest at JBS events in Birmingham, New York City, Chicago, Los Angeles—with two thousand in attendance at the Paladium—and other cities. The Birches were honored at the Society's fifth anniversary dinner at Boston's Sheraton Hotel on July 4, 1964, where Welch presented them with an oil painting of John. Two days later, they attended a large JBS banquet in Atlanta.

In 1960, *The Life of John Birch* was reprinted in one issue of *American Opinion*, with the explanation that both the hardbound and paperbound editions were out of print.[44] The Society's July 1962 monthly *Bulletin* profiled Birch as "one of the greatest young men that America has produced.... His heroism, accomplishments, and nobility of character were to make of him a legend which the Communists could not allow to live." A full-page illustration showed Captain Birch in his uniform, with radiant beams of light around his head, looking over a hill where there was a large white cross and a flag-draped coffin. "You had probably never heard of John Birch before our Society came into the limelight," readers were told. "This is simply because the Communists in *Washington* planned it that way."[45] Around the same time, the Society produced a video version of *The Life of John Birch*, narrated by G. Edward Griffin, Welch's biographer.

In 1964, the JBS placed a sixteen-page Sunday magazine advertising supplement in a number of newspapers, aiming to dispel the mystery surrounding the JBS and John Birch. His portrait in military uniform was featured on the supplement's front page, and readers learned that he "came to the plains of China from far-away America. He came to teach Chinese people of the Christian way of life." His death at the hands of erstwhile allies "was known and mourned all over China, for he had become a symbol of Christianity, of true brotherhood and humility, and of the goodness and strength of America. The cruel murder of Captain Birch was a grim warning by the Red Chinese to all who would oppose their 20th century barbarism."[46]

This kind of hyperbole did not make Birch more accessible or real. The Red Chinese did not intend his murder as a "grim warning." Nor was it true that his death "was known and mourned all over China." Birch's life was not the simple morality tale that Welch would have us imagine. Like the history of America's involvement in China, the truth was more complicated.

16

The Real John Birch

LIFE WAS MADE AGONIZING for the Birch family when Robert Welch and the JBS became notorious in the early 1960s. The radical, fanatic image now associated with John bore no relation to the son and brother they knew and loved. Journalists staked out their house in Macon and harassed them with phone calls at all hours of the day and night. After President Kennedy's assassination in Dallas in November 1963, some people blamed extremists associated with the Birch Society and, by implication, Birch himself. His parents received a letter asking, "How can you live with yourself having raised a monster like John Birch?"[1] The author obviously was unaware that Birch had no connection with the organization that bore his name.

Ethel and George Birch surely were uncomfortable with the fact that Welch smoked cigars and drank alcohol (he favored Manhattans), not to mention knowing that he had abandoned the Baptist faith of his youth. But they remained staunch advocates of the Society to the end of their days. Public vilification of the JBS only made Ethel more steadfast in her support; to reject the Society would have been tantamount to denying her own son. She told a Fort Worth reporter in 1961 that she and her husband were "heartily in accord with the purpose and procedure of the John Birch Society." She believed John was chosen by Welch "for his willingness to give his life for Christ and for his country." As for his thoughts on communism, he "had strong feelings about anything that was subversive."[2]

A *Miami Herald* reporter who interviewed the Birches in 1964 described Ethel as "a plump, pleasant woman with lively blue eyes and a debater's knack for putting a point across." She told him, "What the society stands for is almost exactly what John was trying to do in China.... He stood for freedom." George Birch, "a lean, alert man with close-cropped gray hair," said to the reporter: "People say, doesn't it make me feel bad, hearing John's name smeared? I say, if it'll wake up the people of this country, it's worth it." If John Birch were alive today, the couple was asked, would he become a member of the John Birch Society? "That's a difficult question to answer," replied Mr. Birch. "We don't know, but we think he would. John would have been fighting communism."[3]

Ethel was proud to be an honorary life member and leader of the first JBS chapter organized in Macon. "Many people do not know how great an organization the patriotic John Birch Society is," she wrote for her fiftieth Wooster College reunion in 1965. "It has been terribly misrepresented by the 'liberals' and communist-sympathizers, and communists, but continues to grow in numbers and effectiveness.... We think Mr. Welch conferred a great honor on our son who was murdered by Chinese communists on August 25, 1945 after the war was over and he was on a peaceful mission while still in uniform."[4]

The media's intense scrutiny of the JBS naturally raised questions about the true identity of John Birch. Robert Welch, who never met him, lauded his "single-minded devotion" and his "self-sacrificing life."[5] Those who had known him in China agreed that he was unusually strong-minded and brave. Jesse Williams wrote to Ethel Birch that John was "one of my most valuable men, and certainly without parallel in his unflinching devotion to duty."[6] Bryan Glass, a Southern Baptist missionary son and intelligence officer, told John's mother that he was so admired that "many of his Chinese friends, I am sure, would have been willing to have taken his place when the Communists assassinated him."[7] According to Arthur Hopkins, he had "an amazing grasp of the Chinese language and understood the people, [and] was absolutely fearless, completely unselfish, never thinking of his personal discomfort or danger."[8] Claire Chennault commended him for his "fortitude, courage, and devotion to duty" and called him "the pioneer of our field intelligence net."[9]

James Hart, an OSS officer who met Birch in China, described him as "a very kind and gentle man. John was very serious, but he was witty, too, and had a very fine mind.... Where brave men were common, John was the bravest man I knew."[10] Laird Ogle, who was traveling with Birch at the time of his death, also expressed his respect in a letter to John's mother. There was something about John that attracted others, said Ogle. "He was a wonderful person and carried on his work during the war with conspicuous skill, zest, and success. Also, even tho one did not share his faith, one could not help admiring its depth and clarity in him."[11]

William Miller, the Army lieutenant who buried Birch, conjured a larger-than-life image, eulogizing him as the "most dedicated officer and the finest Christian I had ever encountered." The "soft-spoken but steel willed" man was "a true patriot and a living legend." Miller called himself a lukewarm Catholic, while Birch was a devout Baptist Bible thumper and a missionary at heart." But Birch was not judgmental and admired the courage of Catholic missionaries. "He never denigrated the Chinese, as so many Americans were prone to do." John was "completely selfless and respected by Chinese and Americans alike," said Miller.[12]

Birch was also a stubborn man, said Paul Frillmann, who worked closely with him in Changsha, and "the fact that he spoke Chinese gave him and gave all of us a certain arrogance" at a time when very few foreigners bothered to learn the language. "You feel that because you speak Chinese, you should be given special treatment. This is very unfortunate, but it's almost unavoidable, in the tone of your voice, in the way you approach a problem, a situation." Birch had been overly demanding at the end of his life, thought Frillmann, which suggests, as others observed, that he was suffering from chronic stress and fatigue. To Frillmann, his demise was "not the death of a hero."[13]

One Georgia journalist examined Birch's past as a college student. George Doss's profile in the *Macon News* asserted that his "brilliance, devotion to his fundamentalist religious beliefs, and outstanding war record are beyond question."[14] But a second article highlighted his role in making charges of "heretical teaching" against faculty members at Mercer University in 1939. The thirteen ministerial students involved, including Birch, belonged to a secret organization called the Fellowship

Group. The facts of the heresy trial, wrote Doss, gave credibility to the idea that "the young man for whom the society was named would have approved of its purpose and methods." In addition, Doss saw a pattern of intolerance in the influence of the fundamentalist preacher from Fort Worth: "That John Birch was a disciple of J. Frank Norris is further evidence of his religious extremism and of his kinship to the Welch philosophy and methodology as expressed in his writings, though Norris was never primarily associated with the anti-Communist cause."[15] Calvin Trillin, then *Time* magazine's Atlanta bureau chief, also drew a connection between Welch and Birch on the basis of intolerance, quoting a college classmate who remembered Birch as "an angry young man, always a zealot. He felt he was called to defend the faith, and he alone knew what it was." Conflating religious fundamentalism with political extremism, Trillin concluded that the JBS was appropriately named.[16]

As controversy swirled around the Society, reporters also looked into the circumstances of Birch's death, although they were limited by the fact that the official file was still classified. If Birch had been murdered because he opposed communism, as Robert Welch claimed, it would confirm that the Chinese Communists were enemies masquerading as America's allies during the war. If his death was unintended, on the other hand, it might imply that the CCP hoped to avoid confrontation with Americans in 1945.

Several men came forward, more than fifteen years after the event, with their versions of the story. William P. Weiss, a Los Angeles stockbroker and former OSS intelligence officer, gave Birch the benefit of the doubt. "Certainly John was just as much a hero as any other American soldier who died for his country." When he tried to bluff his way out of a confrontation with the Communists, the problem was inexperience, claimed Weiss. "John Birch was not OSS-trained but was what we called recruited in the field—from the 14th Air Force—because of his linguistic ability."[17]

Gustav J. Krause, former head of the OSS office in Xi'an, was far more critical. He worked with Birch and had seen the reports on his death and photos of his mutilated body. He noted in his diary prior to the incident, "Birch is a good officer, but I'm afraid is too brash and may run into trouble." He was "a real fine gentleman," Krause told a reporter, but "pretty forward and spoke harshly with the Chinese." As for the altercation that led to his murder, Birch "had that [Red Army] commander backed into a corner ... where he almost had to shoot ... to save face among his group.... The men in the patrol agreed that if he'd kept his mouth shut, the Chinese Communist would have never touched him." Krause told *Time* magazine, "Militarily, John Birch brought about his own death."[18] Joseph S. Sample, a Billings, Montana, radio and TV broadcaster who had been with the OSS, also went public to express his doubts. Birch's final mission "should have been routine," thought Sample. But he "chose to bluff his way out of a difficult situation. Harsh words led to insults, and insults to arrogance. Finally, in a fit of rage, the Chinese Communist leader shot Birch." Sample felt there was "no real object lesson in the death and certainly no glory."[19]

It was perhaps to be expected that some former OSS officers were critical of Birch since he had been so unhappy about leaving Chennault's 14th Air Force command when seconded by the OSS. He made no secret of his disdain for their clandestine methods and their ignorance of China when many of them arrived late in the war from Europe. Yet despite this animosity, it also seems clear he had pushed himself too hard for too long. He knew better than to lose his temper with the Chinese, whether they were Communists or not, and was typically patient and diplomatic. In this case, however, his emotional outburst cost him his life.

Because of his prominence, General Albert Wedemeyer gave the most damaging assessment in the *Newsweek* interview where he was quoted as saying Birch's behavior "provoked the attack" on him.[20] Wedemeyer elaborated in a letter to the editor and publisher of the *Monterey Peninsula Herald*. He had met Birch personally on two occasions and "the duties he performed definitely required courage, self-reliance and initiative." Birch did a fine job and in fact was commended by his immediate commanders, including General Chennault. But his actions were not unique; there were a number of small special operations teams of Americans and Chinese equipped with portable radios behind the Japanese lines during the war. "During the day they would hide out and at nighttime they would observe Japanese troop movements or dispositions and then radio reports in to my headquarters." These groups typically were comprised of two or three Americans and perhaps four or five Chinese. In Wedemeyer's opinion, there was no particular reason to single out Captain Birch.

After Japan's surrender, the general continued, American OSS teams were instructed "to report to the nearest rail head, air base or satellite field so that they could be promptly evacuated to Theater Headquarters." Birch was following these orders when he was confronted by a Communist patrol. His arrogance and abusive language "unquestionably provoked the violent measures resorted to by the Communist soldiers," the majority of whom were illiterate and would have responded with violence. "The John Birch murder was not, in my opinion, symbolic of Communist techniques," wrote Wedemeyer. For that reason, he had advised Robert Welch "not to use this incident as one around which to create an image of Communist recalcitrance and methods."[21] Wedemeyer's assessment was all the more credible not only because he had commanded U.S. forces in China but also because he spoke frequently and forcefully about the threat of communism.

Picking up on these various accounts, columnists in the *Atlanta Constitution* and *New York Herald Tribune* wrote that Birch was killed for losing his temper. His commander, who was not identified in the article, was quoted as saying Birch was not "a super-patriot or a fanatic. He was a militant Christian. But he was used up, nervously exhausted and no longer capable of thinking rationally." John's father sent letters to the editors of both newspapers and also wrote to General Wedemeyer questioning the source for his comments and demanded proof of statements that cast his son's judgment in a negative light.[22]

Wedemeyer responded to the senior Birch that the "unfortunate incident which resulted in your son's death was fully investigated and a comprehensive report was submitted to the War Department in Washington." He had spoken personally with Mao Zedong and Zhou Enlai and "received assurances from them that there would never be a recurrence of such action on the part of their troops and that they would punish those who were responsible for the tragic killing of your son."[23] He was adamant that there was no attempt by U.S. military officials to cover up information about Captain Birch's death, as alleged by Robert Welch. "No effort was made on my part and certainly not on the part of the China Theater Headquarters to conceal anything that occurred in that Theater while I was in command from 1944–1946 inclusive." Welch, of course, could argue that the case was hushed up because the report had not been made public.

Wedemeyer admitted to Mr. Birch that he had warned Robert Welch against naming his organization for Captain Birch, concerned that the JBS would become a target for "people who are liberals or sympathetic to or at least soft on Communism." He regretted saying that he had anticipated the very developments that had occurred. "As the father of two sons, I fully understand your desire to protect the memory of your son. I have never questioned his loyalty and his bravery; neither do I question the sincerity and patriotism of Mr. Robert Welch who made the decision to pay tribute to his memory by using his name for the title of his organization."[24]

Others who had known Birch protested the use of his name by the JBS, which, they believed, had transformed him beyond recognition. Curtis Grimes, the OSS civilian with him at the time of his death, moved to Hawaii and became a music teacher after the war. When the Birch Society became so controversial, he told the *Honolulu Advertiser*, "I've kept my mouth shut for 16 years, but I'm going to open it right now." Grimes was "riled up" because the Birch Society was "using the name of John Birch in vain. The society is a political deal. It has distorted the facts about John Birch. If Birch were alive today, he wouldn't allow his name to be used with the Birch Society, not unless he'd gone nuts."

Birch was a devout Christian and the son of missionaries, said Grimes. "He got into the army, as far as I know, principally because of his love of the Chinese people. Birch was a very fine man. You could tell that even in two weeks, which was all the time that I knew him. His thinking was completely straight. Birch was against communism but he would not go for violence and the Birch Society has gone so far right it has gone to an extreme." Grimes was sure that Birch would "not have gone along" with Robert Welch.[25] James Hart agreed that, if he were alive, Birch "would be no more connected today with the John Birch Society than he would be with the Communist movement itself. He was a very straightforward, straight-thinking man."[26]

Audrey Mair, the Scottish nurse who was engaged to marry John, also resented the misuse of his name. Mair was opposed to Chinese communism, her nephew Michael Mair told me, but always said about the JBS, "He wasn't like they've made him."[27] Earnie Johnson, the B-25 airman, was equally firm in believing that Birch had been misrepresented. He was "not a bigot" and "was not a political person," said Johnson. Sometimes the men would purchase wine from French Catholic priests, and while Birch "did not drink, smoke, or sleep with women, he also did not self-righteously criticize those who did." Johnson believed Birch was simply in the wrong place at the wrong time when he was killed. The use of his name by the John Birch Society "disturbed" him.[28]

Marjorie Tooker Whittlesey, the Yale-in-China nurse who fell in love with John in Changsha, also spoke out to defend Birch's reputation. In a letter to the Burlington, Vermont newspaper, she wrote, "He would never have consented to becoming the figurehead and martyr for a new cult with goals so far removed from John's ideal of winning the world for Christ." As for those who questioned whether he was a hero:

> I knew John Birch well in China and know he risked his life many times, rescuing American pilots brought down in enemy territory, and performing dangerous missions behind enemy lines. It was a miracle he didn't die sooner. But the organization formed in his name does him great discredit. He was a missionary first, and then a soldier, and one of the finest young men I have ever known. His one hope, if he should survive the war, was to spend his life as a missionary in Tibet. Whether or not you call him a hero, the world would be better for more men like John Birch, ready to live or to die for their principles, and fewer societies spreading dissension and suspicion under the guise of a good cause.[29]

Not long after Birch's death and years before the Birch Society was founded, Laird Ogle anticipated the use of his name for political purposes, telling his mother, "However deeply and bitterly you—and many others—especially those who were with him at the time naturally feel about it, I believe that it would have been wrong for the press or other public voices to seize upon his death and exploit it in a way that went beyond the very real and clear issue of justice involved. I am sure that John himself would be glad that this did not occur."[30]

John, of course, had nothing to say about the matter, while others—including his mother, William Miller, William Knowland, and Robert Welch—ignored Ogle's plea. Preferring to enshrine Birch as a victim of Cold War politics, all of them read too much back into history. It was as if they held up a warped mirror to American society, believing that the reflection was an accurate picture of the past. The attack on Birch was unjustified but not unprovoked; he was killed not because of his opposition to communism but due to a random act of violence; information about his death was classified because the truth was difficult to explain, not because of subversive elements inside the U.S. government. Welch believed the little-known story of an upright missionary, patriotic soldier, and selfless martyr would inspire and instruct Americans about conspiracy and communism. Instead, Birch's memory was misappropriated and made synonymous with extremist politics.

Birch's odyssey was cut short when he was only twenty-seven years old. He would not live to marry and have children, nor would he fulfill his ambition to remain in China as a missionary. His personal joys and failures, his loves and disappointments, his self-assurance and private doubts, his victories and defeats all had come to naught. With the founding of the John Birch Society, his memory became irrevocably intertwined with right-wing American politics. The anxieties of the Cold War masked and distorted the young man rather than revealing him. No longer was he an authentic American hero, a man of irrefutable "purity of character and nobility of purpose." Instead of being honored for the dedication of his faith and service to his country, the real John Birch became a mirage, much like the American dream for China, shimmering in the distance, always just beyond reach.

Epilogue

A CERTAIN MEASURE OF official government recognition for Birch's valor finally came when Georgia governor Lester Maddox, a populist Democrat, proclaimed John Birch Day on August 25, 1969. The proclamation read: "The State of Georgia and this Administration are unequivocally on the side of the freedom and religious ideals, opportunities and responsibilities which we inherited, and are unalterably opposed to the tyranny and the terror of the criminal conspiracy which has killed John Birch and so many thousands of other young Americans on foreign soil." Birch was "the first known American casualty, in uniform, in the conflict between international Communism and the free peoples of the world." His superiors and fellow officers called him "the most valuable single man in the American forces in China."[1] Maddox stood with his hands on the shoulders of Ethel and George Birch, the three of them smiling broadly, in a photograph marking the occasion.[2]

By the time of this ceremony, however, the John Birch Society had faded from public view, although it still exists today. For many Americans, rising opposition to the war in Vietnam undermined the Society's anti-communist raison d'être. Some of those who shared Welch's conspiratorial view of the world pursued more radical alternatives. On the left, the Black Liberation Army, Symbionese Liberation Army, and Weather Underground (originally called the Weathermen) used bombings and robberies to bring down the capitalist establishment and the U.S. government. On the right, groups like the Minutemen took up arms to oppose global and domestic communist schemes. Members of Posse Comitatus preached militant "localism," opposing any form of government above the county level and refusing to pay federal income tax. Robert DePugh, leader of the Minutemen and a member of the JBS, believed Chinese Communists were massed on the Mexican border, ready to attack the United States.[3]

Robert Welch wanted "misguided dupes, symps or real commies" to be exposed and was willing to use direct action and dirty tactics to accomplish this. He was disruptive and subversive, but stopped short of advocating revolution; what he sought was recognition and respectability for his ideas. His charges of elitism and suspicion of "Insiders" was a revival of old-fashioned grassroots populism. Rather than anarchism, he wanted to turn back the clock to recover traditional values. He envisioned an idealized middle-class defending family values, social morality, and the American way of life without the interference of government.[4]

The Birch Society was an early sign of a fracturing social consensus—a harbinger of the culture wars to come. But Welch did not encourage or anticipate the rise of a new religious right that became a potent force in American politics—and was a movement that John Birch might have actually embraced. For the first time since the battle over evolution in the 1920s, there was a new cause that galvanized religious conservatives—the landmark 1973 Roe v. Wade Supreme Court decision that legalized abortion. Combined with fears about race relations, urban violence, the sexual revolution, and the Vietnam War, the abortion debate convinced devout Protestants and Catholics to cross over and become involved in politics.[5] In the New South and the West, evangelicals alienated by the Democratic Party's liberalism sought a presidential candidate who would defend their moral values. Richard Nixon dubbed this new voting bloc the "silent majority" and told them he had their interests at heart. Jimmy Carter, an evangelical Baptist from Georgia, was leery about linking his personal religious beliefs to social agendas. Ronald Reagan, on the other hand, appealed directly to the religious right for votes. "Make no mistake, abortion-on-demand is not a right granted by the Constitution," said Reagan. Echoing the mantra of Robert Welch, he declared in his first inaugural address, "Government is not the solution to our problem; government is the problem."[6]

After leading the Birch Society for more than twenty-five years, Welch died in 1985, a few years before the end of the Cold War. Larry

McDonald, a member of Congress from Georgia, had been named chairman of the JBS two years earlier. But not long afterward he was a passenger on Korean Air Lines Flight 007, which was shot down by a Soviet jet fighter after the plane entered Russian airspace west of Sakhalin Island. The 269 passengers and crew all perished, and there were those who believed the tragedy could not have been accidental. John McManus, the Society's spokesman and president since 1991, said he was not at all surprised by the attack, "which is why for 25 years we've been calling for the end of recognition of the Soviet Union."[7]

In 1989, the Massachusetts and southern California JBS offices closed and moved to Appleton, Wisconsin, which coincidentally was the home of Joseph McCarthy. Fears of globalization—the so-called New World Order—replaced communism as the contemporary master conspiracy, breathing fresh life into the Society. The JBS experienced another resurgence after the election of Barack Obama, a liberal Democrat, as president in 2008. Fueled by the Internet, conspiracy theories ran rampant.

"The Birchers' politics and their view of American history—which focused more on totalitarian threats at home than on those posed by the Soviet Union and Communist China—has proved remarkably persistent," writes Sean Wilenz, a scholar at Princeton University.[8] The central issue throughout has been a battle over the size and scope of government, especially the federal government. The rapid rise of the Tea Party after the 2008 recession was a response to many of the same concerns that drove the Birch Society fifty years earlier: immigration, encroachment on individual rights, growing trade deficits, and national debt. Fred Koch—father of billionaires Charles and David Koch, both of whom have been associated with the Tea Party—was a founding member of the John Birch Society. Libertarian Ron Paul gave the keynote address at the Society's fiftieth anniversary dinner in October 2008.

The updated agenda of the Birch Society, according to its website, opposes amnesty for illegal immigrants, the national health care law, free trade agreements, the United Nations ("at the hub of a global network working to submerge the independence of all nations in a world government controlled by the elites, including man's reputed contribution to climate change"), and Agenda 21 (the United Nations' plan "to establish control over all human activity"). Today's JBS advocates "the framework of limited government as structured in the Constitution of the United States" as well as the right of states "to retain the power to nullify any and all unconstitutional laws imposed by the federal government on the states." Birchers defend prayer in schools, the right of individuals to keep and bear arms, and the value of family and education.[9]

These issues overlap with the Tea Party's agenda, which has had much more success in electoral politics than the JBS ever did. In October 2013, this rebellious wing of the Republican Party, led by its spokesman Texas senator Ted Cruz, turned to obstruction in an effort to overturn the Affordable Care Act ("Obamacare"). The federal government was partially shut down for two weeks while a vote to raise the national debt ceiling was used as leverage. This effort to restrict government in the name of protecting individual freedoms was entirely consistent with both the principles and tactics once advocated by Robert Welch.

John Birch, who was socially and religiously conservative, might have agreed with some of the positions advocated by the JBS, but he was inclined to give up worldly pursuits. George Birch, in his later years, said in an interview that his son was more concerned with the spiritual side of life than with politics. "He wanted to be a missionary from the time he was 11 years old. . . . If he were still alive, I think he'd be a missionary in China. I think he'd like to see more Christians in the world today, I think he'd like to see more issues settled on a moral basis."[10] As John's brother Robert said even more clearly, "There was no connection between the John Birch Society and John Birch. . . . He was just an American citizen dedicated to serving his country, his God, and the Chinese people."[11]

Much of human history is defined by battles against evil, be it a moral peril, a mortal enemy, or a menacing ideology. In each case the response is to defend a virtuous cause, and this is where the absolutism of religious and political fundamentalism sometimes find common ground. Welch imagined a sense of shared purpose with Birch, but his choice of an avatar was misguided. Throughout Birch's trials and tribulations, he looked to the future with an optimism inspired by his faith.

Welch, who considered himself a rationalist but was driven by demons, fearfully defended the past.

————

After more than two decades of mutual isolation, relations between the United States and China came full circle in 1972 when Nixon stepped off Air Force One in Beijing to shake hands with Premier Zhou Enlai and later that day met with Mao Zedong. It was not until that year that the U.S. government made the classified file on John Birch's death available to the public, in response to a Freedom of Information request. According to the *Washington Post*, the release of the materials was delayed by several days so the disclosure "could not cause embarrassment during President Richard Nixon's trip to China."[12] Although the Birch case seemed like nothing more than a distant historical echo, it was still sensitive enough to make U.S. bureaucrats think twice about how Chinese officials and the American press might react to the story.

It took a politician who had built his early career on anti-communism and was a staunch supporter of Taiwan to make the breakthrough to China. The primary rationale for détente, however, was not acceptance of China on its own terms or for its own sake, but the use of the PRC as a counterweight against the Soviet Union. As Nixon said in a toast to his hosts in Beijing, "It is not our common beliefs that have brought us together, but our common interests and our common hopes."[13] In the world of triangular diplomacy, where realpolitik trumped ideology, this was called "playing the China card." Just as during the Second World War, China was not strong or important enough to be a core concern for the United States. The Chinese, of course, were playing the same game, expecting that relations with the United States would take pressure off their northern border with the USSR, while also hoping that Washington's support for Taiwan could be curtailed.

This strategic calculus did not dampen widespread enthusiasm for reconciliation. After Washington and Beijing established full diplomatic relations in 1979, many Chinese and Americans looked back with nostalgia on the years of cooperation between their two countries during World War II. There was renewed appreciation for the sacrifices made by Americans who fought to defend China against the Japanese. Two

Chinese feature films were made to commemorate Communist rescues of downed American fliers; the history of Sino-American cooperation during the war was celebrated in TV serials and documentaries, news reports, monuments, and memorials. Veterans of the Flying Tigers, 14th Air Force, and Doolittle's Tokyo Raiders returned to China for reunions. A Monument to the Aviator Martyrs in the War of Resistance Against Japan was constructed in Nanjing in 1995, listing the names of 2,186 Americans, 870 Chinese, 236 Russians, and two Koreans. And in 2005, a neglected cemetery in a village northeast of Kunming, where three hundred American and five hundred Chinese airmen who worked together during the war were buried, was rediscovered.[14]

A great deal of this history has been forgotten, as my wife Ellen and I discovered when we traveled to China in June 2013. In Xuzhou, we found a bustling metropolis of several million people, with wide streets and high-rise buildings; the city's bloody wartime history was a distant reality, visible only in old black-and-white photographs. On our first morning, Wang Yutai, a medical doctor, told us about the site where John Birch had been buried; he remembered seeing the grave in 1945 when he was ten years old. His father, a Presbyterian minister, said one of the prayers at Birch's service. Dr. Wang and his colleagues took us to nearby Yunlongshan—a large, heavily forested public park—directly across the street from Xuzhou's impressive archaeological museum. After passing through an archway and climbing wide stone steps for several minutes, we came upon a lovely pavilion, built as a memorial to railway workers who died in the war against Japan. Just above the pavilion in a wooded area on the northern slope of the hill was the location where Birch and two American airmen were once interred. Their tombs were constructed above ground, which would make it easy to remove the remains. But we could find nothing beyond a large cement slab and a few scattered stones that may have been part of the graves. Wang and his colleagues had no information about the circumstances of Birch's death. They assumed he was one of the heroic Flying Tigers.

What later happened to the graves is a mystery, although we know that Birch's remains were not repatriated to the United States. In April 1946, U.S. Army Lieutenant G. Thompson Brown visited Xuzhou, where he had grown up with his Presbyterian missionary parents. He hiked up Yunlongshan and was surprised to happen upon an area where he found the graves of three Americans. The largest tomb had an imposing inscription dedicated to the memory of John Birch, a name that "meant nothing to me at the time," recalled Brown. During a subsequent trip to Xuzhou thirty-five years later, he searched for the graves and markers, but they had disappeared.[15] Most likely, our Chinese hosts agreed, any remains not recovered by the families were removed during the anti-American campaigns of the Korean War. I was unable to gain access to the archives that would have confirmed this.

The Catholic church where Birch's funeral took place still stands. It is a well-maintained, sturdy gray brick building graced with arched entrances. When we visited, interior stone columns reaching up to a series of vaulted ceilings were festooned with red and blue banners printed with Bible verses in Chinese characters. Father Dai, a middle-aged Chinese priest, greeted us warmly and said the church grounds had served as a refuge for many Chinese when the Japanese bombed, invaded, and occupied the city in 1938. He talked about the foreign Jesuits who continued to live in Xuzhou during the war, but there are no records of them or of the funeral service for Birch. Any documents, said Father Dai, might have been destroyed during the Cultural Revolution in the 1960s.

We also traveled with our Chinese hosts to Huangkou, where Birch was shot and the members of his OSS party were taken prisoner. The town lies about thirty miles west of Xuzhou on Highway 310 in Anhui Province, not far across the Jiangsu border. The terrain is flat and a large irrigation canal parallels the road for most of the way. Driving in a Buick minivan, we passed fields of ripening wheat and orchards full of apples and peaches. When we reached the sprawling, nondescript market town, a small, grey brick lookout tower was the only prominent structure remaining from the past that we could find. Birch may have been detained nearby. The town walls had long since been torn down. We learned that the train station where the OSS team arrived on the fateful day in 1945 was razed in 1980. At the new station, we watched a train en route from Guangdong to Yentai. A sleepy local government office displayed a banner warning against the danger of superstitious religion. There were no markers or signs to commemorate the location where an American soldier died. Like so many places in contemporary China, much of the past has been swept aside.

China constantly reinvents itself. Much to the surprise of Western observers, there has been a boom of religious activity, including Christianity, in recent decades. Worship of Chairman Mao and the Communist Party was a substitute for other belief systems, and religion was suppressed as a relic of feudal society in New China. But as Maoism withered away, a broad network of underground churches re-emerged, springing not from the missionary legacy so much as indigenous evangelical Christian movements dating back to the early twentieth century.[16] In keeping with the demands of globalization and, ironically, as a way to help maintain social stability, the Chinese government has allowed a wider practice of Christianity and other faiths.

For some Americans, the resurgence of religion and other reforms led by Deng Xiaoping resurrected the dormant idea that China might follow a path leading to capitalism and liberal democracy. Visions of a vast China market danced in the heads of businessmen, universities scrambled to set up exchange programs, and organizations like the Yale-China Association and the Oberlin-Shansi Association renewed their ties from pre-revolutionary days. The Western liberal vision for China reached its apex with the 1989 democracy movement as the citizens of Beijing marched in the streets to protest inflation and corruption. Students waged a hunger strike that galvanized the movement and grabbed the world's attention. But the Tiananmen Square crackdown of June 3 and 4 left no doubt about the leadership's priorities, and disillusion about prospects for greater openness spread in its wake.[17]

China has since emerged as a new power, challenging long-held assumptions about American primacy in East Asia and beyond. No longer is the relationship that of a supplicant seeking enlightenment from the West. The dilemma for the United States always has been whether to accept China on its own terms, as different as those may be from American values. For the Chinese, the struggle has been whether to embrace foreign ideas that might advance the nation's ambitions for wealth and power but undermine the Communist Party's control. Both nations have compelling reasons to see the other more clearly.

From early on, U.S. relations with China were constructed around the idea that Americans possessed the mandate and the power to transform China.[18] A compulsion to save, rescue, and defend the Chinese went hand in hand with genuine empathy and good will for the Chinese people. In America's emotional and political imagination, China was a cause made all the more potent because it was perceived as an epic battle of good versus evil: heathenism was a moral peril, Japan a mortal enemy, and communism a perverse ideology. The fact that China has been distant and perplexing has not dissuaded Americans from pursuing a dream of making the Chinese just like us. For better and for worse, the impulse to change China stubbornly persists as Americans seek to rescue China for Western-style freedoms, defend China against the enemy of an authoritarian one-party system, and oppose China as a threat to U.S. interests.

John Birch believed in this dream, which turned into a personal nightmare. Righteous anger contributed to, but did not justify, his death. A warrior's martyrdom was not his intent, exposing the aims of the Chinese Communists was not his cause, and representing a conspiracy theory was not his ambition. He was neither a right-wing fanatic nor a patron saint. With a profound sense of moral conviction he had come to rescue and defend the Chinese, first as a missionary and then as a soldier. Instead, like so many other well-meaning outsiders, he became the unsuspecting victim of war and politics, forgotten in China and remembered in America only as a symbol of distorted historical memory.

ACKNOWLEDGMENTS

———◦•◦———

I AM DEEPLY INDEBTED to everyone who has helped to make this book a reality. It is a particular pleasure to acknowledge Lee Hamilton, Bob Hathaway, and the staff of the Woodrow Wilson International Center for Scholars in Washington, DC, where the idea was born while I was in residence as a public policy scholar in 2010. Charles Hayford, Robert Oxnam, and Lyman Van Slyke graciously commented on an early draft. Darren Mulloy kindly reviewed chapters on the John Birch Society. Mary Child provided invaluable editorial advice. Sinan Chu ably assisted with some translations. Ernie Lazar introduced me to important documents on the John Birch Society. Joseph Stoll expertly designed the maps, and Debbie Olson crafted the index. At Oxford University Press, David McBride believed this was a story worth telling, and Kathleen Weaver, Anne Rusinak, and Molly Morrison guided me to the finish line.

A number of people assisted me in understanding the life and legacy of John Birch. First and foremost, I must acknowledge three of his brothers and their spouses: Robert and Jenia Birch, Douglas and Toni Birch, and George Stanley Birch. They generously and unconditionally shared memories, letters, photographs, and newspaper clippings with me. Ruth Birch Sykes, the daughter of John's brother Ellis, also went out of her way to speak with me about the family's history. Several chapters of the book have been enlivened and enriched because of them, and I am most grateful.

Birch fell in love with three women in China and revealed his hopes and dreams to each of them. Jean Whittlesey spoke with me about her mother, Marjorie Tooker Whittlesey; Michael Mair provided information about his aunt, Audrey Mair; and Gloria Leigh told me about her sister, Dorothy Yuen. Edna Chiang, another sister, kindly provided a photograph of Dorothy. It is a privilege to thank each of them.

I need to express my appreciation to many others. Leo Loving gave me access to video interviews he recorded with several people who had known John Birch. Donald Willmott allowed me to quote from his letters, organized by his wife Elizabeth Willmott, describing the outpost in north China where Birch was stationed at the war's end. Tony Heardt located materials written by Earnie Johnson, an airman who knew Birch in China. Bill Leonard recommended sources on Frank Norris and the Independent Baptists. Claire Conner corresponded with me about her book on growing up in Chicago with parents who were ardent Birchers. Christopher Buckley gave me permission to consult William F. Buckley's papers at Yale. Bill Brown, whose grandparents were missionaries to China, introduced me to Wang Yutai, Xia Kaichen, and Li Jianhua, who drove Ellen Lautz and me to the town in China where Birch was shot and killed, showed us the church where his funeral took place, and took us to the site where he was buried.

The librarians and archivists who have assisted my research during the past few years deserve special credit. Sifting through mountains of documents is like panning for gold. I have been fortunate to discover more than a few nuggets because of their dedication and expertise. I especially want to recognize Vickie Bryant at Arlington Baptist College in Arlington, Texas; Martha Smalley and her staff at the Yale Divinity School Library; Eileen Fitzgerald at the College of Wooster; Michael O'Malley at Berry College Memorial Library; Patt Martinelli at the Vineland Historical Society; and Drew Griffith at the Freedom of Information Center and University Archives at the University of Missouri-Columbia. To everyone who has given me permission to quote from unpublished letters and to use photographs, I extend my sincere appreciation.

The encouragement, enthusiasm, and advice of friends and colleagues has meant a great deal to me. It is a pleasure to recognize Nancy Anderson, Andy Andreasen, John Bussey, Mary Bullock, Mike Carroll, Chen Jian, Irv Drasnin and Xiaoyan Zhao, Joseph and Mary Chamie, Lucy Ferris, John Fitzgerald, Michael Gilligan, Kate Hartford, Ellie Hirschhorn, Lynn Joiner, Jan Kiely, Helena Kolenda, Norman Kutcher, Mike and Susan Lampton, Bob Lewis and Maryhelen Hendricks, Nancy Yao Maasbach, Elizabeth Perry, Mark Rupert, Margaret Scott, David Shambaugh, Glenn Shive, Douglas Spelman, Kristin Stapleton, John Stremlau, Hongying Wang, Steve Wasserman, and Pauline Yu.

For cheering me on and helping in many ways, I am enormously grateful to my family: Bryan Lautz and Patricia Silva, Colin and Laura Lautz, Wendy and Bill Horton, and Kathy Lautz. With profound gratitude for her miraculous love and infinite support, this book is dedicated to Ellen Lautz.

NOTES

Abbreviations

JMB	John Morrison Birch
EEB	Ethel Ellis Birch
MTW	Marjorie Tooker Whittlesey
WFK	William F. Knowland
ACW	Albert C. Wedemeyer
RW	Robert H. W. Welch Jr.
CCP	Chinese Communist Party
KMT	Kuomintang (Nationalist Party)
Knowland Papers	William F. Knowland Papers, Bancroft Library, University of California, Berkeley
AFHRA	Air Force Historical Research Agency, Maxwell Air Force Base, AL
JBS	John Birch Society
NACP	National Archives at College Park, College Park, MD
OSS	Office of Strategic Services
PHSA	Presbyterian Historical Society Archives, Philadelphia, PA
PRC	People's Republic of China
RG	Record Group
YDSL	Yale Divinity School Library, Special Collections, New Haven, CT

Archives and Libraries
Note: Unless otherwise stated, John Birch's letters are from the personal collection of Robert G. Birch.

Air Force Historical Research Agency (AFHRA), Maxwell Air Force Base, AL
Arlington Baptist College Heritage Collection, Arlington, TX
Bancroft Library Archives, University of California, Berkeley, CA
Berry College Memorial Library Archives, Mt. Berry, GA
The College of Wooster Libraries, Special Collections; and The College of
    Wooster, Gault Alumni Center Archives, Wooster, OH
Columbia Oral History Archives, Rare Book and Manuscript Library,
    Columbia University, New York, NY
Eugene McDermott Library, Special Collections, University of Texas,
    Dallas, TX
Harvard-Yenching Institute Archives, Harvard University, Cambridge, MA
Hoover Institution Archives, Stanford University, Stanford, CA
Jack Tarver Library, Special Collections, Mercer University, Macon, GA
Library of Congress, Washington, DC
National Archives at College Park, MD
New York Public Library, New York, NY
Presbyterian Historical Society Archives, Presbyterian Church (U.S.A.),
    Philadelphia, PA
Sterling Memorial Library, Yale University, New Haven, CT
Vineland Historical and Antiquarian Society, Vineland, NJ
Washington Memorial Library, Macon, GA
Yale Divinity School Library, Special Collections, New Haven, CT

Introduction

1. Robert G. Birch, interview by author, Macon, Georgia, May 9, 2011;
    EEB to MTW, October 8, 1945, RG 197, Box 7, YDSL. Carl Vinson,
    who graduated from Mercer University in 1902, served in the U.S.
    House of Representatives for fifty years.
2. EEB to her sons, September 12, 1945, reprinted in *The Fundamentalist*,
    September 21, 1945.
3. Edward Witsell to EEB, September 12, 1945, Carton 241, Knowland Papers.
4. Charles B. Stone, September 28, 1945, Carton 241, Knowland Papers.
    Stone later became a member of the JBS's national council.
5. RG 226.147.6.152, NACP. A small exhibit on Birch at the Robins Air Force
    Base Museum of Aviation in Warner Robins, Georgia, includes his camera.
6. Webb Garrison, *Atlanta Journal-Constitution*, January 4, 1987; quoted in
    Miami Herald, October 16, 1964.
7. See D. J. Mulloy, *The World of the John Birch Society: Conspiracy,
    Conservatism, and the Cold War* (Nashville: Vanderbilt University Press,
    2014) for a thoroughly researched and balanced account of the JBS.
    Ernie Lazar has obtained and posted hundreds of Federal Bureau of
    Investigation (FBI) documents on the JBS (including many newspaper
    articles) through Freedom of Information Act requests. See https://
    archive.org/details/ernie1241_jbs.

8. I am grateful to Michael Barkun for his insights on the logic of conspiracy. He is the author of *A Culture of Conspiracy: Apocalyptic Visions in Contemporary America* (Berkeley: University of California Press, 2003).

9. Robert H. W. Welch Jr., *The Life of John Birch: In the Story of One American Boy, the Ordeal of His Age* (Chicago: Henry Regnery, 1954), 2, vi.

10. See Clifford Clark, "John M. Birch: Missionary, Soldier, Hero, Martyr," in *Drama in the Real Lives of Missionaries* (Milford, OH: John the Baptist Printing Ministry, n.d.); James Hefley and Marti Hefley, *By Their Blood: Christian Martyrs of the Twentieth Century*, 2nd ed. (Grand Rapids, MI: Baker Books, 1996), 66–7; William P. Grady, "Bei Shang Wei" [Captain Birch], in *How Satan Turned America Against God* (Knoxville, TN: Grady Publications, Inc., 2005), 473–503.

11. Robert Welch's *The Life of John Birch* is a slim hagiography, and as much about Welch's own political agenda as it is about Birch. Based on Welch's book, the JBS produced a ten-minute video about Birch titled *The Adventures of Captain John Birch* (available at www.jbs.org/videos). The History Channel aired *This Week in History: John Birch* on April 19, 2002. The show was a brief summary of his life and death in China and included an interview with his brother Robert G. Birch. James and Marti Hefley's *The Secret File on John Birch* (Wheaton, IL: Tyndale Publishers, Inc., 1980), a sympathetic portrait written from a conservative Christian perspective, draws on a variety of sources but includes fictitious conversations and has no footnotes or bibliography. A documentary film by Leo Loving, *A Secret War Story: Who Was John Birch?* (Salt Lake City: Loving Images, 2004) features valuable interviews with people who knew Birch, but it does not discuss how Birch's name came to be associated with the eponymous Society.

   The most reliable sources on John Birch are his own letters, many of which have been collected by Robert and Jenia Birch; other letters are held by Douglas and Toni Birch. Birch's correspondence is also located in the papers of Marjorie Tooker Whittlesey at the Yale Divinity School Library; in the papers of William F. Knowland at the University of California, Berkeley; and reprinted in *The Fundamentalist* weekly newspaper. A detailed oral history on Birch's wartime experiences—recorded five months before his death—and other reports quoting Birch are located in the archives of the Air Force Historical Research Agency (AFHRA) at Maxwell Air Force Base in Alabama.

Part One

1. See Orville Schell and John Delury, *Wealth and Power: China's Long March to the Twenty-first Century* (New York: Random House, 2013); and Terrill E. Lautz, "Hopes and Fears of 60 Years: American Images of China, 1911–1972," in *China in the American Political Imagination*, ed. Carola McGiffert (Washington, DC: The CSIS Press, 2003), 31–37.

2. *The Battle of China*, film directed by Frank Capra and Anatole Litvak, 1944.

3. See T. Christopher Jesperson, *American Images of China, 1931–1949* (Stanford, CA: Stanford University Press, 1996); and Harold R. Isaacs, *Scratches on Our Minds: American Views of China and India* (New York: John Day Co., 1958).

4. Pearl Buck to Henry Luce, October 22, 1941, Box 1, Folder 13, Henry Robinson Luce Papers, Manuscripts Division, Library of Congress.

Chapter 1

1. Reginald Heber, "From Greenland's Icy Mountains" (1819), http://cyberhymnal.org.

2. JMB to parents, July 22, 1940, reprinted in *The Fundamentalist*, October 4, 1940. The *Hie Maru* and *Taiyou Maru* were both sunk during the war in the Pacific.

3. See Rana Mitter, *Forgotten Ally: China's World War II, 1937–1945* (Boston and New York: Houghton Mifflin Harcourt, 2013), 98–108.

4. JMB to parents, August 16, 1940, reprinted in *The Fundamentalist*, October 4, 1940.

5. Robert W. Barnett, *Economic Shanghai: Hostage to Politics, 1937–1941* (New York: Institute of Pacific Relations, 1941), 44–46, 73–75.

6. "Reports from Some of our Missionaries," *The Fundamentalist*, September 13, 1940.

7. Donald E. Willmott, email to author, February 17, 2014; Bryan Glass, "John Birch and I," July 9, 2005, http://www.weihsien-paintings.org/NormanCliff/epilogue/DonovanOSS/JohnBirchAndI.htm; and *The Reminiscences of Paul Frillmann*, interviewed by Frank W. Rounds Jr., 1963, Columbia Oral History Archives, Rare Book and Manuscript Library, Columbia University in the City of New York, 323.

8. JMB to parents, August 16, 1940, reprinted in *The Fundamentalist*, October 4, 1940.

9. Fred Donnelson, ed., *Mother Sweet: 51 Years Missionary to China* (Chicago: World Fundamental Baptist Missionary Fellowship, n.d.), 14–15.

10. Donnelson, *Mother Sweet*, 24.

11. G. B. Vick, *The Fundamentalist*, September 20, 1940.

12. "Japanese Terrorized Hangchow for 3 Days," *New York Times*, January 6, 1938.

13. JMB to parents, January 20, 1941.

14. JMB to parents, August 23 and 27, 1940, reprinted in *The Fundamentalist*, October 4, 1940.

15. Timothy Brook, "Christianity Under the Japanese Occupation," in *Christianity in China: From the Eighteenth Century to the Present*, ed. Daniel H. Bays (Stanford, CA: Stanford University Press, 1966), 325.

16. JMB to parents, February 8, 1941.

17. *Re-Thinking Missions: A Laymen's Inquiry after One Hundred Years* (New York: Harper and Brothers, 1932), 3, 28, 326–29.
18. Pearl S. Buck, "Is There a Case for Foreign Missions?" (New York: The John Day Company, 1932), 8, 20, 30.
19. Daniel H. Bays and Grant Wacker, eds., *The Foreign Missionary Enterprise at Home* (Tuscaloosa: University of Alabama Press, 2003), 188.
20. JMB to May Cosman, August 18, 1941.
21. Fred Donnelson, *The Fundamentalist*, April 7, 1939; Fred Donnelson to M. H. Wolfe, *The Fundamentalist*, May 24, 1940.
22. Kepler Van Evera, May 4, 1941, RG 82.61.14, and March 1941, RG 82.60.11, PHSA.
23. Fred S. Donnelson, *Finding Freedom in a Japanese Prison Camp* (Chicago: World Fundamental Baptist Missionary Fellowship, n.d.), 57.
24. JMB to parents, February 8, 1941.
25. JMB to parents, January 20, 1941.

Chapter 2

1. Henry H. Goddard developed tests to measure intelligence for the military during World War I. See Leila Zenderland, *Measuring Minds: Henry Herbert Goddard and the Origins of American Intelligence Testing* (New York: Cambridge University Press, 1998).
2. The College of Wooster Yearbook, 1914–1915; *Miami Herald*, October 16, 1964.
3. George S. Birch, application to the Board of Foreign Missions of the Presbyterian Church, received March 31, 1917, RG 414, PHSA.
4. Ibid.
5. *Cincinnati Enquirer*, November 25, 1914. "September Morn" was painted by French artist Paul Chabas in 1912. It depicts a slender young woman bathing in the waters of a mountain lake at sunrise. Modest by today's standards, the nude painting became a subject of controversy when displayed by an art gallery in New York City. Dismissed as kitsch by critics at the time, the original was purchased by the Metropolitan Museum of Art in New York in 1957.
6. "Historical Sketch," *The Berry School Bulletin*, May 1916.
7. Ethel Ellis, The College of Wooster alumni reports, 1916.
8. *The Berry School Bulletin*, May 1916; *The Berry School Alumni Quarterly*, November 1917.
9. Ethel Ellis, The College of Wooster alumni reports, 1917.
10. Ethel May Ellis, application to the Board of Foreign Missions of the Presbyterian Church, received July 23, 1917, RG 414, PHSA.
11. Applications of George Snider Birch, May 15, 1915, and Ethel May Ellis, October 1913, Student Volunteer Movement Archives, RG 42, Boxes 33 and 52, respectively, YDSL.
12. Ethel Ellis to Mrs. J.B. Howell, May 29, 1917, RG 414, PHSA.

13. See Terrill E. Lautz, "The Student Volunteer Movement and Transformation of the Protestant Mission to China," in *China's Christian Colleges: Cross-Cultural Connections, 1900–1950*, eds. Daniel H. Bays and Ellen Widmer (Stanford: Stanford University Press), 4–21.
14. Board secretary to Ethel M. Ellis, January 10, 1917, RG 414, PHSA.
15. George Birch to Orville Reed, April 30, 1917, RG 414, PHSA.
16. George Birch to Orville Reed, May 22 and 26, 1916, PHSA; George Birch, missionary application, PHSA.
17. George Birch, missionary application, PHSA.
18. Ethel Ellis, missionary application, PHSA.
19. "Vineland Girl Marries Missionary," *Evening Journal*, Vineland, NJ, September 13, 1917.
20. U.S. Consular Registration Application for George S. Birch, Calcutta, India, April 12, 1918, obtained through http://ancestry.com.
21. See Kama Maclean, *Pilgrimage and Power: The Kumbh Mela in Allahabad, 1765–1954* (New York: Oxford University Press, 2008).
22. EEB, The College of Wooster Alumni Bulletin, October 1919. John was named after his paternal grandfather, and Morrison was the maiden name of his paternal grandmother, Elizabeth. She grew up in the north of Ireland and immigrated to the United States when she was sixteen.
23. EEB, "Resume of the Early Life of John Morrison Birch," unpublished, n.d., Robert G. Birch Collection.
24. Ibid.
25. Sam Higginbottom, *Sam Higginbottom: An Autobiography* (New York: Charles Scribner's Sons, 1949), 163, 105.
26. Gary R. Hess, *Sam Higginbottom of Allahabad: Pioneer of Four Point to India* (Charlottesville: University Press of Virginia, 1967), 43.
27. Higginbottom, *Sam Higginbottom*, 167; Hess, *Sam Higginbottom of Allahabad*, 78; George Birch, missionary application, PHSA.
28. Sam Higginbottom to friends, August 27, 1930, Harvard-Yenching Institute Archives, Cambridge, MA.
29. Hess, *Sam Higginbottom of Allahabad*, 43–4. After Higginbottom visited Wooster College, Ethel Birch's alma mater, in 1931, money was raised to send a graduating senior annually to teach and coach athletics for two-year terms in Allahabad.
30. George Stanley Birch, telephone interview with author, May 13, 2011.
31. SS *Trafford Hall* itinerary and passenger list, obtained through http://ancestry.com.

Chapter 3

1. Quoted in Frank DeMaio, *So Rash an Enterprise: The Founding and History of Vineland, New Jersey* (Vineland, NJ: Friends of Historic Vineland, 2011), n.p.
2. Ibid.

3. See Vineland Historical and Antiquarian Society, Vineland, New Jersey, http://www.vinelandhistory.org.

4. George Stanley Birch, telephone interview with author, May 20, 2012. Birch's missing front teeth were used to identify him after his death in China.

5. EEB to Mr. McKee, April 28, 1926, The College of Wooster alumni files.

6. George Stanley Birch, interview by author, Chattanooga, Tennessee, May 20, 2012.

7. EEB, "Resume of the Early Life of John Morrison Birch," Robert G. Birch Collection.

8. George Stanley Birch, telephone interview with author, December 15, 2012.

9. Freeman H. Swartz, "Grow Old Along with Me," *The Alumni News*, Bible Institute of Pennsylvania, March 1937, 11:4.

10. William B. Gatewood Jr., ed., *Controversy in the Twenties: Fundamentalism, Modernism, and Evolution* (Nashville: Vanderbilt University Press, 1969), 50–51.

11. Quoted in Ibid., 50.

12. Ibid., 53.

13. Cryus I. Scofield, "Introduction," *The Scofield Reference Bible*, 2nd ed. (New York: Oxford University Press, 1917), n.p.

14. EEB to alumni secretary, May 20 and May 28, 1926, The College of Wooster alumni files.

15. Jerry Falwell, an Independent Baptist, founded the Moral Majority in 1979 to mobilize political action by conservative Christians. On the diversity and complexity of Baptist life, see Bill J. Leonard, *Baptists in America* (New York: Columbia University Press, 2005).

16. Jeffrey P. Moran, *The Scopes Trial: A Brief History with Documents* (Boston and New York: Bedford/St. Martin's Press), 5.

17. JMB's school paper, September 1931, Robert G. Birch Collection.

18. Robert G. Birch, interview by author, Macon, Georgia, May 9, 2011; George Stanley Birch, telephone interview with author, June 1, 2011. Berry College graduated its first class in 1932.

19. Ethel Birch, "Resume of the Early Life of John Morrison Birch."

20. George Stanley Birch, telephone interview with author, June 1, 2011.

21. Ruth Birch Sykes, interview by author, Macon, Georgia, December 17, 2012,

22. Douglas Birch, interview by author, Asheville, North Carolina, August 31, 2012.

23. Betty Birch (Mrs. M. F. Toms Jr.), quoted in the *Asheville Citizen-Times*, June 14, 1964.

24. George Stanley Birch, telephone interview with author, June 18, 2012.

25. JMB to MTW, March 21, 1945, RG 197, Box 7, YDSL.

26. George Stanley Birch, Robert Birch, and Douglas Birch, interviews by author.
27. Douglas Birch, telephone interview with author, July 6, 2011; George Stanley Birch, telephone interview with author, June 1, 2011.
28. *The Fundamentalist*, November 10, 1939.
29. See Regina D. Sullivan, *Lottie Moon: A Southern Baptist Missionary to China in History and Legend* (Baton Rouge: Louisiana State University Press, 2011).
30. Daniel H. Bays, *A New History of Christianity in China*, (Malden, MA: Wiley-Blackwell, 2012), 93, 123. The Communists ended this anti-Christian campaign in 1936.
31. Ethel Birch, "Resume of the Early Life of John Morrison Birch."

Chapter 4
1. Chauncey Daley, "The John Birch I Knew," *Western Recorder*, General Association of Baptists in Kentucky, Middletown, Kentucky, April 13, 1961.
2. Charles Drake, video interview in *A Secret War History: Who Is John Birch* (Salt Lake City, UT: Loving Images, 2004), documentary film produced by Leo Loving.
3. James Burke, *My Father in China* (New York: Farrar and Rinehart, Inc., 1942), 225–43.
4. George Stanley Birch, telephone interview with author, June 1, 2011.
5. *The Fundamentalist*, November 10, 1939.
6. *Macon Telegraph*, November 15, 1938.
7. Jonathan M. Schoenwald, *A Time for Choosing: The Rise of Modern American Conservatism* (New York: Oxford University Press, 2001), 67–68.
8. E. G. Conklin, "Dismissal of Dr. Henry Fox from the Faculty of Mercer University," *Science*, no. 61 (February 1925): 176–78.
9. *Macon Telegraph*, March 31, 1939.
10. *Macon Evening News*, March 31, 1939.
11. Spright Dowell, *A History of Mercer University, 1833–1953* (Macon, GA: Mercer University Press, 1958), 322–33.
12. Quoted in Sam Hopkins, "John Birch and the 'Unholy 13,'" *Atlanta Journal and Constitution Magazine*, April 23, 1978.
13. Dowell, *A History of Mercer University*, 324.
14. Walter B. Shurden, "The Mercer Heresy Trails of 1939," unpublished paper, 1996, 8, Special Collections, Mercer University Libraries.
15. *Macon Telegraph*, March 31, 1939.
16. Ibid.; *Macon Evening News*, March 31, 1939; *Atlanta Constitution*, March 31, 1939.
17. *The Cluster*, March 31, 1939.
18. Dowell, *A History of Mercer University*, 324–25.
19. *The Cluster*, April 7 and 13, 1939.
20. Shurden, "The Mercer Heresy Trails of 1939," 21.

21. Douglas Birch, interview by author, Asheville, North Carolina, July 6, 2011.
22. Drake, video interview in *A Secret War History: Who Is John Birch?*
23. Daley, "The John Birch I Knew."
24. Douglas Birch, telephone interview with author, July 6, 2011.
25. JB to parents, July 4, 1945.
26. J. Frank Norris, *Inside History of the First Baptist Church, Fort Worth and Temple Baptist Church, Detroit* (Fort Worth: self-published, 1938), 190.
27. Ibid., 194.
28. See Barry Hankins, *God's Rascal: J. Frank Norris and the Beginnings of Southern Fundamentalism* (Lexington: University Press of Kentucky, 1996).
29. "Musical, Inspiring Program Fail to Soothe Legislators," *Atlanta Constitution*, January 31, 1939. Norris's speech was filmed and broadcast over radio. The Hour of Charm All-Girl Orchestra preceded his address with the popular songs "Old Man Mose" and "A Tisket, A Tasket."
30. These communications are reprinted in *The Fundamentalist*, May 12, 1939.
31. Grove Samuel Dow, *Introduction to the Principles of Sociology* (Waco, TX: Baylor University Press, 1920), 211; J. Frank Norris, "Professor Dow and Baylor University," *The Searchlight*, November 11, 1921.
32. Norris, *Inside History*, 10.
33. Norris to JB, April 3, 1939, reprinted in *The Fundamentalist*, April 7, 1939.
34. *The Fundamentalist*, November 10, 1939, April 7, 1939, and June 5, 1942.
35. George Stanley Birch, telephone interview with author, May 14, 2011.
36. *The Fundamentalist*, June 14, 1940. George Norris, standing in for his father who was traveling, introduced Birch as a crusader who had stood up for the fundamentals of the faith when he discovered modernism at Mercer University.
37. Quoted in *The Fundamentalist*, November 10, 1939.
38. Ibid.
39. John Rawlings, telephone interview with author, March 2, 2012.
40. Louis Entzminger, *The J. Frank Norris I Have Known for 34 Years* (Fort Worth: self-published, 1948), 22; *The Fundamentalist*, June 7, 1940.
41. Entzminger, *The J. Frank Norris I Have Known*, 257–59, 253.
42. *The Fundamentalist*, November 3, 1939, and September 15, 1939.
43. *The Fundamentalist*, November 3, 1939; Matthew 28:19 (King James Version).
44. See, for example, Robert H. W. Welch Jr., *The Life of John Birch: In the Story of One American Boy, the Ordeal of His Age* (Chicago: Henry Regnery, 1954), 7.
45. *Forth Worth Star Telegram*, July 1, 1940.
46. *The Fundamentalist*, November 3, 1939.
47. Quoted by Ethel Birch in *Miami Herald*, October 16, 1964.

Part Two

1. JMB to parents, February 8, 1941.
2. JMB to his Aunt Marion, October 9, 1938.
3. Theodore White and Annalee Jacoby, *Thunder Out of China* (New York: William Sloane Associates, 1946), 154; and James Dalby, "Storm from Hell," *Ex CBI-Roundup*, January 1977.
4. Hugh B. Cave, *Wings Across the World: The Story of the Air Transport Command* (New York: Dodd, Mead, and Co., 1945), 104.
5. Claire Lee Chennault, *Way of a Fighter: The Memoirs of Claire Lee Chennault* (New York: G. P. Putnam's Sons, 1949), 236–37. Each Liberty Ship had a cargo capacity of about 10,000 tons.
6. "Big Raids on Japan Seen in Six Months," *New York Times*, May 23, 1942.
7. Warren I. Cohen, *America's Response to China: A History of Sino-American Relations*, 5th ed. (New York: Columbia University Press, 2010), 146.

Chapter 5

1. JMB to parents, October 2, 1941.
2. *The Fundamentalist*, February 6, 1942.
3. JMB to parents, October 29, 1941, reprinted in *The Fundamentalist*, January 30, 1942.
4. JMB to parents, October 6, 1941.
5. JMB to parents, October 29, 1941.
6. JMB to U.S. Military Mission, Chungking, April 13, 1942, Robert G. Birch Collection.
7. JMB to parents, August 13, 1945.
8. JMB to parents, June 24, 1942.
9. Fred S. Donnelson, *Finding Freedom in a Japanese Prison Camp* (Chicago: World Fundamental Baptist Missionary Fellowship, n.d.), 71; 14–16.
10. *The Fundamentalist*, March 8, 1940.
11. Donnelson, *Finding Freedom*, 90–91.
12. The James H. Doolittle Collection, Eugene McDermott Library, University of Texas, Dallas; Craig Nelson, *The First Heroes: The Extraordinary Story of the Doolittle Raid—America's First World War II Victory* (New York: Viking Penguin, 2002); Carroll V. Glines, *Doolittle's Tokyo Raiders* (Princeton, NJ: Van Nostrand Co., 1964); and James M. Scott, *Target Tokyo: Jimmy Doolittle and the Raid That Avenged Pearl Harbor* (New York: W. W. Norton and Company, 2015).
13. Claire Lee Chennault, *Way of a Fighter: The Memoirs of Claire Lee Chennault* (New York: G. P. Putnam's Sons, 1949), 168.
14. James H. Doolittle, *I Could Never Be So Lucky Again* (New York: Bantam Books, 1991), 9.
15. Jimmy Doolittle interview by Phillippe de Bausset, *Paris Match*, August 14, 1965.

16. Ibid.
17. He Yangling [Ho Yang-ling], *Dulite Jiangluo Tianmu Ji* [Doolittle Parachuting on Tianmu Mountain] (Shanghai: Cultural Service Publishing Co., 1947).
18. Donald Smith and Thomas White, NACP, RG 18.384.5.
19. Doolittle, *I Could Never Be So Lucky Again*, 11–12.
20. Doolittle actually was over Tokyo for about six minutes, not thirty seconds. After the raid, he served as an Army Air Forces commander in North Africa and Europe.
21. He Yangling, *Dulite Jiangluo Tianmu Ji*.
22. John M. Birch oral history interview with 14th Air Force Historical Office staff, Kunming, China, March 20, 1945, 862.04-3, Air Force Historical Research Agency (AFHRA), Maxwell Air Force Base, Alabama.
23. Quoted in Scott, *Target Tokyo*, 277.
24. JMB to parents, May 4, 1942.
25. Doolittle, *I Could Never Be So Lucky Again*, 277–79.
26. He Yangling, *Dulite Jiangluo Tianmu Ji*.
27. Doolittle to Frank Norris, May 21, 1943, Arlington Baptist College Archives.
28. JMB oral history interview, March 20, 1945, AFHRA; and JB to parents, April 27, 1942.
29. JMB to parents, April 27 and May 4, 1942.
30. Doolittle interview by Phillippe de Bausset, *Paris Match*, August 14, 1965.
31. "Report of John M. Birch," in Doolittle, *I Could Never Be So Lucky Again*, Appendix 2, 545–46.
32. "Tokyo Reports on Raids," *New York Times*, May 25, 1942.
33. JMB to parents, June 24, 1942, Knowland Papers, Carton 241.
34. Robert H. W. Welch Jr., *The Life of John Birch: In the Story of One American Boy, the Ordeal of His Age* (Chicago: Henry Regnery, 1954), 2.
35. Doolittle, *I Could Never Be So Lucky*, 278.
36. Chennault, *Way of a Fighter*, 169; R. Keith Schoppa, *In a Sea of Bitterness: Refugees during the Sino-Japanese War* (Cambridge, MA: Harvard University Press), 28–30; and "The Japanese in China," editorial, *New York Times*, May 28, 1943.

Chapter 6

1. JMB oral history interview, March 20, 1945, AFHRA; JMB to parents, June 24, 1942.
2. JMB to parents, August 25, 1942; Daniel Ford, *Flying Tigers: Claire Chennault and His American Volunteers, 1941–1942* (Washington, DC: Smithsonian Books, 2007), 329.
3. Thomas G. Trumble, "Thomas Trumble Biography," ca. 1980–83, http://www.usshawkbill.com/tigers/trumble.htm.
4. Ibid.

5. JMB oral history interview, March 20, 1945, AFHRA.

6. JMB to parents, October 7, 1942.

7. Arthur H. Hopkins Jr. to EEB, January 1946, Carton 241, Knowland Papers.

8. JMB telegram to parents, November 2, 1942. Back in Fort Worth, Louis Entzminger later explained to Frank Norris that graduates of a Bible institute had no standing as compared with federally approved divinity schools and seminaries—which Norris jokingly called "cemeteries." As a consequence, Norris agreed to change the name of the Fundamental Baptist Bible Institute to the Bible Baptist Seminary, but this did not happen until 1944. Louis Entzminger, *The J. Frank Norris I Have Known for 34 Years* (Fort Worth: self-published, 1948), 55.

9. Ford, *Flying Tigers*, 21.

10. See Martha Byrd, *Chennault: Giving Wings to the Tiger* (Tuscaloosa: University of Alabama Press, 1967).

11. *The Reminiscences of Paul Frillmann*, interviewed by Frank W. Rounds Jr., 1963, Columbia Oral History Archives, Rare Book & Manuscript Library, Columbia University in the City of New York, 122, 148.

12. J. C. Williams to EEB, March 22, 1946, Carton 241, Knowland Papers; *The Reminiscences of Paul Frillmann*, 323.

13. Chennault to EEB and GB, October 30, 1945, Carton 241, Knowland Papers.

14. "14th Air Force Intelligence Liaison Activity in China, 1944–45," June 18, 1946, 862.609, AFHRA.

15. JMB oral history interview, March 20, 1945, AFHRA.

16. Claire Lee Chennault, *Way of a Fighter: The Memoirs of Claire Lee Chennault* (New York: G. P. Putnam's Sons, 1949), 257–58; "History of Headquarters and Headquarters Squadron, 14th USAF, Kunming, 10 March 1943–6 Jan 1946," 862.071, AFHRA.

17. Wilfred J. Smith interview by EEB, Athens, Ohio, June 18, 1947. For explanations of signals intelligence, photo intelligence, technical intelligence, and human intelligence, see John F. Kreis, ed., *Piercing the Fog: Intelligence and Army Air Forces Operations in World War II* (Washington, DC: Air Force History and Museums Program, 1995).

18. JMB, "Report on East China Trip," April 21, 1943, 862.153.1, AFHRA. The report does not mention anyone who accompanied him.

19. Chennault, *Way of a Fighter*, 258–59.

20. Hopkins to EEB, January 1946; JMB to parents, April 20, 1943.

21. JMB to EEB, December 30, 1943, J. Frank Norris Papers, Microfilm 2148, Arlington Baptist College Heritage Collection.

22. Claire Chennault interview by EEB, Atlanta, Georgia, December 10, 1945, Carton 241, Knowland Papers. V-mail or Victory Mail correspondence was photographed and transported as small microfilmed images in order to reduce the weight and bulk of shipping. The images were printed on small sheets of paper upon arrival overseas.

23. JMB to parents, March 17, 1944.
24. James E. Tull to George Birch, n.d., Carton 241, Knowland Papers. Paul Frillmann, who was Chennault's chaplain, returned to the United States after the Flying Tigers were disbanded and came back to China as an intelligence officer in 1943.
25. Darren Dochuk makes the same point in *From Bible Belt to Sunbelt: Plain-Folk Religion, Grassroots Politics, and the Rise of Evangelical Conservatism* (New York: W. W. Norton and Company, 2011), 47–50.
26. *The Fundamentalist*, March 26, 1943.
27. JMB oral history interview, March 20, 1945, AFHRA. Chennault and Xue developed great respect for one another, but did not meet face-to-face until late in the war.
28. Malcolm Rosholt, one of Chennault's intelligence officers, wrote *Dog Sugar Eight: A Novel of the 14th Air Force Flying Tigers in China in World War II* (Rosholt: Rosholt House, WI, 1977). The lead character is named Jeff Benning, an American in Changsha who was closely modeled on John Birch.
29. *The Reminiscences of Paul Frillmann*, 322–23.
30. Lulu Birkel, October 3, 1941, and A. H. Birkel, October 2, 1941, RG 82.64, PHS.
31. Marjorie T. Whittlesey, *The Dragon Will Survive* (Ft. Lauderdale: Ashley Books, 1991), 29.
32. Ibid., 13; Maude Pettus, interview by author, Stamford, Connecticut, March 15, 2011; Whittlesey, *The Dragon Will Survive*, 15.
33. Lulu Birkel, "Changsha News Letter," January 28, 1942, RG 82.64, PHS.
34. JMB to parents, January 14, 1943.
35. JMB to J. Frank Norris, April 6, 1944, Norris Papers, Microfilm 2150, Arlington Baptist College.
36. Historical Office, 14th Air Force Headquarters, "The Changteh [Changde] Campaign of October-December, 1943," May 20, 1945, AFHRA; JMB oral history interview, March 20, 1945, AFHRA; Smith interview by EEB, June 18, 1947.
37. AGRFTS reports, October 9 and 10, 1944, RG 226.154.190, NACP. After being forced out of Changsha in June 1944, the radio school relocated to Kukong in the south.
38. Hopkins to EEB, January 1946; JMB oral history interview, March 20, 1945, AFHRA.
39. Smith interview by EEB, June 18, 1947; JMB to parents, September 21, 1943.
40. Hopkins to EEB, January 1946.
41. Smith interview by EEB, June 18, 1947; OSS Report, May 20, 1944, RG 226.154.190, NACP; JMB oral history interview, March 20, 1945, AFHRA.
42. JMB oral history interview, March 20, 1945, AFHRA.

43. 14th Air Force Headquarters Historical Office, "The Changteh [Changde] Campaign of October–December, 1943," May 20, 1945, 862.04-3, AFHRA.

44. Ibid.

45. JMB radiogram to Chennault, December 15, 1943, in ibid.

46. JMB oral history interview, March 20, 1945, AFHRA.

47. JMB memorandum, September 30, 1944, RG 226.148.102, NACP.

48. JMB to George Stanley Birch, September 22, 1944.

Chapter 7

1. Marjorie T. Whittlesey, *The Dragon Will Survive* (Ft. Lauderdale: Ashley Books, 1991), 133.

2. Hilary Saunders, *The Red Cross and the White: A Short History of the Joint War Organization of the British Red Cross Society and the Order of St. John of Jerusalem during the War 1939–1945* (London: Hollis and Carter, 1949), 162.

3. Alexander Mair, *Unforgettable: Memories of China and Scotland* (London: Epworth Press, 1967).

4. JMB to Audrey Mair, February 29, 1944, Douglas Birch Collection.

5. Ibid.

6. JMB to Mair, March 14, 1944; JMB to Betty Birch, April 1, 1944.

7. JMB to Mair, March 11, 1944, Douglas Birch Collection.

8. Ibid.; JMB to George Birch, March 11, 1944.

9. JMB to Mair, March 14, 1944, Douglas Birch Collection.

10. JMB to Ethel Birch, March 31, 1944.

11. Ibid.

12. JMB to parents, April 19 and May 21, 1944.

13. Michael Mair, email to author, July 6, 2012; Ruth Birch Sykes, interview by author, Macon, Georgia, December 17, 2012.

14. JMB to Betty Birch, May 16, 1944.

15. JMB to George Birch, April 28, 1944.

16. JMB oral history interview, March 20, 1945, AFHRA.

17. The threat of air attacks on Japan from bases in China provoked a major Japanese offensive, named Ichigō Sakusen (Operation Number One), the largest campaign in the history of the Japanese army. All of the Allied air bases in southern and eastern China were overrun. By late 1944, however, the tide was turning and the enemy started pulling back from the south to wage a defensive war. As Japanese opposition withered away, U.S. bombers flew unopposed without fighter escorts.

18. JMB, "Opening of Liaison Work, East Honan [Henan]," September 30, 1944, AGFRTS 862.6001, AFHRA.

19. Ibid.; William Drummond, interview by EEB, Washington, DC, December 31, 1945.

20. Claire Lee Chennault, *Way of a Fighter: The Memoirs of Claire Lee Chennault* (New York: G. P. Putnam's Sons, 1949), 258–59; Chennault, interview by EEB, Atlanta, Georgia, December 10, 1945.

21. JMB to Betty Birch, April 1, 1944.

22. JMB to MTW, September 22, December 14, 1944, and March 21, 1945, RG 197, Box 7, Marjorie Tooker Whittlesey Papers, Special Collections, YDSL.

23. Earnest D. Johnson, *In Search of Ghosts* (Boise, ID: Jet Publishing Company, 1989), 125.

24. Ibid., 127.

25. Ibid., 131–32.

26. Whittlesey, *The Dragon Will Survive*, 165–66.

27. Ibid., 14.

28. Ibid., 169, 173.

29. Whittlesey, "J.B.," unpublished manuscript, n.d., 1, RG 197, Box 10, YDSL; JMB to MTW, n.d. (spring 1944?), quoted in ibid., 10.

30. Whittlesey, *The Dragon Will Survive*, 174.

31. Quoted in ibid., 174–76.

32. JMB to MTW, March 21, 1945, RG 197, Box 7, YDSL.

33. Whittlesey, *The Dragon Will Survive*, 181; JMB quoted in ibid., 189.

34. Quoted in ibid., 189–90.

35. JMB to MTW, August 11, 1945, RG 197, Box 7, YDSL.

36. JMB to Yuen, February 27, 1944. See C. O. Lamp, *Gentle Tigress* (New York: Leisure Books, 1980) for a semifictional account of Dorothy Yuen's life in China during World War II.

37. Dorothy Yuen Phipps, video interview, June 10, 2000, Sun City, Arizona, produced by Leo Loving.

38. JMB to Dorothy Yuen, February 27, 1944, Robert G. Birch Collection.

39. Dorothy Yuen to EEB, May 1948, Robert G. Birch Collection.

40. JMB to Yuen, May 9, 1945.

41. Yuen to EEB, May 1948.

42. Ibid. Dorothy Yuen married Colonel Richard H. Wise, an American officer she worked for in China, in 1948. After divorcing him, she married Harald Leuba, and after his death married Clifford Phipps. She died in 2010.

43. JMB to Yuen, August 13, 1945.

44. Yuen to EEB, May 1948.

Chapter 8

1. JMB to J. Frank Norris, April 6, 1944, Microfilm 2150, Norris Papers, Arlington Baptist College Heritage Collection.

2. Quoted in Claire Lee Chennault, *Way of a Fighter: The Memoirs of Claire Lee Chennault* (New York: G. P. Putnam's Sons, 1949), 309.

3. Albert C. Wedemeyer, *Wedemeyer Reports!* (New York: Henry Holt and Co., 1958), 277; Albert C. Wedemeyer, "Relations with Wartime China: A Reminiscence," *Asian Affairs* 4, no. 3 (January–February 1977): 199–200.

4. Wedemeyer, *Wedemeyer Reports!*, 197–98.

5. Ibid., 267–69.
6. Ibid., 278.
7. Quoted in Keith E. Eiler, "The Man Who Planned the Victory: An Interview with Gen. Albert C. Wedemeyer," *American Heritage*, October/November 1983 (reprinted online at http://www.americanheritage.com/content/man-who-planned-victory).
8. Quoted in John J. McLaughlin, *General Albert C. Wedemeyer: America's Unsung Strategist in World War II* (Havertown, PA: Casemate Publishers, 2012), 125.
9. Theodore White and Annalee Jacoby, *Thunder Out of China* (New York: William Sloane Associates, 1946), 165.
10. Hopkins to EEB, January 1946.
11. JMB oral history interview, March 20, 1945, AFHRA.
12. Tien-Chi Hsu, May 1988, CACW, 865.309-1, AFHRA.
13. Ken Daniels, *China Bombers: The Chinese-American Composite Wing in World War II* (Stilllwater, MN: Specialty Press Publishers and Wholesalers, 1999), 18–20.
14. Maochen Yu, *OSS in China: Prelude to Cold War* (New Haven and London: Yale University Press, 1996), 171.
15. See Milton E. Miles, *A Different Kind of War: The Little-known Story of the Combined Guerrilla Forces Created in China by the U.S. Navy and the Chinese during World War II* (Garden City, NY: Doubleday, 1967); Frederic E. Wakeman, *Spymaster: Dai Li and the Chinese Secret Service* (Berkeley: University of California Press, 2003).
16. Oliver J. Caldwell, *A Secret War: Americans in China, 1944–1945* (Carbondale and Edwardsville: Southern Illinois University Press, 1972), 73.
17. Chennault, *Way of a Fighter*, 257.
18. Miles, *A Different Kind of War*, 483.
19. AGFRTS Report, August 1944, RG 226.154.190, NACP.
20. Francis B. Mills, with John W. Brunner, *OSS Special Operations in China* (Williamstown, NJ: Phillips Publications, 2002), 66.
21. See Miles, *A Different Kind of War*, 488.
22. Chennault, February 4, 1945, Intelligence Files, 1943–45, 862.609-1, AFHRA.
23. Wilfred Smith, interview by EEB, Athens, OH, June 18, 1947.
24. Chennault to JMB, February 13, 1945, Intelligence Files, 1943–45, 862.609-1, AFHRA.
25. Dorothy Yuen to RGB, March 5, 2001.
26. JMB oral history interview, March 20, 1945, AFHRA.
27. Smith, interview by EEB, June 18, 1947.
28. JMB oral history interview, March 20, 1945, AFHRA.
29. Ibid.

30. Ibid. Wilfred Smith said Birch "embarrassed me terribly, when he told me he would rather be a buck private in the 14th Air Force than a major in the OSS, and sent a radiogram to that effect that was seen by everybody." Smith, interview by EEB, June 18, 1947. Chennault also mentions Birch's message in *Way of a Fighter*, 260.

31. JMB oral history interview, March 20, 1945, AFHRA. At the CIA's headquarters in Langley, Virginia, there is a book with the names of OSS officers who died in the line of duty during World War II. The names of five men killed in China are listed, but John Birch is not one of them, perhaps because he was on detached service to the OSS from the 14th Air Force.

32. "Revised Copy of Crow Plan," August 1, 1945, RG 226.148.102, NACP.

33. JMB to George Stanley Birch, August 13, 1945. Birch hoped his brother George Stanley would be able to join him in China after the war. Instead, he and his wife Alice spent twenty-one years in northern Nigeria and fifteen years in Jamaica as Christian missionaries.

34. JMB to parents, September 21, 1943.

35. Smith, interview by EEB, June 18, 1947; JMB to parents, September 21, 1943; Edwin James to EEB, January 29, 1946.

36. JMB to parents, August 13, 1945.

37. Smith, interview by EEB, June 18, 1947.

38. Donald E. Willmott, "A 'Mish Kid' in the OSS in Wartime China, 1944–1945," unpublished ms., n.p., March 2014. A closer airstrip named Drill Field was deemed too dangerous because of enemy activity in the area.

39. Ibid; "History of the SI Branch, OSS, China Theater," October 1945, RG 226.154.3333, NACP. Some Korean dissidents fled to China after Japan annexed their country in 1910. Aside from the Korean Liberation Army, a small number of leftists established the Korean Volunteer Army with the CCP's assistance in Yenan. Still others, including Kim Il-sung, were with the Soviet Army in Manchuria. Chong-sik Lee, "Korean Communists and Yenan," *The China Quarterly*, vol. 9 (1962): 182–192.

40. Willmott, "A 'Mish Kid' in the OSS."

41. Ibid. Willmott writes that six weeks after Japan's surrender, the Americans at the R2S base were ordered to destroy all of their equipment—electric generators, radio equipment, and a complete weather station—before they were evacuated. Permission was given for General Wang to keep a jeep.

42. Richard Rudeloff, *CBI Roundup*, October 2005, 11–12, http://www.cbi-history.com/part_vi_10th_weather_sq4.html.

43. JMB to MTW, March 21, 1945.

44. Ibid.

45. JMB to Frank Norris, April 6, 1944, item 2150, Microfilm of Norris Papers, Arlington Baptist College Heritage Collection.

46. Daniel H. Bays, *A New History of Christianity in China* (Malden, MA: Wiley-Blackwell, 2012), 146.
47. JMB to Betty Birch, March 22, 1945.
48. JMB, "War Weary Farmer," April 1945, Robert G. Birch Collection.
49. Dorothy Yuen to EEB, May 1948, Robert G. Birch Collection.
50. JMB to Betty Birch, March 22, 1945.
51. JMB, "War Weary Farmer," April 1945.
52. JMB to Betty Birch, March 22, 1945.
53. JMB to MTW, March 21, 1945, RG 197, Box 7, YDSL.
54. JMB to parents, April 19, 1944.
55. JMB to Mair, March 11, 1944, Douglas Birch Collection; JMB to George Birch, March 11, 1944; JMB to George Stanley Birch, September 22, 1944; JMB to Betty Birch, March 16 and 22, 1945.
56. Quoted in Whittlesey, *The Dragon Will Survive*, 192.
57. MTW to JMB, October 18, 1945, RG 197, Box 7, YDSL. Tooker also wrote, "I'm glad you are not here to deal with the color problem. There has been a lot of feuding between the black and white American troops, stabbings, shootings, hand grenades, and even an organized machine gun resistance."

Part Three

1. See Kenneth Shewmaker, *Americans and Chinese Communists, 1927–1945: A Persuading Encounter* (Ithaca, NY: Cornell University Press, 1971.)
2. Jing Li, *China's America: The Chinese View of the United States, 1900–2000* (Albany, NY: SUNY Press, 2011), 42–44. Mao and Zhou received no response to their letter to Roosevelt.
3. See Ronald H. Spector, *In the Ruins of Empire: The Japanese Surrender and the Battle for Postwar Asia* (New York: Random House, 2007).
4. JB to MTW, March 21, 1945, RG 197, Box 7, YDSL.

Chapter 9

1. JMB to parents, August 13, 1945.
2. JMB to MTW, August 11, 1945, RG 197, Box 7, YDSL.
3. Donald E. Willmott, "A 'Mish Kid' in the OSS in Wartime China, 1944–1945," unpublished ms., n.p., March 2014.
4. JMB to Betty Birch, March 22, 1945, Robert G. Birch Collection; JMB to MTW, March 21, 1945; EEB to MTW, June 14, 1945, RG 197, Box 7, YDSL.
5. Earnest D. Johnson, *In Search of Ghosts* (Boise, ID: Jet Publishing Company, 1989), 164.
6. Oliver J. Caldwell, *A Secret War: Americans in China, 1944–1945* (Carbondale and Edwardsville: Southern Illinois University Press, 1972), 180–83; James Hart, Courier-Journal, Louisville, Kentucky, April 5,

1961. Drill Field was closer to the R2S base than the Valley Field airstrip where Willmott and others had landed.

7. John S. Thomson, "Account of the Death of Captain John Birch," September 14, 1945, RG 226.168.16, NACP; Jeremiah J. O'Connor, "Death of Captain John Birch, 0-8889028, AC," Office of the Theater Judge Advocate, November 13, 1945, Albert Wedemeyer Collection, Box 87, Folder 2, Hoover Institution Archives.

8. Mark Peattie, Edward Drea, and Hans van de Ven, eds., *The Battle for China: Essays on the Military History of the Sino-Japanese War of 1937–1945* (Stanford, CA: Stanford University Press, 2011), 190–96.

9. OSS radiogram, August 17, 1945, RG 226.148.6.87, NACP.

10. Ronald H. Spector, *In the Ruins of Empire: The Japanese Surrender and the Battle for Postwar Asia* (New York: Random House, 2007), 7–9.

11. OSS radiogram, August 18, 1945, RG 226.148.6.87, NACP.

12. Curtis Grimes, Laird Ogle, and Albert Meyers, "Report on the Death of Capt. Birch and Detention of His Party," November 7, 1945, Albert Wedemeyer Collection, Box 87, Folder 2, Hoover Institution Archives. (This report also appears in RG 226.182.17.98, NACP.)

13. Ibid.

14. "Testimony of Tung Chin-sheng (or Tung Fu Kuan) [Dong Qinsheng]," August 28, 1945, RG 226.168.16.225, NACP.

15. "OSS Special Operations S.O.P.," RG 226.154.196.3333, NACP.

16. Grimes, Ogle, and Meyers, "Report on the Death of Capt. Birch." The Communist troops in the area belonged to the New Fourth Army but originally came from the Eighth Route Army.

17. "Testimony of Tung Chin-sheng [Dong Qinsheng]"; and "Statement of 1st Lt. Tung Chin-sheng," October 3, 1945, RG 226.168.16.225, NACP.

18. Thomson, "Account of the Death of Captain John Birch."

19. "Report of Sixth Route [Nationalist] Army Headquarters on Death of Captain John Birch," August 30, 1945, RG 226.168.16.225, NACP; Thomson, "Account of the Death of Captain John Birch"; William T. Miller report to Albert Wedemeyer, September 1, 1945, Albert Wedemeyer Collection, Box 87, Folder 2, Hoover Institution Archives.

20. "The Man Who Buried John Birch," *Amarillo Daily News*, July 6, 1962.

21. Miller to ACW, September 1, 1945.

22. After the war, Miller had brief postings in Washington, DC, Panama, and Bolivia before leaving the Army in 1947. He earned a master's degree in biology at Stanford University, and then lived and worked in the Caribbean. William Miller, video interview by Karen Keith, November 22, 1997, Tulsa, Oklahoma, produced by Leo Loving.

23. "The Man Who Buried John Birch," *Amarillo Daily News*, July 6, 1962.

24. William T. Miller, "How the Chinese Killed John Birch," *Life*, May 12, 1961, 128.

25. Miller to ACW, September 6, 1945, RG 226.168.16.225, NACP.

26. William T. Miller, "Georgia on My Mind," September 1977, unpublished article, Albert Wedemeyer Collection, Box 87, Folder 2, Hoover Institution Archives.
27. Miller to ACW, September 1, 1945.
28. Ibid. In addition to 1.2 million Japanese military in Manchuria in China's northeast, there were 750,000 in Korea and at least 700,000 in various parts of Southeast Asia. Spector, *In the Ruins of Empire*, 26.
29. Robert H. W. Welch Jr., *The Life of John Birch: In the Story of One American Boy, the Ordeal of His Age* (Chicago: Henry Regnery, 1954), 73, 127.
30. *The Fundamentalist*, September 21, 1945; *Fort Worth Telegram*, November 22, 1945. The building with John Birch Memorial Hall on the ground floor no longer stands.

Chapter 10

1. Curtis Grimes, *Behind China's Red Screen*, unpublished ms., n.d., Walter Judd Papers, Box 187, Folder 6, Hoover Institution Archives, copyright Stanford University.
2. Eugene Warner, "Operational History of *Das Neue Deutschland*," October 1, 1945, http://www.psywar.org/dnd.php; Donald Willmott, "A 'Mish Kid' in the OSS in Wartime China, 1944–1945," unpublished ms., n.p., March 2014.
3. Smith, interview by EEB, June 18, 1947.
4. Laird Ogle, interview by EEB, New York City, March 1946, Carton 241, Knowland Papers.
5. Grimes, *Behind China's Red Screen*.
6. Grimes, Ogle, and Meyers, "Report on the Death of Capt. Birch," November 7, 1945; Thomson, "Account of the Death of Captain John Birch," September 14, 1945.
7. Grimes, *Behind China's Red Screen*.
8. Grimes, Ogle and Meyers, "Report on the Death of Capt. Birch"; Grimes, *Behind China's Red Screen*.
9. Grimes, Ogle, and Meyers, "Report on the Death of Capt. Birch."
10. Ibid., 9.
11. Grimes, *Behind China's Red Screen*.
12. Laird Ogle, interview by EEB, March 1946.
13. Grimes, Ogle and Meyers, "Report on the Death of Capt. Birch."
14. Ibid.
15. RG 226.148.6.87, NACP.
16. *The Revolutionary: Sidney Rittenberg*, documentary film produced by Stourwater Pictures in association with Irv Drasnin, Bainbridge Island, Washington, 2013, DVD.
17. David D. Barrett, *Dixie Mission: The United States Army Observer Group in Yenan, 1944* (Berkeley: Center for Chinese Studies, University of California, 1970), 73.
18. Zhu De to William Donovan, January 23, 1945, RG 226.148.6.87, NACP.

19. See Lynn Joiner, *Honorable Survivor: Mao's China, McCarthy's America, and the Persecution of John S. Service* (Annapolis, MD: Naval Institute Press, 2009).

20. W. J. "Pete" Peterkin, *Inside China, 1943–1945: An Eyewitness Account of America's Mission in Yenan* (Baltimore: Gateway Press, 1992), 64–65; Barrett, *Dixie Mission*, 81–82. A mess hall and recreation center was named in Whittlesey's honor at Yenan. He was not related to Steven Whittlesey, who married Marjorie Tooker after the war.

21. Zhu De to ACW, September 15, 1945, Albert Wedemeyer Collection, Box 87, Folder 2, Hoover Institution Archives.

22. The following account of Joseph Baglio's rescue was recorded by Henry C. Whittlesey, "Baglio's Walk Out," in Peterkin, *Inside China, 1943–45*, Appendix C, 129–41.

23. Frey stayed in China for the rest of his life and died there in 2004. "Ranshao ban shiji de Zhongguo qing: Huainian Baiqiu'en shi de Dafu Fulai" [Mid-century China in Flames: Commemorating the Bethune-like Dr. Frey], Xinhua News, March 25, 2005, http://news.xinhuanet.com/newscenter/2005-03/25/content_2742918.htm.

24. William Taylor, *Rescued by Mao: World War II, Wake Island, and My Remarkable Escape to Freedom Across Mainland China* (Madison, WI: Silverleaf Press, 2007), 251, 268, 290–92, 296.

25. Francis B. Mills with John W. Brunner, *OSS Special Operations in China* (Williamstown, NJ: Philips Publications, 2002), 490.

26. OSS memorandum, May 27, 1945, RG 226.145.212.3520, NACP.

27. Francis Coolidge, "Analysis of Spaniel Mission," September 13, 1945, RG 226.148.6.87, NACP.

28. Carolle J. Carter, *Mission to Yenan: American Liaison with the Chinese Communists, 1944–47* (Lexington: University of Kentucky Press, 1997), 77–79; *New York Times*, January 17, 1945.

29. Coolidge, "Analysis of Spaniel Mission." For another account of the Spaniel incident, see Maochen Yu, *OSS in China: Prelude to Cold War* (New Haven and London: Yale University Press, 1996), 220–23.

30. RG 226.198.3368, NACP.

31. Ibid.

Chapter 11

1. Claire L. Chennault, "Unauthorized Transactions with Chinese Authorities," June 3, 1945, Box 81, Folder 1; Wedemeyer to Mao, July 30, 1945, Albert Wedemeyer Collection, Box 82, Folder 22, Hoover Institution Archives.

2. "Minutes of Meeting Held at Ambassador Hurley's Home, August 30, 1945," Albert Wedemeyer Collection, Box 82, Folder 2, Hoover Institution Archives. (Also held in RG 226.148.6.87, NACP.) The seven-page transcript was classified "Top Secret." Mao and Zhou were accompanied by an unnamed woman interpreter; Hurley and

Wedemeyer were joined by General Maddocks, General Olmsted, Captain Eng, and Lietenant Boyle. All of the following quotations of Mao, Zhou, and Wedemeyer come from this document.

3. Patrick J. Hurley, *Foreign Relations of the United States, 1945*, vol. 7 (Washington, DC: Government Printing Office, 1969), 542–43.

4. ACW to Mao Zedong, August 31, 1945, Albert Wedemeyer Collection, Box 82, Folder 2, Hoover Institution Archives.

5. Ibid.

6. General Xu Yongzhang to ACW, September 13, 1945, RG 226.168.16.225, NACP. The Nationalists saw the Birch incident as evidence of the CCP's real intentions as well as an opportunity to sow doubts in the minds of the Americans. Even the Japanese took an unusually active interest in the case, noted the 14th Air Force director of intelligence, possibly viewing the incident as a chance "to stir up dissension among the opposing forces." Memo from Colonel J. M. Murphey, RG 226.198.3368, NACP.

7. Zhu De to ACW, Albert Wedemeyer Collection, Box 87, Folder 2, Hoover Institution Archives.

8. Hu Qiaomu, *Hu Qiaomu Huiyi Mao Zedong* [Recalling Mao Zedong] (Beijing: People's Press, 1994), 83.

9. William Stueck, "The Marshall and Wedemeyer Missions: A Quadrilateral Perspective," in Harry Harding and Yuan Ming, eds., *Sino-American Relations, 1945–1955* (Wilmington, DE: Scholarly Resources, Inc., 1989), 99.

10. Zhu De, August 10, 1945, RG 226.148.87, NACP.

11. Suzanne Pepper, *Civil War in China: The Political Struggle, 1945–49* (Berkeley: University of California Press, 1978), 10–11.

12. ACW memos of August 12 and 14, 1945, Albert Wedemeyer Collection, Box 83, Folder 40, Hoover Institution Archives.

13. See Steven I. Levine, "On the Brink of Disaster: China and the United States in 1945" in *Sino-American Relations, 1945–55*, 3–13.

14. Zhu De to ACW, September 15, 1945, Albert Wedemeyer Collection, Box 87, Folder 2, Hoover Institution Archives.

15. Statement of 1st Lt. Tung Chin-sheng, October 3, 1945.

16. W.J. "Pete" Peterkin, *Inside China, 1943-1945: An Eyewitness Account of America's Mission in Yenan* (Baltimore, MD: Gateway Press, 1992), 104, 106.

17. Maochen Yu, *OSS in China: Prelude to Cold War* (New Haven and London: Yale University Press, 1996), 221–23.

18. Ren Donglai, "Baiqi Shijian yu Kangzhan houqi Meiguo yu Zhonggong Guanxi de Qifu." [The Birch Incident and the Fluctuation of U.S.-CCP Relations after the Anti-Japanese War], conference paper presented in Guiyang, China, December 8, 2011.

19. Quoted in Yu, *OSS in China*, 222–23.

20. *Zhonggong Zhongyang Wenjian Xuanji* [Selected Documents of the CCP Central Committee, 1945], vol. 15 (Beijing: Zhongyang dangxiao, 1989–92), 179–80.

21. Zhu De to ACW, September 15, 1945.

22. *Zhonggong Zhongyang Wenjian Xuanji*, vol. 15, 263.

23. The story of Lieutenant Colonel Peter Dewey has some remarkable parallels with the John Birch case. Dewey, an American officer with the OSS in Vietnam, was shot and killed in Saigon on September 26, 1945 by the Viet Minh, who were fighting the French and British. He was the first U.S. soldier to be killed in Vietnam. The Vietnamese Communists were hoping for American support at this time. Ho Chi Minh was so distressed by the incident that he wrote a letter to Truman, promising to identify and punish those responsible, but this never happened. See Dixee R. Bartholomew-Feis, *The OSS and Ho Chi Minh: Unexpected Allies in the War Against Japan* (Lawrence: University Press of Kansas, 2006), 288–99.

24. Jeremiah J. O'Connor, "Death of Captain John Birch," Office of the Theater Judge Advocate, November 13, 1945, Albert Wedemeyer Collection, Box 87, File 2, Hoover Institution Archives.

25. Yu, *OSS in China*, 235–37.

26. Ren, "Baiqi Shijian yu Kangzhan houqi Meiguo yu Zhonggong Guanxi de Qifu."

27. Constantine Brown, "This Changing World," *Washington Evening Star*, November 15 and 17, 1945.

28. "Chinese Reds Slew American Army Officer," *Los Angeles Times* (AP), November 22, 1945.

29. *Shanghai Evening Post and Mercury*, November 23, 1945. The story also mentioned the deaths of two foreigners in Shanghai, H. A. Reeks, a British attorney, and Louis Fabre, head of the former French Concession police force. Both committed suicide.

30. *Macon Telegraph*, November 22, 1945.

31. Adeline Gray to W. P. Anderson, November 17, 1945, reprinted in S. C. Lyons, *His Name Was John Birch* (Dry Branch, GA: self-published, 1968), 30.

32. EEB quoted Gray in her letter to MTW, November 23, 1945, RG 197, Box 7, YDSL.

33. Adeline Gray, *Macon Telegraph*, November 22, 1945.

34. Robert H. W. Welch Jr., *The Life of John Birch: In the Story of One American Boy, the Ordeal of His Age* (Chicago: Henry Regnery, 1954), 74.

35. Xu Yongzhang to ACW, RG 226.198.3368, NACP.

Part 4

1. Quoted in Simei Qing, *From Allies to Enemies* (Cambridge, MA: Harvard University Press, 2007), 133.

2. Chen Jian, *China's Road to the Korean War: The Making of the Sino-American Confrontation* (New York: Columbia University Press, 1994), 11, 216; Warren I. Cohen, *America's Response to China: A History of Sino-American Relations*, 5th ed. (New York: Columbia University Press, 2010), 184.
3. Chen Jian's *China's Road to the Korean War* is an excellent study of the Chinese decision-making process.
4. Quoted in Jing Li, *China's America: The Chinese View of the United States, 1900–2000* (Albany, NY: SUNY Press, 2011), 63–64.
5. Dean Rusk, "American Friendship for the Peoples of China," speech to the China Institute, New York, May 18, 1951. The U.S. government used Peiping rather than Peking (or Beijing)—which means "northern capital"—to show that China's government was illegitimate.
6. Robert H. W. Welch Jr., *The Life of John Birch: In the Story of One American Boy, the Ordeal of His Age* (Chicago: Henry Regnery, 1954), 126–27.

Chapter 12

1. EEB to MTW, October 7, 1945, RG 197, Box 7, YDSL.
2. EEB to Dorothy Yuen, May 12, 1948, Robert G. Birch Collection.
3. Quoted in S. C. Lyons, *His Name Was John Birch* (Dry Branch, GA: self-published, 1968), 10. Lyons was a businessman and a coordinator for the John Birch Society in Georgia.
4. EEB to MTW, October 8 and November 2, 1945, RG 197, Box 7, YDSL. William Borden was a Yale University graduate and missionary in China and Egypt who died from meningitis in 1913 at age twenty-five. He was famous for renouncing his claim to the family's fortune and giving it to the China Inland Mission.
5. EEB to MTW, November 7, 1945, RG 197, Box 7, YDSL.
6. MTW to parents, October 30, 1945, RG 197, Box 3, YDSL.
7. Mary Tooker to MTW, November 8, 1945, RG 197, Box 3, YDSL.
8. JMB to MTW, March 21, 1945, RG 197, Box 7, YDSL.
9. JMB to EEB, March 21, 1945.
10. Douglas Birch, interview by author, Asheville, North Carolina, August 31, 2012.
11. Marjorie Tooker Whittlesey, "J.B.," unpublished manuscript, n.d., 1, 10, RG 197, Box 10, YDSL; MTW to Ian (no surname), February 16, 1946, RG 197, Box 17, YDSL.
12. Marjorie T. Whittlesey, *The Dragon Will Survive* (Ft. Lauderdale: Ashley Books, 1991), 199; Jean Whittlesey, interview by author, Berkeley, California, February 11, 2011.
13. Ethel Birch's account of these trips appears in Lyons, *His Name Was John Birch*. John Thomson, the son of missionaries who taught at Nanjing University, went on to have a distinguished career in the CIA. His brother James Thomson was a well-respected specialist of U.S.-East Asia relations at Harvard and Boston University.

14. EEB to Clayton Bissell, December 17, 1945, Carton 241, Knowland Papers.

15. Chennault, interview by EEB, Atlanta, Georgia, December 10, 1945; Claire Lee Chennault, *Way of a Fighter: The Memoirs of Claire Lee Chennault* (New York: G. P. Putnam's Sons, 1949), 260; Paul Frillmann and Graham Peck, *China: The Remembered Life* (Boston: Houghton Mifflin, 1968), 290.

16. ACW, May 5, 1968, Albert Wedemeyer Collection, Box 115, Folder 10, Hoover Institution Archives, copyright Stanford University.

17. EEB to MTW, November 23, 1945, RG 197, Box 7, YDSL. As explained in the previous chapter, there were various news reports about Birch in the weeks after his death.

18. Ibid.

Chapter 13

1. Quoted in Tang Tsou, *America's Failure in China* (Chicago: University of Chicago Press, 1963), 509.

2. WFK, *Congressional Record—Senate*, September 26, 1949 (reprint in Knowland Papers).

3. *New York Times*, November 28, 1945; quoted in Tsou, *America's Failure in China,* 509. Hurley's resignation letter appears in *The China White Paper, August 1949*, vol. 2 (Stanford, CA: Stanford University Press, 1967), 581–84.

4. WFK, *Congressional Record—Senate*, September 5, 1950, 14204–14205. Knowland did not reveal Miller's name, but Miller later told Wedemeyer that he was the source for the information about Birch's death.

5. *Saturday Evening Post*, April 25, 1953; *Time*, January 14, 1957.

6. See Gayle B. Montgomery and James W. Johnson, *One Step from the White House: The Rise and Fall of Senator William F. Knowland* (Berkeley: University of California Press, 1957); and Joyce Mao, "Asia First: China and American Conservatism, 1937–1965," PhD diss., University of California, Berkeley, 2007. After a failed bid against Edmund Brown for the governorship of California—expecting that the office would be a springboard to the presidency—Knowland left politics and succeeded his father as publisher of the *Oakland Tribune*. In 1974, deeply in debt and facing a second failed marriage, he drove to his summer cabin in Sonoma County and took his own life with a gun.

7. Quoted in Montgomery and Johnson, *One Step from the White House*, 97.

8. Walter H. Judd, *Congressional Record—House*, November 25, 1947, 10856; Walter H. Judd, *Saturday Evening Post*, October 11, 1952.

9. WFK, *Congressional Record—Senate*, December 4, 1950 (reprint in Knowland Papers).

10. WFK, *Congressional Record—Senate*, September 5, 1950, 14204–14205.

11. *Macon Telegraph*, September 6, 1950.

12. WFK to EEB, September 9, 1945; and EEB to WFK, September 14, 1950, Carton 241, Knowland Papers.

13. *Congressional Record—Senate*, September 15, 1950, 14879–81.

14. EEB to James Burke, May 1, 1947, Carton 241, Knowland Papers.

15. "Replacement of General MacArthur," *Congressional Record—Senate*, April 12, 1951 (reprint in Knowland Papers).

16. Harry S. Truman, "Report to the American People on Korea," April 11, 1951, http://www.pbs.org/wgbh/amex/macarthur/sfeature/officialdocs03.html.

17. EEB to Harry Truman, April 17, 1951, Carton 241, Knowland Papers. (Uppercase in the original.)

18. "Text of General MacArthur's Address to Joint Meeting of Congress," *New York Times*, April 20, 1951.

19. "Inquiry into the Military Situation in the Far East, Senate Committees on Armed Services and Foreign Relations," 82nd Congress, May 11, June 11, and June 13, 1951 (Washington, DC: Government Printing Office, 1951), 544, 2301–02, and 2526–27. I am grateful to Darren Mulloy for bringing these hearings to my attention.

20. O'Connor, "Death of Captain John Birch," Office of the Theater Judge Advocate, November 13, 1945.

21. Frillmann to EEB, n.d. [1946?], Carton 241, Knowland Papers.

22. Hopkins to EEB, January 1946, Carton 241, Knowland Papers.

23. Charles B. Stone to U.S. Air Force Chief of Staff, November 2, 1946, Carton 241, Knowland Papers; Claire Chennault to George Birch, October 30, 1945, Box 7, YDSL; Witsell is quoted by Ethel Birch in S. C. Lyons, *His Name Was John Birch* (Dry Branch, GA: Self-published, 1968), 17.

24. EEB to Carl Vinson, December 4, 1947, Carton 241, Knowland Papers; EEB to MTW, November 23, 1945, RG 197, Box 7, YDSL; EEB to James Burke, May 1, 1947.

25. WFK to Thomas Finletter, December 4, 1950 and January 5, 1951; Finletter to WFK, December 30, 1950, Carton 241, Knowland Papers.

Chapter 14

1. Robert H. W. Welch Jr., *The Life of John Birch: In the Story of One American Boy, the Ordeal of His Age* (Chicago: Henry Regnery, 1954), v. Knowland was unable to give Welch access to the classified file on Birch's death. It does not appear that the two men ever met in person.

2. RW to Ethel and George Birch, July 20, 1953, Carton 241, Knowland Papers.

3. EEB in S. C. Lyons, *His Name Was John Birch* (Dry Branch, GA: self-published, 1968), 20.

4. Robert Welch, *One Man's Opinion* (magazine), February 1956. Welch published *One Man's Opinion*, which was renamed *American Opinion* in 1958 and became *The New American* in 1985.

5. See G. Edward Griffin, *The Life and Words of Robert Welch: Founder of the John Birch Society* (Thousand Oaks, CA: American Media, 1975).

6. Robert Welch, *The Road to Salesmanship* (New York: The Ronald Press, 1941).

7. Quoted in Griffin, *The Life and Words of Robert Welch*, 151–53, 155.

8. Robert A. Taft, address to Republican Party State Convention of Maine, Portland, March 31, 1950, quoted in *The Papers of Robert A. Taft* (Kent, OH: Kent State University Press, 1997), 149.

9. Quoted in Clarence E. Wunderlin, *Robert A. Taft: Ideas, Tradition, and Party in U.S. Foreign Policy* (Lanham, MD: Rowman and Littlefield, 2005), 145–46.

10. Robert Welch, *American Opinion*, April 1958, 19.

11. *The Blue Book of the John Birch Society*, 24th ed. (Appleton, WI: Western Islands Press, 2012), 109.

12. Robert H. W. Welch, *May God Forgive Us* (Chicago: Henry Regnery Co., 1952), 77.

13. The biographies of Syngman Rhee and Chiang Kai-shek were published in *One Man's Opinion*.

14. Welch, *The Life of John Birch*, vi, 119, 126–28.

15. Ibid., 2. Among other exaggerations and errors, Welch wrote that Birch was a perfect student who made only A's in college; that he completed a two-year course of study at the Baptist Bible Institute in Fort Worth in only one year; that he learned to speak fluent Chinese in only six or seven months; and that he was engaged to a Red Cross nurse at the Yale-in-China hospital in Changsha.

16. Ibid., 72–73, 2, 94.

17. Ibid., 115–16.

18. "Testimony of Tung Chin-sheng [Dong Qinsheng]," August 28, 1945. Since Welch did not have direct access to Dong's testimony, this quote most likely was provided in one of the documents collected by Ethel Birch.

19. *Saturday Evening Post*, January 22, 1955, 30. Welch was probably unaware of newspaper reports published in 1945 about Birch's death, although Ethel Birch would have seen these stories.

20. RW to Kohlberg, June 7, 1954, Alfred Kohlberg Papers, Box 17, Hoover Institution Archives. Welch said *The Life of John Birch* sold thirty-five thousand copies during its first year.

21. EEB, The College of Wooster Alumni Records, June 1955.

22. J. Allen Broyles, *The John Birch Society: Anatomy of a Protest* (Boston: Beacon Press, 1964), 27.

23. *The Blue Book*, 145, 151–52.

24. RW to William Buckley, February 23, 1960, MS 576, Box 12, William F. Buckley Jr. Papers, Yale University Library.

25. *The Blue Book*, 141, 46.

26. *The Blue Book*, 45–46, 49–50, 137, 151; RW to David Roemer, November 20, 1959, quoted in Griffin, *The Life and Words of Robert Welch*, 270.

27. EEB to William Grede, December 6, 1965, Archives of the Wisconsin Historical Society; Slobodan M. Draskovich to Revilo P. Oliver, November 23, 1965, University of Wyoming, American Heritage Cener, posted on the website of Ernie Lazar, https://sites.google.com/site/jbs9004.

28. See Arnold Forster and Benjamin R. Epstein, *Danger on the Right* (New York: Random House, 1964).

29. Robert Welch, "A Touch of Sanity," *The Robert Welch Presentations* (Appleton, WI: John Birch Society, 1965), DVD.

30. Forster and Epstein, *Danger on the Right*, 14, 37–39.

31. "Birch Society Gains Back Founder's Boast," *Washington Post*, February 6, 1965.

32. *American Opinion*, January 1962.

33. Welch, *The Life of John Birch*, 95, 98–99. Welch mentioned nothing about the significant centralization of federal power under Abraham Lincoln during the Civil War.

34. *American Opinion*, July–August 1958 and July–August 1961.

35. Robert Welch, "An Introduction to the John Birch Society," *The Robert Welch Presentations* (Appleton, WI: John Birch Society, 1961), DVD.

36. Samuel L. Brenner, "Shouting at the Rain: The Voices and Ideas of Right-Wing Anti-Communist Americanists in the Era of Modern American Conservatism, 1950–1974," PhD diss., Brown University, 2009, 469, 476, 483, 424.

37. *Life* magazine editorial, May 12, 1961, 32.

38. RW to Alfred Kohlberg, December 26, 1959, Kohlberg Papers, Box 200, Hoover Institution Archives.

Chapter 15

1. Robert Welch, *The Politician*, 266–67. A copy of the original version appears on the website of Ernie Lazar at https://archive.org/details/foia_Welch_Robert_The_Politician_manuscript.PDF. The most incendiary words in *The Politician* were deleted from the version published by Robert Welch in 1963.

2. Jack Mabley, "Bares Secrets of 'Red-Haters': They Think Ike Is a Communist," *Chicago Daily News*, July 26, 1961. The articles and editorials from the *Santa Barbara News-Press* and *Los Angeles Times* were reprinted in the *Congressional Record—Senate*, March 20, 1961, 4017–28.

3. *Los Angeles Mirror*, April 15, 1961; *New York Herald Tribune*, April 15, 1961.

4. *Time*, March 10, 1961.

5. *New York Herald Tribune*, May 1, 1961.

6. *Life*, May 12, 1961, 124–30.

7. Ibid., *32*.

8. *New York Herald Tribune*, April 4, 1961.

9. Ibid., April 9, 1961. See D. J. Mulloy, *The World of the John Birch Society: The World of the John Birch Society: Conspiracy, Conservatism, and the Cold War* (Nashville: Vanderbilt University Press, 2014), 110–17 for a discussion of the JBS campaign to impeach Earl Warren.

10. *New York Herald Tribune*, April 23, 1961.

11. *New York Herald Tribune*, July 29, 1962, and November 16, 1961; J. Edgar Hoover, *Investigation of the Assassination of President John F. Kennedy* (Washington, DC, Government Printing Office, 1964) vol. 5, 101.

12. Richard Nixon, "Nixon Tells Why He Opposes Birch Society," *New York Herald Tribune*, March 16, 1962. Earlier in March, the California Republican Assembly adopted a resolution, offered by Nixon, which called the Birch Society "dictatorial and totalitarian" and asserted that Welch has "rendered immeasurable harm to the cause of individual liberty." *New York Herald Tribune*, March 5, 1962.

13. William F. Buckley, "Goldwater, the John Birch Society, and Me," *Commentary*, March 1, 2008.

14. William F. Buckley, "The Question of Robert Welch," *National Review*, February 13, 1962, 83–88.

15. Barry Goldwater, letter to editor, *National Review*, February 20, 1962.

16. *National Review* received over one thousand letters expressing disappointment, concern, shock, and outrage over Buckley's "desperate," "savage," and "fanatical" attacks on Welch and the JBS. He was accused of becoming an anti-anti-communist. See William F. Buckley Jr. Papers, Yale University, MS 576, Box 1.

17. John B. Judis, *William F. Buckley Jr.: Patron Saint of the Conservatives* (New York: Simon and Schuster, 1988), 200.

18. Quoted in the *Washington Post*, July 17, 1964.

19. William F. Buckley Jr. Papers, Yale University, MS 576, Box 3.

20. "Main Street McCarthyites," *Macon News*, March 31, 1961.

21. "Investigate the John Birch Society," *New York Herald Tribune*, April 1, 1961.

22. Gene Gisley, "John Birch Society: The Extreme Right," *Ventura Country Star-Free Press*, March 16, 1961. The author wrote that John Birch was a one-time missionary, but misidentified him as a U.S. Navy captain.

23. Darren Mulloy, telephone communication with author, June 25, 2013.

24. *New York Herald Tribune*, March 31, 1961.

25. Robert Welch, Memo to Members of Our Council and a Few Other Friends, April 1, 1961, in William F. Buckley Jr. Papers, Yale University, MS 576, Box 14.

26. *San Diego Union*, April 1, 4, and 14, and May 4, 1962; JBS *Bulletin*, May 1962.

27. *Newsweek*, December 4, 1961. For a detailed discussion of the Walker case, see D. J. Mulloy, *The World of the John Birch Society*, 42–57.

28. "Inquiry into the Military Situation in the Far East, Senate Committees on Armed Services and Foreign Relations," 82nd Congress, May 11, June 11, and June 13, 1951 (Washington, DC: Government Printing Office, 1951), 544; 2301–2302; 2526–27. The hearings are discussed in Chapter 13.

29. Wedemeyer, *Wedemeyer Reports!* (New York: Holt, 1958), 366–69; WFK, *Congressional Record—Senate*, April 12, 1951 (Reprint).

30. Wedemeyer, *Wedemeyer Reports!*, 369.

31. ACW to RW, September 5, 1961, Albert Wedemeyer Collection, Box 115, Folder 9, Hoover Institution Archives, copyright Stanford University.

32. RW to ACW, October 7, 1961, Albert Wedemeyer Collection, Box 115, Folder 9, Hoover Institution Archives. There were news reports about Birch at the time of his death, but they did not receive much attention.

33. ACW to RW, October 14, 1961, Albert Wedemeyer Collection, Box 115, Folder 9, Hoover Institution Archives, copyright Stanford University.

34. *American Opinion*, July–August 1961, 6; Robert Welch, "An Introduction to the John Birch Society," *The Robert Welch Presentations* (Appleton, WI: The John Birch Society, 1961), DVD; *American Opinion*, April 1961, 2.

35. "*Ladies of the Press* Meet Robert Welch, Founder of the John Birch Society," WOR-TV Channel 9, New York, October 24, 1963, transcript in William F. Buckley Jr. Papers, Yale University, MS 576, Box 26.

36. *New York Times*, January 17, 1965.

37. Stanley Mosk and Howard H. Jewel, "The Birch Phenomenon Analyzed," *New York Times*, August 20, 1961.

38. Robert Welch, "A Touch of Sanity," 1965 speech, *The Robert Welch Presentations*.

39. Art Buchwald, "The Orlov Plan," *New York Herald Tribune*, December 12, 1961.

40. "Satire on Birch Society Barred from Ed Sullivan's TV Show," *New York Times*, May 14, 1963.

41. "The John Birch Society," music and lyrics by Michael Brown, 1961, used by permission of Alley Music Corporation and Trio Music Company.

42. A. J. Liebling, "The Candy Kid," *New Yorker*, May 20, 1961.

43. Claire Conner, *Wrapped in the Flag: A Personal History of America's Radical Right* (Boston: Beacon Press, 2013), 33, 38, 41–43, 60–61.

44. Robert Welch, *American Opinion*, March 1960.

45. JBS *Bulletin*, July 1962 (emphasis in original quote).

46. JBS advertising supplement, *St. Louis Globe-Democrat*, September 1, 1964, provided by the FOI Center and University Archives, University of Missouri-Columbia.

Chapter 16

1. Robert G. Birch, interview by author, Macon, Georgia, May 11, 2011.
2. Quoted in the *Fort Worth Star-Telegram*, March 29, 1961.
3. *Miami Herald*, October 16, 1964.
4. The College of Wooster Alumni Records, July 7, 1965.
5. Robert H. W. Welch Jr., *The Life of John Birch: In the Story of One American Boy, the Ordeal of His Age* (Chicago: Henry Regnery, 1954), 106.
6. Jesse Williams to EEB, March 22, 1946, Carton 241, Knowland Papers.
7. Bryan Glass to EEB, January 30, 1946, Carton 241, Knowland Papers.
8. Arthur Hopkins to EEB, January 1946.
9. Claire Lee Chennault, *Way of a Fighter: The Memoirs of Claire Lee Chennault* (New York: G. P. Putnam's Sons, 1949), 259.
10. James Hart, *Courier-Journal*, Louisville, Kentucky, April 5, 1961; James Hart to EEB, March 7, 1947, Carton 241, Knowland Papers.
11. Laird Ogle to EEB, January 30, 1946, Carton 241, Knowland Papers.
12. Miller, "Georgia on My Mind," September 1977; quoted in "The Man Who Buried John Birch," *Amarillo Daily News*, July 5, 1962.
13. *The Reminiscences of Paul Frillmann*, interviewed by Frank W. Rounds Jr., 1963, Columbia Oral History Archives, Rare Book and Manuscript Library, Columbia University in the City of New York, 408–09; Paul Frillmann and Graham Peck, *China: The Remembered Life* (Boston: Houghton Mifflin, 1968), 289–90. Frillmann says Chennault wanted him to write the untold story about Birch and the other intelligence liaison officers in China, but he begged off, saying he was reluctant to do so since he and Birch had both been missionaries. Because the Communists now were claiming that all missionaries were imperialist spies, Frillmann was worried that his story could be used to persecute Christians in China. *The Reminiscences of Paul Frillmann*, 406.
14. George Doss, "Birch was Brilliant Young Man with Outstanding War Record," *Macon News*, March 24, 1961.
15. George Doss, "John Birch was Leader in Charges of Heresy Against Professors," *Macon News*, March 27, 1961.
16. Calvin Trillin, "Who Was John Birch?," *Time*, April 14, 1961.
17. "Birch's 'Hero Death' Stirs New Controversy," *Los Angeles Times*, April 3, 1961.
18. "Ex-OSS Officer Defends Birch as American Hero," *Macon Telegraph* (Associated Press), April 3, 1961; "Who was John Birch?" *Time*, April 14, 1961.
19. "Birch Death Story Told by Broadcaster," *Los Angeles Times*, April 2, 1961.
20. *Newsweek*, December 4, 1961. Also discussed in Chapter 15.
21. ACW to Allen Griffin, December 11, 1961, Albert Wedemeyer Collection, Box 115, Folder 9, Hoover Institution Archives, copyright Stanford University.

22. Quoted in the *Atlanta Constitution*, December 5, 1962; George Birch to ACW, December 10, 1962, Albert Wedemeyer Collection, Box 115, Folder 10, Hoover Institution Archives.

23. The CCP's investigation determined that the Communist detachment had acted in self-defense. Mao and Zhou expressed regret but never said they would punish those responsible for the death of Birch.

24. ACW to George Birch, December 24, 1962, Albert Wedemeyer Collection, Box 115, Folder 10, Hoover Institution Archives, copyright Stanford University.

25. "Honolulu Man Tells Details of John Birch's Death, Blasts Birch Society" and "John Birch Death Witness Raps Society," *Honolulu Advertiser*, August 29, 1961.

26. "Louisvillian Says John Birch Would Shun Group," *Courier-Journal*, Louisville, KY, April 5, 1961, provided by FOI Center and University Archives, University of Missouri-Columbia. James Hart, an OSS officer who met Birch toward the end of his life, wrote a two-part series on "The Violent Death of John Birch," as told to Bill Surface in *Saga: The Magazine for Men* in July and August 1961. Hart's sensationalized account freely mixed fiction with fact.

27. Michael Mair, email to author, July 6, 2012.

28. Earnest D. Johnson, *In Search of Ghosts* (Boise, ID: Jet Publishing Company, 1989), 130; Earnest Johnson, video interview, Boise, Idaho, May 20, 2000, produced by Leo Loving.

29. MTW letter to editor, *Burlington Free Press*, Burlington, Vermont, n.d., RG 197, Box 7, YDSL.

30. Laird Ogle to EEB, January 30, 1946.

Epilogue

1. Proclamation, Executive Department, State of Georgia, signed August 19, 1969.

2. *Atlanta Constitution*, August 21, 1969.

3. Neil A. Hamilton, *Militias in America* (Santa Barbara, CA: ABC-CLIO, 1996), 13.

4. See Lisa McGirr, *Suburban Warriors: The Origins of the New American Right* (Princeton, NJ: Princeton University Press, 2001).

5. See Darren Dochuk, *From Bible Belt to Sunbelt: Plain-Folk Religion, Grassroots Politics, and the Rise of Evangelical Conservatism* (New York: W. W. Norton and Company, 2011).

6. Ronald Reagan, "Abortion and the Conscience of a Nation," *The Human Life Review* (Spring 1983), http://humanlifereview.com; Ronald Reagan, "First Inaugural Address," January 20, 1981.

7. "John Birch leaders call Soviet action 'murder,'" Associated Press, September 2, 1983.

8. Sean Wilentz, "Confounding Fathers: The Tea Party's Cold War roots," *New Yorker*, October 18, 2010.

9. The John Birch Society, http://www.jbs.org/action-projects, accessed October 16, 2013.

10. David Beasley, *Atlanta Journal Constitution*, April 1, 1984. Ethel Birch died in 1977 and George Birch in 1992.

11. Quoted in *This Week in History: John Birch*, The History Channel, television broadcast, April 19, 2002.

12. Wesley McCune, "John Birch: Did He Seek Death?," *Washington Post*, August 6, 1972. The records of the OSS, which were declassified in the 1990s, are available at the National Archives in College Park, Maryland.

13. "Transcripts of Toasts by Nixon and Chou at Dinner," *New York Times*, February 26, 1972.

14. John Pomfret, "Rediscovering the Ties that Bind," *Washington Post*, June 13, 1998; "Cemetery for U.S. 'Flying Tigers' Found in China," Xinhua News Agency, August 8, 2007, http://www.chinadaily.com.cn/china/2007-08/30/content_6069567.htm.

15. G. Thompson Brown, *Legacy: Frank A. Brown of China* (Atlanta: self-published, 2004), 142–43.

16. See Daniel H. Bays, *A New History of Christianity in China* (Malden, MA: Wiley-Blackwell, 2012).

17. See Richard Madsen, *China and the American Dream* (Berkeley: University of California Press, 1995).

18. See Jonathan Spence, *To Change China: Western Advisors in China, 1620–1960* (New York: Little, Brown and Company, 1969).

INDEX

Note: Entries using "JMB" refer to John Morrison Birch; "JBS" refers to the John Birch Society. Page numbers appearing in italics refer to photographs.